Getting an IT
Help Desk Job

FOR

DUMMIES®

A Wiley Brand

Getting an IT Help Desk Job

FOR DUMMIES®
A Wiley Brand

by Tyler Regas

FOR DUMMIES®
A Wiley Brand

Getting an IT Help Desk Job For Dummies®

Published by: **John Wiley & Sons, Inc.,** 111 River Street, Hoboken, NJ 07030-5774, www.wiley.com

Copyright © 2015 by John Wiley & Sons, Inc., Hoboken, New Jersey

Published simultaneously in Canada

For general information on our other products and services, please contact our Customer Care Department within the U.S. at 877-762-2974, outside the U.S. at 317-572-3993, or fax 317-572-4002. For technical support, please visit www.wiley.com/techsupport.

Wiley publishes in a variety of print and electronic formats and by print-on-demand. Some material included with standard print versions of this book may not be included in e-books or in print-on-demand. If this book refers to media such as a CD or DVD that is not included in the version you purchased, you may download this material at http://booksupport.wiley.com. For more information about Wiley products, visit www.wiley.com.

Library of Congress Control Number: 2014958353

ISBN 978-1-119-01898-8 (pbk); ISBN 978-1-119-01899-5 (ePDF); ISBN 978-1-119-01897-1 (ePub)

Manufactured in the United States of America

10 9 8 7 6 5 4 3 2 1

Contents at a Glance

Table of Contents

Introduction

. . . .

Technology as a whole, is the foundation of a strong and energetic job industry brimming with a seemingly neverending supply of jobs. Most IT help desk jobs are on a form of help desk, but there is a lot of diversity in roles, including consulting, a customer facing help desk, and internal technical support team member. If you're looking to get in on the ground floor of technology, the IT help desk operation is one of the more diverse segments to exploit.

When you look at the landscape of technology, however, you may wonder if it's even possible to become proficient. There's so much to know, and new technologies are being introduced every year. Windows XP ran for ten years, and now it's jumped from Windows 7 to 8.1 to the upcoming Windows 10 in just a few years. Mobile phone OS like Apple iOS, Google's Android, and even BlackBerry 10 evolve radically with each new version. This isn't even counting the rapid growth and expansion in all other IT technologies, telecommunications, software, web services, and countless other segments. How can anyone keep up with all of it?

You, however, are a rock star. You are a nerd, and nerds now rule the world. You live, eat, drink, and breathe technology. You can, and you do, keep up. It's not easy, but then again, what is? On the other hand, it is healthy to understand that you do not know everything and you'll need some help on occasion. That is why this book exists. With this book, you don't need to tax your nerd brain with the effort of finding work; you just need to use the tools provided.

Using this book, you can develop a sense of purpose, discover your area of strength, expand your knowledge base, become a better you, and become a better employee at the same time.

About This Book

Getting an IT Help Desk Job For Dummies introduces you to the world of IT help desk operations and how to prepare or improve yourself for employment in this world. With this book as your guide, you will learn

- ✔ All about the help desk
- ✔ The different paths you can take on your road to the help desk
- ✔ The array of different certifications that are available to you
- ✔ What a day is like for each kind of role in the support industry
- ✔ Why selecting the help desk is the best choice when getting into IT
- ✔ What the federal government has to say about how awesome IT is
- ✔ About the kind of education that can help you in your quest for work
- ✔ More about optional forms of education
- ✔ The inner workings of the nerd mind and how to apply it to help people
- ✔ The manifold arena of post-education that is known as certifications
- ✔ The good, the bad, and the functional of getting certifications
- ✔ How to make yourself a better nerd outside of education
- ✔ Effective tools for expanding your technical prowess
- ✔ New platforms and new ways of experiencing technology
- ✔ Everything you need to know about being a help desk nerd
- ✔ The core elements that make up working as a consultant
- ✔ What it's like to work inside a company, small or large
- ✔ The ins and outs of providing technical support to customers
- ✔ How to brand yourself using the Internet as your toolbox
- ✔ How to develop a winning cover letter and the ultimate resume
- ✔ How to survive the grueling interview process
- ✔ What to do and what not to do when interacting with decision-makers
- ✔ Why it's critical to treat people nicely
- ✔ How to properly manage the post-interview process
- ✔ How interesting lists of information can really be

After you decide that you want an IT help desk job — or, if you already have one, decide whether you want to keep working in IT — how do you advance yourself?

That's why this book exists. This book is designed to empower you, give an extra boost to your already active nerd gene, help you find the job you want, build on that foundation, and develop a long-lasting career in IT that makes you happy and fulfilled.

Foolish Assumptions

Getting an IT Help Desk Job For Dummies is written in a way that's fully accessible for beginners, for people who don't currently hold an IT help desk job, and for those who are looking to get their first job. However, I did have to make a few assumptions while writing this book, or I would not have had enough space to get you the information you need while not making this book 1,000 pages long. Here are my assumptions:

✔ You're familiar with computers, such as those that run Windows, Mac OS X, and maybe even Linux. I assume that you can work with icons, the keyboard, and a mouse and that you have all of the basic skills for using a computer. In addition, I assume that you are generally far more familiar with computers and technology than most people (or you would be hard pressed to support them).

✔ You're familiar with using the Internet and its resources, such as search engines, searching for jobs using online jobs boards, and purchasing various kinds of products.

✔ You have a smartphone or tablet and/or related mobile devices, can find, install, and use apps on those devices, and know how to manage those devices.

✔ You know something about the basic mechanics of getting a job. If not, please see *Job Hunting For Dummies*, 2nd Edition, by Max Messmer (yes, one of Wiley's books) to get up to speed.

Icons Used in This Book

Throughout the margins of this book are little round pictures known as icons. Here's what those icons signify:

The text next to this icon offers tips for completing tasks or for making your job easier. You'll want to take advantage of these nuggets of wisdom!

Pay special attention when you see this icon. It points out information you'll want to make sure to remember.

This text warns you of things that can go wrong . . . very wrong!

Beyond This Book

The fun doesn't stop with this book. You will find the following goodies online:

- ✔ **Cheat Sheet:** You can find this book's Cheat Sheet online at www. dummies.com/cheatsheet/gettinganithelpdeskjob. See the Cheat Sheet for checklists that can help you throughout the entire process of finding, preparing for, and following up on jobs.

- ✔ **Dummies.com online articles:** You can find companion articles to this book's content online at www.dummies.com/extras/ gettinganithelpdeskjob. The articles deal with what you need to know, finding the right job, landing the right job, and a bonus list of things you should never, ever say to an interviewer.

- ✔ **Updates:** If this book has any updates after printing, they'll be posted to www.dummies.com/updates/gettinganithelpdeskjob.

Where We Go from Here

Like other *For Dummies* books, *Getting an IT Help Desk Job For Dummies* is a reference. That means you can read it in the order that makes sense to you. You can flip through to stumble upon scads of helpful info, or you can use the table of contents and index to zero in on exactly the topic you're looking for.

You also have the option to read this book like a book, from beginning to end. This approach can be valuable for two reasons. One, if you're new to the world of the help desk, reading through the entire book can give you layers of context that you may not have been previously aware of. Two, if you're working to learn a new skillset so that you can advance from your current position, this book will give you insight into the arena of IT help desk operations and how people work together and also grants you clarity where before there was none.

If you want to know what you need to work in IT, check out Part II. If you need to jump straight to information on what type of IT help desk job is right for you, look no further than Part III. If you want help getting your cover letter and resume materials all ship-shape, then move to Part IV.

Good hunting!

Part I

So You Want to Be an IT Help Desk Engineer

In this part . . .

- ✔ Discover your job options so that you can get find the IT help desk job that's right for you.

- ✔ Get the inside scoop on what a help desk engineer does on a day-to-day basis so that you can determine which career path is right for you.

- ✔ Find out what a position at a help desk can lead to so that you can plan accordingly.

- ✔ Visit `http://www.dummies.com` for great Dummies content online.

Chapter 1

Embracing IT Help Desk Jobs

In This Chapter

▶ Establishing a better understanding of how companies use the help desk

▶ Developing an awareness of your options for positions

▶ Understanding the tools you'll need to get work

*I*t's time to get a job, and you're quite talented with technology, so where do you go? How do you find one? How do you verify that you know what you need to know in order to take a position? How do you understand what your potential pay will be? How do you determine your options? You go online and look at what the IT job industry offers and find an enormous selection of positions and little understanding about what most of the jobs entail. Now what do you do?

You start by reading this chapter. In this chapter, I break down a number of things like what a help desk is, how important the help desk is to industry, a look at the IT job market, and more. In short, the information in this chapter starts you on a path to discover whether a career in IT suits you. In general, if you have any technical aptitude at all, then it's likely an IT position will be a positive step forward for you. IT is a strong industry with lots of opportunity for advancement.

This chapter has an element of looking inside yourself, as if the content inside these pages is a looking glass for personal introspection. You discover more about the IT industry and likely more about yourself. It is also the aim to help you feel a sense of confidence in yourself as you recognize more and more information, learning that you are not alone in the way you think and that you probably know quite a bit more than you may think.

What Is a Help Desk?

Literally, the *help desk* is a desk people can go to for help. Yes, that definition isn't exactly helpful, but in general terms, the help desk is an organization inside of a corporation that is part of the IT department that is designed to assist users with their computer needs.

I use simple terminology throughout this book to describe the people who run the help desk as *engineers* and the people who do not as *users.* For example, the engineer installs a printer driver update for the user.

The overall scope of what is termed help desk is frequently wider than just engineers helping users, though this rule isn't strict. Some help desks are tightly controlled and have a very limited role. You will find these limited roles in larger organizations that either work on government contracts or must comply with various laws and regulations.

The core aspect of a help desk, however, is to provide users with the resources they need to use technology as tools to perform their work for the corporation. Yet, because you are living in the world of IT, even this core purpose is complicated. As in *The Matrix,* you can choose the Red Pill or the Blue Pill, each taking you on a different path.

Why Technical Support Matters

There is a long legacy of personal computing history that illustrates the growing need for technical support. Way back in 1976, on April 1 for that matter, a small company called Apple created what is widely regarded as the first Personal Computer, or PC.

Despite the fact that all computers used by people are technically Personal Computers, that's not how things worked out when it comes to terminology. When most people talk about a *PC,* they are referring to a computer running Microsoft's Windows operating system. The term PC was popularized by IBM, which produced the IBM PC line of computers that ran PC DOS to compete in the nascent personal computer market. To the contrary, if it's an Apple product, then it's a *Mac.* For sheer nerdliness, when discussing Linux, the popular open source operating system, the machines are usually called *Linux Boxes.*

A whole new world

The Apple I was popular among the technical people of the time, but Apple's market share really exploded with the Apple][line, which became popular in homes and in schools. IBM was more popular on the business end of the market, because companies knew and respected the IBM name. Apple, in turn, eschewed the strict business orientation of IBM's PC and pushed the development of easy-to-use computer software that was attractive. The late '70s and early

'80s bore a vast number of different platforms, most popularly the Atari line, Radio Shack's own Tandy line, the ridiculously popular Commodore C64, Texas Instrument's TI 99/4a, and Sinclair's ZX line, all of which, except Apple and the IBM PC, were wiped out.

In 1984, Apple unleashed the Macintosh on the market. A radically different computer, the Mac used a mouse to move icons around a virtual desktop. Instead of typing cryptic commands, users pointed and clicked to make the computer act. In 1985, the Apple Writer hit the market and fostered a mass movement for desktop publishing. Due to its ease of use compared to the IBM PCs of the day, popular applications like Aldus's PageMaker, the new printer, and a graphical environment, Apple established the Macintosh as a computer for design and creative types.

In the meantime, IBM's PC compatibility standard was pushing all other competitors out of the marketplace. Manufacturers who were building computers to support other standards started getting in line with IBM as they saw the writing on the wall. Apple had already set its well-forged path and was strong enough to avoid getting on the IBM bandwagon, but the only maker of significant market share remaining was the plucky little Amiga. Sadly, Amiga was unable to continue pushing the envelope with technological advances and was pushed out of the market by 1996.

By 1997, however, Apple was in trouble, steadily losing market share to IBM and the clone makers Dell, HP, Compaq, Packard Bell, and many others. The clone market dramatically pushed down part costs through vigorous competition to produce the latest and greatest while remaining compatible with the PC standard. Apple was on the ropes with machines that were far more expensive and lacked compatibility with the IBM standard. It looked like IBM, with Microsoft Windows and IBM's own OS/2 (which lasted until 2001 with the release of OS/2 Warp 4.52) designed specifically for business and was compatible with Windows programs, was winning.

Apple's then CEO, Gil Amelio, turned to previously ousted Steve Jobs in an attempt to get his advanced NeXT operating system for a new generation of Apple Macintosh computers. In a twist best served by various biographies, Amelio was pushed out, Jobs was brought back in as iCEO, and NeXT was absorbed into Apple. Jobs then went on a spring cleaning event, clearing much of what he deemed useless from the projects roster, and pushed for Apple to renew its presence in the computer market. The result of his and others efforts was the iMac, released in 1998, a colorful little all-in-one that would mark an enormous shift in personal computing history.

Apple had, in one fell swoop, pronounced that beige was out, candy colors were in, and if you wanted to be cool, you would never go beige. The move from beige as default component color would not, however, really take hold until the release of Mac OS X in 2001 that would start the fundamental change at Apple, and thus in the rest of the PC industry. On the IBM PC front, however, it was business as usual, though competition for advancement wasn't lacking. Those changes, however, were more technical than esthetic. AMD, a former subcontractor for Intel, started out on its own and began marketing competing CPUs, the heart of any PC.

AMD had already started to make x86 CPU clones back in 1991, but in 1996, the company unveiled its K5 processor. The K stood for Kryptonite, the only substance that could harm Superman, which in this case was Intel. AMD

(continued)

(continued)

was first to develop a mass-produced 64-bit CPU, but Intel quickly followed with its own, and the Intel Pentium was a hard product name to beat. AMD never did overtake Intel as CPU market leader, but it remains a staple of low-end systems and a favorite of so-called over-clockers.

By the mid-2000s, most IBM PC clone makers had been absorbed into the big cloners, such as Dell and HP. Even HP took over Compaq, and Packard Bell went bust in the United States, mostly over very poor reliability and technical support issues. Japanese PC makers were also flooding the market with innovative new designs and lower price points, among them Sony, Acer, and Toshiba. By this time, Windows was considered the de facto desktop standard with the very popular Windows XP, and even IBM's OS/2 was now gone. It was no longer a fight for hardware, but the operating system, and the only two standing were now Microsoft's Windows and Apple's Mac OS X.

Then something remarkable happened. While Intel and AMD were fighting it out on the PC side, Apple was fighting with IBM and Motorola over advancing development of the PowerPC

CPU, the core of Apple's Macintosh computers. The PowerPC was running too hot and could be sufficiently cooled only in Apple's hot new PowerMac Pro towers, all aluminum towers packed with power for the creative types that loved Mac OS X's ease of use and designer-centric interface language. Apple wanted to put faster CPUs into its laptops and desktop systems, but it had no way to keep them from burning to a crisp.

It was at this point Apple decided that in order to stay in the market and not have to close shop, it would do something unheard of. Apple changed its entire lineup to run on Intel's x86 CPU architecture and dumped the PowerPC. In a way, Apple had done this before. It had killed off the 68k line to move to the more powerful PowerPC chips, and it was one of the smoothest transitions in computing history. This time, the transition wouldn't go quite as smoothly, but in the end, all Apple products now run on Intel-based chips, just like PCs running Windows. Contrary to theories at the time, however, Apple still licenses Mac OS X to run only on Apple computers and only using approved hardware components.

Heads in the Clouds

Aside from a number of watershed events in the last decade, such as the advent of the iPod and iPhone, the precipitous rise and fall of the netbook market, the surprise dominance of Apple iPad, and the long and hard push by Google to crack and ultimately dominate the mobile phone market, only one thing has taken hold and likely won't let go: ease of use. Computers of all kinds are everywhere. People carry them around in the form of laptops, tablets, and smartphones. People use them at ATMs, in cars, in airports, and in other places. Computers guide humans via GPS, show them TV and movies in the living room, and protect homes and offices. Computers are every-where, and the differences between Windows and Mac OS X are getting less important.

Back in the day, it was all about the applications. Now it's all about access to tools on the Internet. Millions upon millions of people use Gmail, Yahoo!, and MSN for email, Twitter and Facebook for social networking, and the Internet in general for all manner of information, shopping, banking, and whatnot. People use the Internet on phones and tablets, too, and even on some watches and in their eyes via Google Glass. Business cannot operate without access to the Internet, and countless productivity services are available for all manner of business operations. If you take away the Internet from people, they generally start to complain rather quickly. The Internet has become an indispensable tool in their daily lives.

With the growth of Mozilla's Firefox and Google's Chrome web browsers that run on Windows, Mac OS X, Linux, and other less popular operating systems, the OS you use has become unimportant. That means that it doesn't really matter whether you use a Mac or a PC for the most part. Certain applications are still exclusive to either Windows or Mac OS X, but most of the big programs are made for both, including Microsoft's own Office. Compatibility is not really much of an issue any more, but the platforms remain different enough to warrant cross-training for technical support staff.

Why Companies Care about Technical Support

The history of the personal computer market speaks for itself when determining why companies care about technical support, but the reasons are far more nuanced than just a collection of market shifts. Technical support started very early in the PC market. Back in the 1970s and early '80s, there was no history for people using technology. If a company wanted users to be happy with its products, everything had to be documented and described, and in many cases, support had to be offered.

Companies care about technical support for a number of reasons, most of which revolve around the bottom line. Without satisfied customers or employees who can perform work, companies aren't left with much to generate revenue from, such as working products or people to create them.

It behooves any company to provide comprehensive support to users inside and out. This seems like a great time to list those reasons:

- ✔ **Providing a sense of security:** Companies do well when their users and customers feel like they can go somewhere to get help when needed. Not everyone is a technical genius, and it's nice to know that someone can help out when problems arise.

✔ **Guaranteeing consistency:** When offering consumers a product, it helps to keep as many of them as happy as possible. When managing internal systems, it helps to make sure everything is working as expected and meets all requirements of IT policies.

✔ **Keeping a close watch on bugs:** No developer likes to offer broken software to users, and a crack technical support team is key to keeping close tabs on any bugs. Watching trends through ticketing systems helps establish a form of triage for issues to be fixed.

✔ **Acting as a another conduit for customer service:** Technical support is one of the primary faces of any company that provides products or services to consumers, and, as such, companies must provide customer services that please consumers.

✔ **Providing customer satisfaction statistics:** A helpdesk is a perfect source for collecting information about how customers feel about both services and products offered by a company. Never waste an opportunity to gather statistical data; just try not to annoy paying customers.

Having a solid understanding of these principles will help guide you on your quest. Having a good 10,000 foot view of how companies view IT operations is critical to understanding why companies make decisions about how IT is used to forward a company's needs and wants. Ultimately, everything a company does reflects the need to generate revenue. It will serve you well to remember that.

The IT Help Desk Job Market

You are looking at joining one of the most stable and consistent growth industries on the planet. Information Technology lives at the core of almost every business on Earth. Literally billions of computers are in the hands of people every day, and massive networks crisscross the globe, providing the backbone of the Internet. As these computers get smaller and the networks get faster, there needs to be a standing nerd army to make it all work.

While development and cloud-computing represent the two hottest segments of the IT job market, there will always be a need for technical support. According to the Bureau of Labor Statistics, annual pay rates range from $48,900 for computer support specialists to $79,680 for computer systems analysts, and 123,000 positions will be added by 2022. As it stands, there are 722,400 people in computer support specialist positions in the United States. Here's how salaries break down in detail:

✔ Lowest 10 percent: $34,930

✔ Lower 25 percent: $44,530

✔ Median: $59,090

✔ Upper 25 percent: $76,450

✔ Highest 10 percent: $96,850

IT help desk jobs are important to corporate America as a whole for several reasons:

✔ **Rapid growth:** Like other IT positions, IT help desk positions are grow-ing at double digits and are one of the biggest growth sectors in the stag-nant American job market.

✔ **Rapid change:** The skills needed for IT help desk positions are chang-ing at an outrageous pace. Not only are new gadgets, software, and SaaS products announced on a regular basis, Windows, Mac OS X, and Linux are improving rapidly, and new technologies are being introduced a few times a year.

✔ **High turnover:** As with many service-based job categories, IT has a lot of turnover. People move from one job to another because they get an offer for better pay, get to work with technologies they prefer, get the opportunity to work with newer technologies, get better perks or a cooler workplace environment, or want to work with certain people. People also move from internal to external help desk positions, take on freelance work, or take a job with a consulting agency.

✔ **Prospecting:** While it's not exactly awesome, some headhunters and HR departments like to ping people for non-existent positions, just to get a sense of what kind of draw they can command. It is what it is. Just be aware that because a job is posted doesn't mean there's an opportunity on the other end.

Two, Two, Two Career Paths in One!

IT is such a complex field that even the career directions you can choose from are complicated! Take the Red Pill, and you are magically transported to the external help desk. Take the Blue Pill, and you inexplicably appear on the internal help desk. While both these paths are all about engineers helping users with technical stuff, they are fundamentally different from each other.

External help desk

Your company, MacroFirm Systems, makes CompuFriend, an application that turns users' computers into best friends. The help desk here is provided as a resource to users of CompuFriend. The users you assist will not be located in your office, so you will spend most of your time helping people by using a phone, a ticketing system, email, online chat, or even remote access.

Aside from the work-a-day tasks you perform assisting users with CompuFriend over the phone or in online chat, all the while updating support tickets, you fulfill other job requirements. You may be tasked with combing through old tickets to find helpful solutions to add to the knowledge base. You may investigate problems with software license piracy.

Internal help desk

Your company, Swanky Media Partners, is an advertising agency that creates campaigns for a number of important clients. This help desk is available only for the use of company employees of SMP. The users you assist will be located in the Swanky offices and a few satellite locations that are securely connected to the home office.

When you help users, you will sometimes answer questions over the phone or through email, but you will mostly assist them at their desks. Some companies use some form of service ticket management system, but they will mostly be seen only by the engineers who create them on behalf of the users. Aside from dealing with user problems or questions, you may also manage servers, update passwords, test and install application patches, create accounts and configure systems for new users, and manage company assets, among many other possible tasks.

The difference

In this example, the external help desk is outward facing and is generally dedicated to CompuFriend's users. In fact, MacroFirm even has its own internal IT help desk that deals only with internal systems. Engineers who work the external help desk help only users of the software that MacroFirm makes but not users inside MacroFirm. External help desk engineers spend the majority of their time supporting users of the product.

Swanky's internal help desk's engineers wear a number of different hats and perform a number of different jobs during the typical day. Swanky, as an advertising agency, has users that use Windows for administration, HR, and in IT, but it also has lots of Mac OS X systems for all of the creative people and to handle creative asset pipeline management. Swanky even has a small A/V (audio/visual) studio in its home office, all of which runs on Mac OS X.

Deciphering Job Titles

When considering a job in IT help desk, it is clear that you need to make a choice early on as to the direction you will take. Certain roles are common to the IT Help desk. While I describe the generic elements of the roles here, you might want to look to Chapter 2 where you can walk in the shoes of various engineers and see how they work on a day-to-day basis.

As you rifle through the job listings on Monster, craigslist, or any of the other dozens of job sites on the Internet, you will see a lot of different names for what looks like the same job. They can be cryptic, but all you need is the key. Table 1-1 can help you figure out what the job titles really mean.

Table 1-1	Deciphering Job Titles
Placement in Job Title	*Potential Terms*
Optional	Junior or senior
First	Desktop or help desk
Second	Can sometimes include support
Third	Technician, engineer, analyst, or specialist

You get the idea. Various companies use their own title variations, but they all generally mean the same thing. The key is in the first term of the title.

- ✔ If it's a *desktop* position, then it will most likely be for an internal help desk role.

- ✔ If it's a *help desk* position, then it will most likely be for an external help desk role.

Following that, the second term of the job title is generally optional, but you will see the word *support* on some ads. The third term, however, is generally interchangeable when coupled with the desktop or help desk terms. Here are some examples taken from Table 1-1:

- ✔ Junior desktop analyst
- ✔ Help desk support engineer
- ✔ Desktop support specialist

Unless you have senior-grade skills, it's not a good idea to apply for a *senior* position. Check the job description to see what the company is really looking for and don't base your impressions on the title alone. Check as many ads as possible. Even check ads that have titles that are peripherally appropriate. You never know. You may just find a hidden gem.

What You'll Need to Get an IT Help Desk Job

The IT industry is something of a mixed bag of nuts when it comes to job requirements. Aside from the countless positions and job titles, you must know a vast array of tools, services, platforms, and disciplines. Fortunately, these disciplines are typically divided into smaller, easier-to-manage chunks, so you can focus your studies.

Studies don't necessarily require attending college, either, but I strongly urge you to consider getting your degree. As I'm sure you've heard many times, people with a college degree make, on average, $1 million more during their lifetime.

Then, the question becomes how you get there and what you need to know in order to make it happen.

Swimming in Acronym Soup

Technology is full of all kinds of interesting and confusing lingo. It can almost seem like a completely alien form of English at times. You should know several acronyms that are associated with technical skills, and many are used for certifications, such as MCSE, CNE, A+, and so on. You may know some terms like USB, SD, or CEO, but even if you do, you are probably not aware of many others.

It's important to understand that being a nerd does not mean knowing all acronyms, but Table 1-2 lists a few acronyms you'll want to know.

I'm not kidding when I say "some." There are hundreds more acronyms, and for all manner of technologies. It's rather overwhelming, to be honest, but it's not impossible to navigate. As you scan through ads, you will see these and other acronyms. Do your best to make yourself familiar with many of these certifications and make sure to carefully read the ads as you seek work.

Of course, I'm just touching the tip of the iceberg here. I dig deep into certifications in Chapter 5.

Table 1-2	Acronyms to Know
Acronym	*What It Stands For*
MCP	Microsoft Certified Professional
MCSE	Microsoft Certified Systems Engineer
MCDST	Microsoft Certified Desktop Support Technician
MOS	Microsoft Office Specialist
CCA	Citrix Certified Administrator
RHCT	Red Hat Certified Technician
CCNP	Cisco Certified Network Professional
CHDP	Certified Help Desk Professional
CHDM	Certified Help Desk Manager
CFST	Certified Field Service Technician
ACSP	Apple Certified Support Professional
A+	CompTIA's basic systems knowledge certification (good to have)

Chapter 2

A Day in the Life of a Help Desk Engineer

*O*ne of the downsides of getting a new job is that you've never done it before. Sure, you know how to work with technology, but this is a *new* job. No matter how much experience you actually have, you will have never experienced this new position. Experience is, after all, one of the legendary chicken or the egg questions of all time. In order to get a job, you need experience, but you can get experience only from a job.

Or can you?

Technology is a fundamentally different subject than almost anything else on the planet. Unlike most skills, you can translate your personal experience with technology into a well-paying job. Try getting a $50,000 entry-level job as a cook, a mechanic, or a hair dresser. You'll have to work your way up, which will take years. The IT help desk is a fantastic place to use your existing experience on a real job where you can quickly and efficiently learn all new technologies, all of which give you a leg up as you move up in the industry.

You can do a lot to develop an awareness of what work will be like, but not much is more effective than going for a kind of virtual ride-along, which is what I give you in this chapter. This chapter certainly isn't the only help you'll get from this book, but I believe it will be a huge hand up for you to get a real sense of what a day in the life of a nerd-for-hire is like.

So, What's the Plan?

In this chapter, through the magic of the printed word, I transport you into three positions to grant you some of the experience of working in each role. Think of this chapter as an out-of-body experience without all of the hard work of becoming enlightened.

As you can likely imagine, not every day will be exactly like the days covered here. These are meant to give you a clear idea of a generic day in the life of the three roles I cover here: the desktop engineer, the consultant, and the help desk representative.

One of these will feel familiar or comfortable to you, and that will help you understand the path you will take. Don't stop here, though! You'll definitely want to look to Chapter 3 to get a better understanding of why starting in the IT help desk is an excellent choice for advancement in your chosen career.

Day 1: The Systems Analyst

You work at Swanky Media Productions, an advertising agency. Your official job title is systems analyst, but you may as well be Lord of All Technology as you find yourself working on a seemingly endless cascade of tasks and problems. The scope of your work is widely varied. Your superiors will likely assign your tasks based on your proven ability to deliver and your word. So, when asked whether you know something, be honest.

Good morning!

Wake up, sleepy head! It's time to get up and get ready to go to work. At Swanky, they don't have a tight dress code, but you can't go to work without taking good care of yourself. Your appearance, even under a lax dress code, will be important, so you can't slack off (even when you look like a slacker).

You head out in order to arrive at work ahead of your scheduled start time of 9 a.m.

Checking in: Part I

Traffic was kind to you this morning, and you made it in at 8:50 a.m. You head up to the IT office, tap your Dr. Who bobble head (it's the eleventh doctor), fire up your desktop system, and log in.

Swanky's HR department demands tracking time for all employees, so you log in to the time-tracking system and check in for the day. You then fire up your mail client — the office standard is Microsoft Outlook 2011 — and check your email. You have a few pieces you'll need to look at, but you have something else to do first.

Punching tickets

The first thing you do every morning is check tickets.

Swanky's IT department switched from a local ticketing system to a Software as a Service (SaaS) solution back in 2010, so you fire up Google Chrome and log in to your Zendesk account to check for any new tickets. There are three, but they have already been assigned. You check on two tickets that have already been closed without a resolution to see whether anything can be done to resolve them, but nothing new presents a solution. You send an email to your supervisor requesting additional information from the development team in hopes of providing a fix.

It's nice to be thorough, though. That's when the phone rings.

Oh, my copier!

Marty from the Finance department has called, and he needs help getting a new copier installed. You tell Marty that you will be over shortly and hang up. All hardware installations are supposed to be approved by IT and go through a detailed process to make sure that the selected product meets the needs of the target department, that the IT department can support it, and that the bean counters will actually pay for it. You didn't know about the new copier, so you need to clear up that detail first.

You walk the few steps over to your manager's office and, because the door is open, pop your head in. "I just got a call from Marty in Finance that he has a new copier," you say.

Linda peeks over the top of her three-screen setup that dominates her desk and is the envy of all IT nerds. "Oh, yes. That was processed and is all good, but I forgot to mention it. Can you handle that?" she asks.

This is one of those times when you will succeed or fail, and failure is not an option. You can choose to tell her "no problem" and go do it, or you can say, "I've never worked on those before" and get some help. You opt for a third option. "I'm not sure. Which model is it?" you ask.

"It's just another Xerox WorkCentre 7845," she replies.

"Ah, no problem then. I've got this," you say, relieved. As part of the IT team, you have helped to install two dozen of these in the offices and now know them rather well.

You head on over to Finance, check in with Marty, verify that the copier is there and is as expected, and create a new install ticket using your mobile phone. You then spend the next two hours getting it all set up, plugged in, added to the network using the correct subnet set aside for printers and copiers. You make sure that it's updated, verify that the driver for Windows systems is on the IT file server, and help a handful of users get connected.

Before you're done, however, Bruce calls you over and tells you that he cannot find the new copier. You take his seat and start to process through the issue. You discover that his Windows desktop is a PITA (a Pain In The A**) that, despite being correctly configured, still refuses to see the copier on the network. Because Bruce is a technophobe, you avoid discussing the details and manually add the copier to the available list, verify that drivers are installed, and set the new copier as the default for Bruce so that he doesn't have to figure out how to select it.

Lunch break!

The morning was busy and involved an unexpected installation, but you were on the job. Lunch ends up being uninteresting, however, as you take it at your desk. Lunch at your desk allows you the time needed to process every-thing required to close out the copier install, though. In between bites of your sandwich, you update the installation ticket, add the new copier's serial number and install date to the asset tracking spreadsheet, and add a note to Linda that an update to the copier drivers is available in Zendesk. Any new drivers need to be tested to make sure that nothing breaks before they are pushed into production.

While you are at it, you also create and close a quick ticket for helping Bruce and answer a few emails from the morning. As you work on these items alone, the other IT team members move in and out, each working on their own items. You mention the new copier installed in Finance, and the other team members ask you about other things. It's a loose but seamless exchange of information that helps keep everyone up-to-date on the goings-on inside Swanky.

Checking in: Part 2

Because you were working while eating lunch, you never checked out. You don't need to check back in, but you do make a note in your timesheet that you took a working lunch. If you don't, HR gets a little weird, so it's best to take the minute required to update your timesheet.

A tale of two locations

You get a call from Cassandra who is located in one of the satellite offices. She's not seeing all of the typefaces available on the font server and is on deadline to get a project done. You could hop in your car and drive the 30 minutes it would take to get there, but that would be a waste of time. Instead, you remotely access her computer from your desktop system and take a look.

It turns out that all creative users at the satellite office are having the same problem and that the font server probably needs a reboot. The satellite office uses older equipment and some consumer electronics instead of enterprise-grade gear, and, despite complaints from the IT department, approval hasn't yet been given to upgrade the site. Because much of the satellite's systems are not standardized, the office experiences more frequent outages.

The reboot of the font server doesn't fix the problem, so you ask Cassandra to alert the office that it will be without Internet access for up to five minutes while you restart the router, an old Linksys. Cassandra tells you that most people are out to lunch and that the ones still in the office are prepared, so you process the restart of the router from the remote web-based administration page.

After a few minutes, you are able to log back into the router admin page and verify that Internet access has been restored. You then log back into Cassandra's desktop, check Internet access, open a terminal and ping the font server, and then check to make sure that the missing typefaces are now accessible. Everything seems to work. Cassandra thanks you, and you hang up. You then create and close a service ticket for the incident in Zendesk.

Taking stock

After all the immediate fires are either being extinguished by others or are already out, you have some time to catch up on some of the ongoing projects. One of the least interesting is the computer monitor asset update. In the earlier days of the company, only computers were cataloged, but the bean counters want to keep track of all assets, so monitors were added to the asset-tracking requirements.

Almost as fun as it sounds, it's time for you to hit the floors and add some more monitors to the asset-tracking list. You have already collected around 80 serial numbers, but you are far from done. Because all PC gear in Swanky is Dell, all you need is the serial number and service tag. To complicate things, you also need to collect the serial number of the computer system the PC is connected to so that the users can be identified as having been allocated that complete system.

It's not entertaining or interesting or even challenging, but it must be done, so you do it.

Maintenance and such

After collecting another 30 monitors for asset tracking, you must move on to a few other things before the day comes to a close. While it used to be a huge issue, nowadays setting up new systems for new employees is a simple affair. Instead of spending a few hours on each system to manually configure them, you can now attach a new system to the imaging system, boot up the imager, and copy a ready-to-eat, out-of-the-box system directly to the hardware in 15 minutes.

You can connect two systems at a time and have six machines to prepare: two Windows machines, one iMac, and three Apple MacBook Pro systems. You get the key to secure storage from Linda, check out the needed systems, log their serial numbers and other details in asset tracking, and trolley them over to the workbench. You unbox them one at a time, placing sticky notes on each with the name of the intended user and where in the office they will be located (each desk has a floor and location ID matched with Ethernet access and power) and plugging them in.

While two are imaging at one time, you create installation tickets for each one in Zendesk and hand the check-out sheet to Linda for verification. Total time to image six machines is about an hour and twenty minutes, including time to document them and make sure everything is neatly labeled. You are all set to start installing the desktop systems when Kathy shows up and asks whether you need help. What luck! You split up the machines, install them, and leave a Welcome packet on each desk with the name of the new employee in large, black letters on the cover page on each keyboard.

Documentation master

The day is coming to a close and you've performed a lot of tasks, but you aren't done yet. To close out each day, you check to make sure that you have closed tickets for all new and completed tasks for the day and that you don't have any new emails waiting that need answers. You hop into the internal

Wiki to update the documentation for copier installation to include a walk-through of the manual connection you had to perform on Bruce's machine. It may be that all engineers know how to do it, but it never hurts to have the process documented in case someone new has never done it.

Checking out

That's it. You finish your last Coke for the day and check out in your timesheet. It's time to head home, play some CS:GO or Team Fortress 2, drink a beer, and go to sleep, only to wake up the next day to do it all over again.

Day 2: The Consulting Magician

In this example, you work for NifTech Consultants as a systems engineer. You do have a desk, but most of your time is spent at client sites where you perform various tasks. You are a consultant, and your services are sold to companies who do not have their own internal IT department. Much like the last job, you will be asked to wear many hats, but you will wear them in many different places, possibly in a single day.

Wake up!

Ah. Morning again. It's nice to wake up after a refreshing night's sleep, have a quick breakfast, shower, and get gussied up for a day of work.

Some consultancies offer uniforms to their engineers, but NifTech is not one of them. NifTech is one of the old school consultancies that morphed into a Managed Services Provider (MSP) in the mid-2000s, but some of the old ideals have stuck. As such, you must wear a button-down shirt and a tie, slacks, and nice shoes.

The daily standup

You arrive at the office at 8:10 a.m. in time to grab the last donut and get a cup of coffee when the meeting starts. Every morning starts with a quick meeting where the dispatcher and General Manager (GM) check with all engineers to see where things are at. Because work as a consultant is fluid and dynamic, the assignments can change all the time, all dependent on client needs.

Because problems are worked on in the field, this is not the place to tell your GM that you have issues left unsolved from the day before. The general rule is that if you can't figure out what the problem is or identify a possible solution in 15 minutes, you need to get some outside perspective. This is when you call the dispatcher and ask for assistance from anyone who is available.

Right now, however, it's time to hit the road.

Getting assignments

Of course, you get the roadblock. The dispatcher calls you out at the end of the standup and asks you to head over to The School sometime today to deal with some indeterminate issues. The dispatcher already knows that you have regular visits scheduled for The Office and LA Law, so he asks you to evaluate the circumstances before heading out so that he can communicate with the other clients as needed.

The triage game

After you receive your assignments, you just need to figure out how quickly The School needs you, so you sit down at your desk, look up the number on your mobile phone, and call them. Sally answers the phone.

"Sally, good morning. This is [INSERT NAME] from NifTech. I understand you're having a problem," you ask (friendly, identifying, and to the point).

"Oh, yes! Thank you for calling. We're having a problem with the projector down in the auditorium. There's a presentation at 11 a.m., and we can't get it to work," she says.

"I understand. I'll be over within the hour," you soothe.

Now that you have determined that the issue is urgent, you head over to the dispatcher and inform him that he may need to inform the other clients that you may be delayed. The only thing left before you leave is to walk through the possible problems, so you will be prepared.

The projector is attached to the ceiling, so it's operated by remote control. There is a rolling platform at the school, so you already have a way to reach the actual projector. Because Sally didn't say what the actual problem was, it consumes time to ask, and nontechnical people should not be imposed upon to determine the cause of issues outside of their expertise, you just have to figure out what it may be and have what you need in case.

So, it could be the remote needs batteries, so you take four AAA and four AA batteries from the store room. It could also be the lamp, so you collect a replacement from The School's part shelf in the store room (noting it in inventory, of course). Because the computers connect to the projector over the network, it could be the Ethernet cable, so you take a spare with you, just in case.

Client 1: Getting schooled

You arrive at 9:40 a.m. and clock into The School's time log from your mobile phone. You head over to the office to check in with Sally, who is pleased to see you, and you head directly over to the auditorium. Sally, at your request, will inform Mr. Slump that you are working on the problem in case he wants to stop by. That ends up not being necessary because he is already in the auditorium.

"Good morning, Mr. Slump," you call out. Leaning over a small folding table with a laptop open on its surface, he grumbles, pecks at a few keys, and then looks up. Nothing happens.

"This darn thing isn't working," he exclaims, gesturing at the projector.

"I understand, sir. I'd be glad to take a look at it," you say calmly. You drop your bag at the foot of the table, grab a nearby folding chair, and sit down. You then unpack your laptop, a notepad, and pen and then start pulling out the bits you brought. You do them one at a time, calling out what they are for each one.

"AA and AAA batteries . . . an Ethernet cable . . . a replacement bulb for the projector," you say. You use this as a way to indicate to the client that there is nothing to be worried about and that you have thought of everything. Mr. Slump isn't impressed.

"How long will this take?" he demands, making a point of looking at my chair while you're looking at him as if to suggest you're being lazy.

"Oh, not long. I should have a good idea of what the problem is in a few minutes. Certainly no more than 15," you respond cheerfully, opening your laptop and logging in.

First things first, you check to see whether the projector is on. A power light is located on the back. You can see that it is on and is glowing green. Just to be sure, you press and hold the Power button on the remote. As it should, the light turns red after a few seconds. You press Power again, and after a few seconds, it turns green again. Power is not the issue.

"We have a very important meeting this morning, and it will reflect poorly on you if we have to move it because of this stupid thing," Mr. Slump spits.

"It won't be much longer, sir. It looks like I've almost got it," you respond neatly.

At your laptop, you start a console session, and, after consulting the client's technical documentation, you ping the projector's IP address on the network. It is responding. You then try logging into the projector's web-based administration panel, and that works just fine. An alert in the projector dashboard tells you that the bulb is burnt out, so now you know what the problem is.

"Well, there it is. The bulb has burnt out and needs to be replaced," you state.

"Oh great," Mr. Slump exclaims. "How long will that take? I don't think we have any." You ignore this outburst and hold up the replacement lamp you brought along.

"Won't take long at all," you say.

Lunch break!

After having worked on a few other issues and logging them in ConnectWise so that they can be correctly billed to the client, you leave The School just before lunch time. Because you drive your own car on all calls, you also log the mileage from the office to The School. As is standard practice, only distance *to* the client is billed for, though some consultancies do pay engineers for the time they are on the road.

You stop at a local burger shop and have lunch while updating the technical documentation to The School so that other engineers know when the projector's lamp was last changed and to indicate that the remote uses two AA batteries. Once done, you head out so that you can get to the next client on time.

Client 2: The Office (Hint: It's not a sitcom)

The Office is a regular client who you are scheduled to visit two days a week. Normally, you take the first half of the morning, but the call at The School shifted things. Fortunately, the dispatcher called both The Office and LA Law to inform them that you would be arriving later. Because you visit both sites regularly, you have no outstanding issues to deal with at either site.

After checking in on ConnectWise and entering mileage from the burger shop to The Office, you start working on your tasks. You do a walkthrough of the entire office, around 50 users, checking in with everyone not talking on the phone to see how things are. Nothing is out of sorts, so you head back to the server room and your little desklet to perform some more work on the replacement mail server configuration. The handoff to the new Exchange server isn't scheduled for another month, but it's easier to have everything in place well in advance.

You wrap things up in no time and check out to move on to the next client.

Client 3: LA Law

The law offices of LA Law are located in LA, and they practice law. LA Law offices are particular in that they use legal software and have additional strictures for the security of client and legal documents. As such, you are required to produce additional documentation about your activities when checked in at LA Law.

Despite these differences, the process at LA Law is much the same as The Office. You check in with everyone who is available at their desks and in offices. LA Law is a little larger than The Office and has around 70 employees. Again, nothing is out of sorts, so you move on to your other tasks. Again.

LA Law has been growing for the past few years and has projected that it will have 100 employees and lawyers in the next year, so it is starting an in-house IT department. As part of your tasks, you are preparing a wide range of documentation and guides so that the nascent IT team can take over in as short a period as possible.

In the meantime, you are still required to perform all duties that LA Law contracts from NifTech, so the hand-off work is in addition to your other duties. In fact, you have two machines that you need to prepare for new employees. You begin to prepare these machines when you receive a call.

Emergency!

Another client has no Internet service, and the engineer on site is having trouble getting it working again. Because your duties today are established, you are frequently called on to help with problems that pop up, just like at The School this morning. Before heading out, you explain the situation to your contact at LA Law and let her know to call the dispatcher if anything happens.

You time out of LA Law in ConnectWise and head over to the other client site. You check in when you arrive and open the service ticket created by the other engineer. After you confer with her, it is decided that she will keep working on the network aspect of the problem, and you will contact the ISP (Internet Service Provider) to see whether the problem is on its end. You will also take notes and assist as necessary.

Between the two of you, you discover that it is, indeed, the ISP's issue and start working on a solution. Because you are on-site and able to provide detailed information to the ISP's techs, you are able to get the issue resolved quickly. In this case, you act as a proxy for the client and communicate with service providers for them. While the client pays for your time, it doesn't pay you for the service.

This situation makes it all the more important to treat the service providers with respect and patience, even if they don't offer you the same courtesy. Ultimately, it is the client's decision if it will change service providers, but as long as you always take the high road, your opinion will always hold more weight.

All done

The day is done. All regular clients have been visited and verified stable, and all emergency calls have been handled to the satisfaction of the clients. You have documented all of your billable time and have leveraged your resources when the need was present.

Day 3: The Help Desk Rep

In this example, you work for MacroFirm, the makers of the popular CompuFriend application. In your new position as senior support representative, you are the team leader for a handful of junior representatives. It's your job to help your charges help users with Tier I issues and to take on Tier II issues that are escalated to your ticket queue.

Sleeping in

What a great day! Because you don't have to go to work until noon, you get to sleep in. Of course, that doesn't leave you much time in the evening to have personal time, but you also don't get home really late at night, either. Your shift runs from noon until 8:30 p.m., and it's this staggered shift arrangement that allows MacroFirm to offer 24/7/365 support with different teams.

Tickets for brunchfast?

Okay, so it's not breakfast because you eat around 11 a.m., but it is your first meal of the day. Like your first meal, the first thing you do when you clock in at MacroFirm is to start checking on your ticket queue. In an external technical support environment, the ticket queue is the lifeblood of the operation. In most cases, tickets are automatically created by customers when they fill out a form on the website or start a support chat.

The only time you create tickets for users is when they call in for support. Of course, because most technical support teams are broken out into teams that cover specific areas of support, it's generally easy to create new tickets. CompuFriend offers both monthly and annual rates and has versions for consumers and businesses, so the default organizational split is between public and corporate support teams, though billing support is shared between the two.

You work for the Windows technical support team on the consumer side of the operation.

Taking the call

Not long after you clock in and have a quick standup with your team, you get a call transferred in from sales. The customer used an old trick to bypass long wait times for standard support and went directly to sales. Because sales usually has much shorter hold times, some people use this trick as a way to get to technical support without having to wait. Not many people do this trick, however, so it is tolerated. The call was transferred to you because your team is occupied and has individual wait times of more than 45 minutes. After you have verified that he is a valid customer, you proceed to helping him.

"As I said before, I just paid for your CompuFriend thing and can't get it installed. This software is terrible, and I hate it," the customer says.

"I'm sorry you're having trouble with the installation process," you reply, ignoring the inflammatory comment. "Can you walk me through the steps you are taking?"

"I run the thing, and it gives me this scary dialog like it's a virus," says the customer curtly.

"I apologize, sir, but I'm new here, so if you could give me a step by step of what you've done so far, I'm sure I can help you out," I say, knowing that sometimes it helps to make the customer think they're helping you.

"Fine," he says.

After you've won some trust from the customer, he tells you everything he did. From his description, you are able to figure out what the problem is. He's up and running before you get off the phone. You create a ticket for the process, run through the required information, collect the required information, and give him a ticket number. Of course, the ticket is also sent to the customer via email because most people don't write the number down.

Support via Instant Message

Some people who need support and don't like to wait on the phone for an agent use the support chat offered by many companies. MacroFirm is one of those companies. As part of your job description, you monitor the chats of your team members so that you can help them perform their job with the least amount of overhead, while maintaining positive relations with customers.

In a standard technical support environment, a single engineer can support up to five customers at one time with minimal discomfort to the user. Existing support chat systems automatically create service tickets for users that engineers connect with and verify the validity of those customers, reducing the amount of time an engineer must spend on these aspects of the job.

Of course, it stands to reason that engineers should take on only as many clients as they feel they can effectively support at any one time, which is where you come in. If you feel that an engineer has bitten off more than he can chew, you can make note and talk with him when he's next available.

It goes without saying that, as a Tier II engineer, you will answer any questions that Tier I engineers have for you as they assist customers and take over any chats that require a more experienced engineer for resolution.

Tickets for snack

As a technical support technician for MacroFirm, most of your day is spent handling support for customers, and much of your work time is spent dealing with service tickets. It generally never ends because tickets are everything when it comes to providing resolution to issues for clients.

Lunch break!

Lunch is a time when you can unwind and take a break from the support grind. It's also a great time to catch up with your team or just to do some team-building. Support teams work better when the members of the team are comfortable with each other and don't feel shunned when asking questions or for assistance.

More tickets, please

When you get back from lunch, it's time for more tickets, emails, phone calls, and chat sessions. This is the standard day for a technical support engineer, and it does take some getting used to. You, however, do benefit from being a team leader in that you get to spend more time mentoring junior engineers and dealing with more advanced problems for customers.

You also get to do some cool things that your lesser counterparts don't.

Remote control magic

It's nearing the end of your day when you get a notification that another customer needs your help. This time, the customer is on the phone and has requested the help of a supervisor. This is when you're called into action. You take over the call in a hand-off procedure where you are on the line with both the customer and the junior engineer at the same time.

"Thank you, George. Hello, Mrs. Frail, I'm [INSERT NAME], and I'll be helping you from here," you say.

"Oh, thank you both so very much," she says. George is disconnected.

"I've looked over the details of your issue and would like to ask whether I can remotely access your computer," you say, once we are alone.

"Dear, you just do whatever it is you need to. I don't understand these things," she says.

"I understand, ma'am. What I'll be doing, with a little help from you, is to operate your computer from where I am. All you need to do is click a link and a button. Do you think you can help me with that, Mrs. Frail?" you ask.

"Yes, I think so."

After verifying that she receives email on that computer and sending her the link, you are able to gain remote access to her computer and help her install CompuFriend. Because it's the end of your day and the other shift has already started filtering in, you take a few extra minutes to help her log in to her account and add her family to her contacts.

The roundup corral

After you are all done for the day and before you clock out, you join up with your manager to talk about how the day went. This time is taken each day so that the process can be improved and employees can be regularly evaluated. CompuFriend is the lifeblood of MacroFirm, and if it goes unsupported, it will stop making money. In order to mitigate any losses due to poor customer support, the company employs support engineers to make sure that customers are kept happy and (yes, this is cynical) paying.

This time is also the opportunity to talk about your team and its strengths and weaknesses. You and your manager will be able to discuss and employ methods to improve things or leverage your methods for the benefit of other teams.

Signing off

Your day is over, and you're heading home. It's time to goof off, catch a movie, drop into the bar with a few friends for drinks, or just read a good book.

How's That Sound?

I know that outlining the day of an external technical support engineer isn't all that exciting, but it remains one possibility when seeking work as an IT help desk engineer. You balance the things that you want to do with the positions that are available in your area and take the best possible job with the best possible company. That is, in effect, how it all works.

Chapter 3

Why Starting at the Help Desk Is an Awesome Choice

In This Chapter

▶ Getting to know the U.S. job market

▶ Understanding the nuances of making your own opportunity

▶ Discovering how to make your mark, protect yourself, and expand your horizons

*O*ne of the questions people will likely ask themselves is "Where can I go from here?" I answer this excellent question in this chapter. For individuals interested in IT as a career path, starting at the help desk is a great way to develop a real foundation in how IT departments work and how businesses use technology.

IT is really the core of almost all business done in the world today. As a member of the IT department, you will not only build up your technical skill, but you will also learn much about how the industry your company operates in works.

In this chapter, I answer the question about where you can go in IT, but I also describe a number of the raw components you will need to see your goals from 10,000 feet. While all of these ideals are covered in much greater detail throughout this book, I feel you will benefit from the following summaries so that you can see the forest for the trees.

What the Bureau of Labor Statistics Has to Say about All This IT Stuff

There may not be a lot of love for the U.S. government these days, but it is really good at one thing: collecting statistics. The Bureau of Labor Statistics, or BLS, is a government agency that tracks how people work in the

United States of America, and that information is ridiculously detailed — so much so, that you can trace the rise and fall of almost any kind of job.

Figures 3-1 and 3-2 are two charts from the BLS that show how active the IT industry is for analysts and support staff. Note the various industries that are most active, and you can get a sense of the secondary knowledge that a firm grasp of can only help when it comes to securing a position.

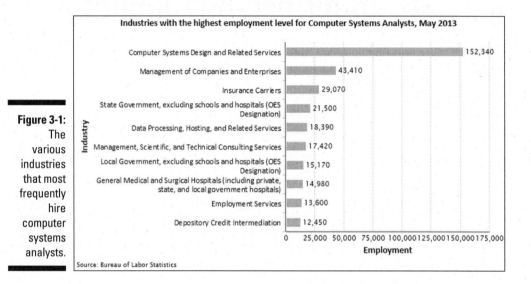

Figure 3-1: The various industries that most frequently hire computer systems analysts.

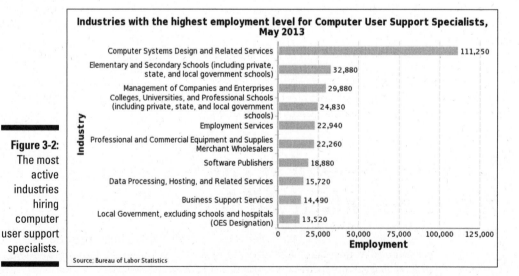

Figure 3-2: The most active industries hiring computer user support specialists.

The simple truth, easily understood without charts and math and whatnot, is that everyone in just about every industry uses technology and, therefore, must be supported. Technology is enabling and supportive, but not necessarily reliable if left unmanaged.

If you'd like to see for yourself, check out the BLS website:

```
http://www.bls.gov/ooh/computer-and-information-technology/computer-support-
                    specialists.htm
```

As Entry-Level Jobs Go . . .

All manner of entry-level positions are available, but very few have the growth potential and availability of the IT industry. While it's not great to have to get an entry-level job, everyone has to start somewhere. Getting an IT job is generally easier than other professional employment opportunities, which I cover in detail in Part II.

The overall idea is simple. You go to school to get an education. Later in your education, you begin to find out what disciplines interest you and for which skills you have aptitude. Some people are good with math. Others are good in sports or physical strength. Still more have talents for history, writing, science, engineering, chemistry, biology, and many other disciplines. For you, it is technology that consumes you.

On your own time, you develop and expand your expertise in technology, but personal interests are rarely strong enough to push one to learn enough to get a job (though it does happen). Education fills the gaps, and you codify your talents for the technical arts. You know computers inside and out, and, when working a job as an analyst of support engineer, you can solve most problems or answer questions in short order.

You are establishing a foundation that will serve you well as your rise in the ranks. Just be aware that it takes time and consistent, solid effort with a range of other elements blended in for good measure.

Creating Opportunities

Sir Francis Bacon once said, "A wise man will make more opportunities than he finds." Pay heed to these critical words. Opportunity will not simply land in your lap, at least not often. That means you need to make as much opportunity as you can.

You can make opportunity for yourself outside of education by pushing to learn more associated technologies.

Keep in mind, though, that if you are skilled at systems administration, it may not be a good idea to start teaching yourself advanced programming. There's nothing wrong with knowing how to program, but it is an utterly different discipline and will derail your efforts to improve as a systems administrator.

You can make opportunity for yourself in your education by seeking courses that add to your base and finding educators with whom you have an affinity. While taking associated courses is a logical course of action, it is just as much an expectation that you take whatever instructor you are given. This expectation isn't necessarily true. Because you select the courses, you also have some room to choose your teacher.

Sit in the classes. Talk to your teachers. Don't just take what you are offered. It's not always the best choice for you.

Finally, you can make opportunity for yourself when you start working. Do everything you are asked, volunteer to work on things that need to be done, and never be afraid to say, "I don't know." This is where you will gain critical and valuable on-the-job training in technologies that aren't taught in school.

Forging a path for yourself is a deeply important aspect of your career. You are your best and most effective advocate, and the best way to leverage your own talents is to use and improve them. Never, ever stop moving forward and be positive, and you will be the captain of the ship that is your life. Corny, but true.

Making an Impact

There are two fundamental ways you can make a real impact when you start your career. The first is the most obvious. If you work hard, you will help people with their issues involving technology. It may not seem like much, but lots of nontechnical types will benefit from your efforts.

Therein lies the second. If you help people and do it with a smile and an empathy for them, you will make an impact at their level. You will make human connections that you can take with you, even if you move to another position.

Don't forget to use LinkedIn, the Internet's most trafficked professional networking website, but repetition is the core of education, so I'll say it here. Don't forget to use LinkedIn and take extra care to retain contact with people you have connected with in the workplace.

It may seem counterintuitive, but making friends and forging those personal interactions is critical to becoming an engineer. Everyone is different, and while technology may come easy to you, it's not everyone's cup of tea.

Don't Rock the Boat, But . . .

Making friends is great, but not everyone will want to be your friend. Don't ignore this fact. It may be surprising, but not everyone will want to be nice to you, help you help them, or be concerned for your future. It is a cruel and real fact of life that not everyone is nice, and a deep understanding of this fact is super, *super* important.

It is not your job to fix people.

Your job is to fix technology for people. You will forget this distinction at your own peril. You are also not an instructor (with exception to actual user training courses). Think of the automobile mechanic who works on your car. He may be nice to you and fix something for you, but he doesn't teach you how to fix your car, and he doesn't try to fix you as a person.

It is not just users that you need to be wary of. You must also understand the people you work with and work for. As the newbie, you will be starting at the bottom of the totem pole, and IT departments are not unlike wolf packs. It has a hierarchy that you must figure out before you start working your way through.

Amazingly enough, your boss (sometimes called a *direct report*) may not be the alpha of your IT wolf pack. Make sure to feel everyone out, get to know them, engage in social events like lunches or beers at a local bar, and tolerate their pranks.

Don't drink too much. Have a beer, but if you are the new face in the crowd, leave early to avoid getting sauced. Make an excuse, if you must, but don't tell a lie that may come back to bite you. My personal favorite is to establish the myth of a helpless, intermittent friend who conveniently needs technical help. "I promised a friend I'd help them with his website /email/ smartphone." This kind of excuse leverages your colleagues' empathy. Of course, when you become the boss, you'll now be able to recognize when your subordinates are using your old excuses!

Don't just be a shrinking violet, though. Take part, follow instructions, but don't test boundaries — at least not yet. You are setting yourself up for the long game, so you need to be patient and take cautious, calculated steps that will move you forward.

Profiling for Technical Support Professionals

Nobody likes the sound of the word *profiling* as it has negative connotations, but as a human, you profile things all day long. It's all rather automatic, as you navigate your daily life. You make snap judgments as a way to help you make decisions and protect yourself. It's just the way life works, and there's nothing sinister or artificial about it. In fact, profiling really comes in handy when you're working with loads of different people who all need help and have their own expectations about how bad their problem is and how soon they'll be rescued.

Not everyone, however, is good at profiling. Some people can just read others and see who they are right away. You may or may not be that kind of person, so if you aren't, the following sections can help you understand the kinds of users you'll be encountering.

People are like snowflakes; no two are alike. The same goes for users. The following is a general guide to help you understand the generic types of users, but don't pigeonhole entire swaths of people. Always treat people with individual respect and dignity and recognize that they are unique. Also, do your best to remember each person's needs and types to reduce the chances of making a mistake you may regret.

The Luddite

This individual isn't exactly a Luddite (one who shuns technology), but he simply doesn't grasp the concepts of general computing. A Luddite is often a professional, such as businessperson, lawyer, doctor, administrator, or the like. Some Luddites can even be officers in a corporation, although it isn't common (see the next section on the Chairperson).

Most of the skills a Luddite has learned are by rote. He merely repeats steps, and if something changes, he is immediately lost (for example, an update changes a desktop icon or modifies a dialog box).

Treatment: You must be patient with the Luddite and visually verify all aspects of his issues. In order to win over a Luddite, you must be able to identify with his issues so that he feels that you understand him and aren't just an arrogant support desk engineer.

After you identify a Luddite, one of your first steps should be to initiate a remote session. The less the client must describe to the engineer, the more comfortable he will feel.

If it helps, you can tell a Luddite that it's okay for him to leave his desk to complete other tasks while you work on his problem. Many Luddite types will appreciate not needing to be included in the process.

As soon as you ID a Luddite, permanently install the remote client so that he never has to click on anything again to get remote support.

The Chairperson

The Chairperson's focus is on business, logistics, and operations. Her technology skills are fair to median, but she views technology (her desktop computer, laptop, BlackBerry, and so on) as means to an end. When it doesn't perform, she gets frustrated.

Chairpersons come in two types:

✔ The In-Your-Face Type I does everything on her own as she generally can't rely on others to get it done to her satisfaction.

✔ The Through-A-Proxy Type II uses her assistant for everything, even direct human contact.

Treatment: It pays to be deferential to these people because they are likely the ones who sign your checks. They likely have an expectation that their service will be better than others. They also expect to come first.

When dealing with Type Is, focus primarily on reducing their need to interact with you or the system. If you need extra help or more time, inform Type Is and give them an ETA. (If you don't, they'll ask for one.)

If you are working with Type IIs, determine the type of their assistant and work with them on that level.

The Lounge Chair

If there is a laidback, easygoing individual, it's The Lounge Chair. A Lounge Chair is cool with everything, is generally self-confident, understands your issues, and realizes that he is not the top of the heap.

The Lounge Chair is often very easy to deal with and likes to joke around after he gets to know you a little. In fact, this lounge lizard may lull you into a state of relaxation that you cannot afford. From the moment you're on the phone or in IM with this person, you are his best pal.

Treatment: Consider this individual's relaxed state to be a dangerous rabbit hole of distraction and proceed quickly to a solution, avoiding as much small talk as possible. Focus on the task at hand and work through it. Resist the urge to chatter, but maintain at least some small interest in what he is talking about, or he will feel ignored.

The Stress Level

This character comes in two primary forms: Alpha Stress Level and Proxy Stress Level. Whether the Stress Level is feeling pressure from the job or she is a high-level executive's assistant who passes that pressure on, she must have any issues dealt with in a timely fashion, preferably last week. The Stress Level is generally a high strung folk with a classic Type A personality.

Treatment: Do not, under any circumstances, attempt to send this person somewhere to distract her. While it may not be helpful or pleasant, you must engage the Stress Level in the solution in order to win her over. Do as much as you can to focus on the problem and a possible solution as quickly as possible and then explain it to her from a 10,000 foot perspective while you are working on the solution.

If you can manage to show the Stress Level that you can figure things out, calm her down, and fix the problem all at the same time, she will develop a begrudging respect for you. Winner!

The Professor

This persona is your friend, but in a rude, condescending way. The Professor is always right and knows far more about technology than the entire support team put together. Any problems this individual has must be the fault of the support team or source from a hardware failure.

The Professor is often indignant about not having administrator access to "his" system and looks on the need to call for assistance with great loathing and disdain. The Professor's MO is to explain all the technical (to him) things he has done to try to identify and solve the problem.

Treatment: First, don't interrupt the Professor while he is listing all of the steps he has tried so far. This information can be helpful, either in determining whether he actually knows something or that he doesn't. Once you are clear that you know what he has tried, you can proceed.

Do not, under any circumstances, explain how the technology works to this personality. In fact, speak to him as if he is just another engineer. This approach may cause him to start respecting you as you treat him like an equal. At no time shall you reveal to him that the problem was user error, even if it was.

The Perfect User

This personality is the perfect client. The Perfect User is attentive, kind, and accommodating and will speak well of you to the ends of the Earth. You make a point of checking in on the Perfect User, making sure that she is happy and fixing any issues as quickly as you can, even though she says she can wait. It is this small set of people who make your day.

Treatment: You will naturally try to help the Perfect User as much as you can. Do not, however, take her for granted. It is her praise that she liberally spreads around the office that fosters and grows your cachet in the office and causes more Perfect Users to be born. Cultivate your Perfect Users, and you will soon have several more.

Solving Support Desk Scenarios

One of the more interesting uses of the user profiles is a kind of game where you can insert one or more types into various scenarios to work out how you can manage them. Try various combinations and see what you would do. How would you triage the problems? How would you allocate resources? How would you approach the users? It's actually quite fun to work out different schemes, and the more you use this tool, the better you'll get.

Here are a few scenarios to get you started:

- ✓ **Standard desktop installations:** This scenario is the most common and straightforward. These users have a static, desktop machine, and everything is clearly documented.

- ✓ **New user account creations:** New employees in an organization often have specific operational questions, such as what software to use for a specified task or help with email.

- **Returning users:** These users can be a special case, depending on company policies regarding data retention.

- **Travelling users:** In most cases, these users will be able to get on the Internet so that you can initiate a remote session. Travel adds a layer of additional stress, so keep that issue in mind.

- **Travelling users in very remote location:** Very remote locations can cause connectivity issues, so prepare users for possible disconnection.

- **Travelling users with no Internet access:** IT help will have to be done entirely over the phone, so be prepared to step through everything in detail. Make sure to walk through the steps on your own system or a virtual machine, which helps you visualize what you are walking them through.

- **Visiting VIPs:** Treat with kid gloves. Seriously. With in-house VIPs, you can establish a rapport. You cannot with visiting VIPs. Don't even try.

- **VIP users in general:** Take good care of them and reduce or limit their need to interact to get a solution.

- **Visiting presenters:** These people often ask for extra bits and services, which you may or may not have or offer. Be careful, though. If they are from a partner of your company, treat them like visiting VIPs.

- **B.Y.O.D.s or Bring Your Own Devices:** Many companies have BYOD policies or just don't bother to care that employees use their own devices for work. BlackBerry, Android, iPhone, and Windows Phone all support some form of enterprise management, but you may still have to limit what you will support. It's also critical to pay attention to possible security issues.

- **Standard server:** Most server administration is handled remotely because it's far easier than plugging in a crash cart to each physical machine. For a server room, a *crash cart* is a media cart with a monitor, keyboard, and mouse on it that you can push around and connect to any server you need to access.

- **Custom services:** Sometimes users will call seeking support for a third-party service that is not generally supported. Most companies have some form of policy to control support resources allocated for such occasions, but most of the time, if you can help them, you probably should.

- **Anything else:** Create your own scenarios. It's fun! Just take care to always pay attention to what's going on around you so that you can help identify what could help you in the future.

Branching Outside Your Comfort Zone

Getting outside of your comfort zone is one of the most powerful tools you have. School will not teach you everything, and you most likely don't have the financial resources to acquire large swaths of enterprise-grade technology so that you can teach yourself. Unsurprisingly, if you had enough money to buy the stuff, you probably wouldn't be getting an entry-level position on a help desk. (In Chapter 6, I go over some gear that you can acquire on a meager budget that you will be able to train on.)

You can do lots of other things, however. You can add a few things to your regular regiment on a daily and weekly basis that will help you stay on top of current technologies and trends and expand your skillset. One thing, however, will be an invaluable tool, but to use it, you must come to grips with your own limitations. You must learn how to say, "I don't know."

Reality dictates that human beings do not know everything. Some humans may know a lot, but nobody can know everything there is to know. Accept this limitation as reality, and you can say the words. When you can say to someone you work with that you don't know something, you open the door to learn it. Rest assured, if a company has a technology in place, someone there knows how to use it.

Go to that person. Tell him how awesome he is and that you would like to start working on sharing his awesome.

 Just be careful. Some people are the jealous type and don't want to share. Sometimes, if you're unlucky, they won't have to share. This is like reading your Wolf Pack and knowing the hierarchy. Know the people you work with, but keep pushing out your borders.

You can do it.

Advancing from Zero to CTO

A career in IT provides an amazingly diverse series of paths to advancement over many other entry-level careers. You can get very few jobs without any prior experience (aside from being a nerd, of course) that offers so many potential doors to open. The vast majority of entry-level positions are mere stopgaps so that you can earn money while you are going to school.

Just think of any entry-level job and try to imagine how far you can go:

- ✔ Get a job as a waiter or on the kitchen staff in a restaurant or fast food joint, and you will earn little and have little opportunity for advancement. You could become a shift leader in a few months or years.

- ✔ As an office worker, you can become a more advanced office worker, a receptionist, or even a team leader. After that you may manage more and more office workers and possibly become a VP of a section of office workers after years of dedication.

- ✔ As a junior mechanic, you can learn how to be a better mechanic, work on nicer cars, maybe open your own shop, and work on more cars.

- ✔ If you go into plumbing, you will be a plumber, and as you grow in your profession, you will still be a plumber. You may be an amazing plumber, but it's still plaster, pipes, toilets, and whatnot.

The term entry-level is misleading because it suggests that you can start at the bottom of the ladder and work your way up. Unfortunately, most service industry positions offer very little opportunity for diversity. If you want to get a better paying job that has real potential for growth, you'll need to get a degree first. Try getting a job as a doctor, lawyer, scientist, or even an engineer without having spent four years in college and earning a degree in that field.

This is what makes Information Technology so special. All you need is a good grasp on how technology works and the ability to help others use it effectively to get an entry-level position. You can even work in the IT industry while you are going to school to enhance your skills.

Part II
What You Need to Know

Five Helpful Certifications

- ✔ **A+:** CompTIA's A+ certification grants those who earn it credentials that indicate a wide-ranging awareness of both hardware and software concepts and practical applications of that knowledge in an entry-level IT setting.

- ✔ **NETWORK+:** CompTIA's Network+, or just Net+, is applied for those who can show competency in networking hardware and software. While it has a small amount of overlap from the concepts covered in A+, the Net+ cert is more specific to networking and associated concepts.

- ✔ **PROJECT+:** CompTIA's Project+ certification is earned through testing that shows that the test taker is familiar with the concepts and practical application of project management. This certification is not a complex one to earn, but it can be very helpful.

- ✔ **SERVER+:** Similar to the A+ certification, the SERVER+ certification program validates the recipient has demonstrated compensated competency in hardware, software, operating systems, and technological concepts that relate to server operations.

- ✔ **Microsoft Certified Professional (MCP):** Unlike the other individual certificates, the Microsoft Certified Professional is a group of certifications and an umbrella of support and services from Microsoft. Once you pass your first qualifying test (not all tests qualify, such as the Microsoft Technology Associate), you become a Certified Professional, but you are generally working toward building a portfolio of certifications for a specific discipline.

See the article "How to Get and Keep That IT Help Desk Job" at www.dummies.com/extras/gettinganithelpdeskjob.

In this part . . .

✔ Discover the education and attitude needed to land and keep an IT help desk job.

✔ Explore helpful certifications and training programs in the IT help desk field.

✔ Find out ways to keep your original inner nerd happy and current.

✔ See the article "How to Get and Keep That IT Help Desk Job" at www.dummies.com/extras/gettinganit helpdeskjob.

Chapter 4

The Education and the Mindset

In This Chapter

▶ Getting to know yourself, your options, and your capabilities

▶ Discovering the manifold aspects of the college education and beyond

▶ Finding out that learning is never the end of learning

*O*ne thing that is critical to any future is education. You cannot skip schooling of some kind. You cannot bypass higher education and expect to become a real success. Statistically, very few people who lack a formal education become very successful. The self-made man is a Hollywood trope based on a few industrious people from the last turn of the century.

In order to create the perfect platform from which to launch yourself, you need the foundation that only a good education can provide. I cannot be more clear. Did I mention getting an education is really, really important? You may hear this message a few more times in this chapter.

In this chapter, I talk about the forms of education that you can get, the time you will need to commit, and the skills they can give you. I strongly suggest that you don't skip this chapter.

Learning Your Way to Success

A solid education, no matter what type, is a powerful tool that you will use for the rest of your life. Self-education is an excellent skill to expand your personal horizons, but nothing beats a formal education.

For the first 18 years of almost everyone's life, much of your time is dedicated to school. Moving on to higher education isn't difficult, but it's not for everyone. Thankfully, a number of options exist.

The basics of schooling

Most people go to school. School starts early. You progress through grade school, middle school, and then graduate high school only to move on to college and yet more school. School, school, school!

According to Superintendent Tom Torlakson of the California Department of Education, the following is the Golden State's promise to its citizens:

> *California will provide a world-class education for all students, from early childhood to adulthood. The Department of Education serves our state by innovating and collaborating with educators, schools, parents, and community partners. Together, as a team, we prepare students to live, work, and thrive in a highly connected world.*

A formal, basic education gives you a wide range of essential skills. Depending on the state you grow up and attend school in, you are typically exposed to English, math, biology, history, physical education, as well as various other classes like home economics, music, and the arts.

Higher education: Going comp sci

Before you leave high school, you will likely be working toward going to college for higher education. Knowing that you want to seek a career in technology, you will probably select computer science as your major. A computer science major is a good thing. Just know that, in almost any collegiate program, you will be required to take a selection of classes that are not technological in nature alongside those courses that will help move you toward your career goals.

Any and all education is good. The more you know, the better you can be, so education is worth your time and effort. Choosing comp sci is also good for your bank account, at least when you get work after earning a degree. Table 4-1 shows the top 10 colleges offering strong comp sci programs.

It shouldn't be all that surprising that California is home to many of the top schools in this list. California is also home to the single, largest enclave of nerds, Silicon Valley, and hosts a very large number of technology-based corporations. Irvine, often considered one of the best cities in America to live in, also has a large number of data centers.

You may not, however, want to fiddle around for four years to get a bachelor's degree.

Table 4-1	Top Ten Colleges Offering Strong Comp Sci Programs		
Rank	**School Name**	**Starting Pay**	**Midcareer Pay**
1	University of California, Berkeley	$82,000	$141,400
2	California Polytechnic State University, San Luis Obispo (CalPoly)	$67,000	$125,000
3	University of California, Santa Barbara (UCSB)	$68,000	$120,200
4 (tie)	Stanford University	$90,000	$120,000
4 (tie)	University of California, Irvine (UCI)	$64,200	$120,000
6	Massachusetts Institute of Technology (MIT)	$82,400	$117,500
7	Virginia Polytechnic Institute and State University (Virginia Tech)	$66,700	$117,000
8	Cornell University	$70,000	$116,500
9	University of California, San Diego (UCSD)	$70,000	$115,000
10	Rutgers University – New Brunswick	$63,000	$114,500

Source: PayScale.com

AA versus BS: Fight!!

College offers two stops along the way to graduation. You can either earn an associate's degree in two years, or you can push for a bachelor's degree in four. Common wisdom dictates that, with a college degree, you will earn $1,000,000 in your lifetime. You would think that an associate's degree would earn you at least $500,000.00 more over your lifetime, but that's not entirely accurate. Take a look at Table 4-2 from the Bureau of Labor Statistics.

As you can see from Table 4-2, earnings rise with greater degrees until professional, where doctoral degrees take a slight dip. You can also see that an associate's degree will only get you $777 a week on average, while a bachelor's degree averages just over $1,100 a week. These numbers clearly indicate that you will earn just less than half from only two years of higher education.

Table 4-2	Earnings and Unemployment Rates by Educational Attainment	
Education Attained	*Unemployment Rate in 2013 (%)*	*Median Weekly Earnings ($)*
Doctoral degree	2.2	1,623
Professional degree	2.3	1,714
Master's degree	3.4	1,329
Bachelor's degree	4.0	1,108
Associate's degree	5.4	777
Some college, no degree	7.0	727
High school diploma	7.5	651
Less than a high school diploma	11	472

Note: Data are for persons age 25 and over. Earnings are for full-time wage and salary workers.

Source: Current Population Survey, U.S. Department of Labor, U.S. Bureau of Labor Statistics.
http://www.bls.gov/emp/ep_table_001.htm

Yet, education isn't everything, and even though the trend has declined somewhat, IT positions often pay more than other entry-level positions in other industries. While there are no guarantees, with just a few years of experience as a consultant, the right keywords on your resume, and a high school diploma or an associate's degree, you can get work that pays upward of $25 an hour, slightly higher than the median $19 an hour.

Vocational training

Vocation training differs from higher education in that you generally learn a skill in a procedural manner from hands-on practice taught by skilled practitioners. Higher education aims to teach you how to understand the fundamental structure of broader disciplines. Think of it like the difference between someone teaching you how to fish using a fishing pole and common accessories versus someone teaching you the history, theory, and fundamentals of fishing and then expecting you to figure out how to do it on your own.

It's the difference between a taught skill and a skill developed through critical thinking based on knowledge. You could start working with a blacksmith to learn the trade of metalworking and you will learn a lot, but you won't have a deeper understanding of how metal alloys are made or work, how to use math to modify alloys, or the fundamental chemical processes taking place and what the result might be. This comparison may suggest that you won't learn as much from a vocational program as from a "real" college program, but the Association of Career and Technical Education (ACTE) doesn't believe that.

As quoted from the ACTE website regarding post-secondary training, the following suggests otherwise:

- ✔ Four out of 5 secondary CTE graduates who pursued postsecondary education after high school had earned a credential or were still enrolled two years later.

- ✔ A person with a CTE-related associate degree or credential will earn on average between $4,000 and $19,000 more a year than a person with a humanities associate degree.

- ✔ Twenty-seven percent of people with less than an associate degree, including licenses and certificates, earn more than the average bachelor degree recipient.

The last two points are most telling. From ACTE's research (it's been around since 1926, in case you were wondering), someone who has earned credentials from a vocational training program can significantly increase his annual pay over that of an individual who has a degree from a two-year course. What's even more telling is, regarding the last point, that a large percentage of people who do not have college educations earn more than those who have achieved a bachelor's degree. Isn't that interesting!?

That extra earning potential comes from collected skill and expertise, or what used to be called *on-the-job training*. Apprenticeships have all but disappeared from the American job landscape and have been replaced by postsecondary education centers like ITT Technical Institute and Brandman University and hundreds of smaller, more localized programs all over the United States. You've likely even seen the TV commercials where a nice person tells you how the dental assistant job market is exploding, and he can help you get on board. Call now. Operators are waiting.

It may seem cheesy, but Career and Technical Education (CTE) is a valid form of education and frequently takes less time than college programs that teach much the same thing. One huge bonus is that this form of education often costs a great deal less while still being able to draw from the same federal support resources for financial assistance and grants. In addition, many of the schools now offer both online and on-campus courses, and sometimes a mix of both.

In the Army

In 1944, the Servicemen's Readjustment Act, better known as the G.I. Bill, was signed into law. The bill offered World War II veterans a wide range of services and resources in order to facilitate their reintegration with society. The G.I. Bill has proven to be one of the most successful federal programs ever created and fostered the growth of one of the most successful generations, the Baby Boomers.

Later came the Veterans Educational Assistance Program and the Montgomery G.I. Bill, which covered veterans after the U.S. military became an all-volunteer force in 1973. After 1985, the Montgomery version of the bill took over for the VEAP and is still active to this day. Under the updated bill, enlisted persons would have the option to pay $100 a month from their first year of service into a fund. Once honorably discharged, veterans would be able to draw tuition allowance and a monthly stipend for up to 36 months for education or training.

Like any other bill, the G.I. Bill is complex and has a lot of additions, options, limits, and stipulations, so don't count on our description to be the ultimate resource. There are a number of chapters, extensions, and amendments that change a bunch of elements, add new resources, and whatnot. It's a good idea to make sure you fully understand all of the resources you will have when you need it.

Applying the Vulcan Mindset

This section isn't about identifying your particular position in this matrix. It's about developing a wide ranging understanding of where IT people come from. The amazing benefit of this understanding is that you will gain a far greater feel for what it takes to be an IT expert.

Think of working through this material like meeting a new person from a distant land. They are new and intriguing, and you want to learn as much as you can about where they are from and who they are. As you learn from them, you learn more about your world and all of the wonders it can contain.

IT is much the same kind of journey, but instead of seeking out wonders from other cultures, you seek out technological marvels created by the hands and minds of human beings. It's an extraordinarily wondrous field to be a part of and a seeming neverending fountain of exciting new technological breakthroughs.

The Born Nerd

Those who are born with technical aptitude are like people who are born to play the piano, play tennis, become a diplomat, or be a brilliant trial lawyer. Born Nerds are people who have both an innate understanding about technology and have been raised in an environment that encourages expressions of interest in technology.

The Born Nerd learns new things, explains complex technical subjects, and solves most problems of a technical nature with ease. The Born Nerd enjoys working with technology, digging into systems, fiddling around with stuff, breaking down and building up systems, and slurping up news on the latest new stuff to break onto the scene.

The Born Nerd can be an introvert, but not always. He can work well with people, but not always. Just like everyone other human on the planet, countless shades of color are in the Born Nerd ecosphere. Not every Born Nerd will want to enter the IT job market, but he likely will in some fashion.

The Natural Nerd

Similar to the Born Nerd, the Natural Nerd is innately skilled at working with technology, but doesn't necessarily have the interest. The Natural Nerd is born of the technology age and has handled this stuff since babyhood. Technology comes naturally to the Natural Nerd, and she may not be able to explain why. The Natural Nerd, however, likely has another interest in life that isn't exactly IT-related, so she probably isn't interested in an IT career. Musicians, photographers, and graphic artists are frequently Natural Nerds.

I mention the Natural Nerd only to make sure that I cover as many bases as possible.

The Forged Nerd

The Forged Nerd often has an innate understanding of technology but doesn't quite qualify as a Born Nerd. The Forged Nerd is either pushed into having to deal with technology or gets drawn in by some other influence.

One common form of Forged Nerd is the Reluctant Office Nerd. Frequently, in small offices, the person who shows the most aptitude for technology of any kind is often pressed into service as the impromptu IT guy.

On the other hand, the Forged Nerd can be built by a person who is keen to teach himself about technology in order to gain entry into a new job market or just to make friends. Some people climb mountains to prove they can meet challenges. Others teach themselves how to compile programs, build a media server, or construct a secure wireless network without having understood

---

Build it, break it, fix it

When I was a child, I would break my toys. Soon, I would build new things from Lincoln Logs (now you know how old I am), and then those logs would end up back in the bucket to later be used to create something new, but the toys I broke would never work again. This frustrated me. I missed my toys, but I always felt compelled to understand how they worked. After a time, I began to see how they worked by taking them apart and figuring out how to put them back together again.

As the late '70s progressed and I found technology, I discovered I could break something without really breaking it and still understand how

it worked. BASIC programs, after all, were very easy to break. I typed game after game into my Tandy — Radio Shack TRS-80 from computer magazines — and saved them to cassette. To make a long story short, I taught himself how to learn how things worked to the point where I could make them work again.

In my early twenties, I started building custom PCs and repairing laptops. All of this happened because I used to break my toys. Discovering how things work is a healthy habit, and it helps build critical thinking, process memory, and troubleshooting skills.

---

how it all works. Like the self-made success, these people will attack it until they have mastered it to their satisfaction.

However the knowledge is gained, the Forged Nerd generally has the spunk and determination to learn something, even if it doesn't come to him easily.

The Master of Analytics

Some people have a talent for analyzing things. Such people tend to be good at math, especially geometry, trigonometry, and other high-level mathematics. Life for the Master of Analytics is like a game of chess, and they see several moves in advance. Analytical people also tend to lead very ordered lives. Everything has to be in just the right place, and God forbid you ever forget to put a tool back or commit the crime of losing something.

Process and policy are very important to the Master of Analytics. Just like the physical objects the Master of Analytics enjoys control over, she also enjoys control over behavior. An ordered world is a predictable one.

While many of the values of the Master are desirable, it can sometimes go too far. Structure and control is good, but it can be taken to an extreme that will turn people off. It's best for the Master to be master of her own urges.

The Empath

Empathy is possibly one of the least represented values in IT. There are countless examples of complaints about how IT people just don't understand users and are rude and mean.

The Empath is the diametric opposite of this common trend and understands how users feel. The Empath can place himself into the user's shoes and is able to shape his approach to the user to suit whom he is helping. The Empath puts the user at ease and doesn't make him feel stupid or inadequate.

Empathy may be a rare innate talent, but it can be trained into just about anyone. You don't have to be a trained therapist to treat people with respect and avoid saying inflammatory or hurtful things. An empathic individual will listen to everything he is told, indicate that he understands in the appropriate places, take notes to make sure that everything is clear, and gives a reasonable estimate as to how long the work will take.

Don't mind the mundane

Some people are just built to withstand the monotonous. It can be a gift. They just sit or stand there and do the same thing over and over. They can manually enter hundreds of lines of data, patch hundreds of Ethernet cables, sort through dozens of spare parts, reimage dozens of machines, and catalog serial numbers of an endless number of assets all day long, and never stop smiling. They are good at doing repetitive tasks and never seem to complain.

As the old saying goes, patience is a virtue, and it pays to be patient when you can manage boring tasks with ease.

Chapter 5

Education and Certifications

. . . .

In This Chapter

▶ Examining your education and training options

▶ Getting a grip on the real costs of a higher education

▶ Understanding the nuances of certifications

. . . .

*B*ecause most people who get into IT don't necessarily have a
college degree in computer science or business management, certifications become a powerful tool in developing an individual's credentials.
Unfortunately, experience is no longer sufficient for hiring managers to deem
an applicant worthy of further vetting to fill a particular position.

In this chapter, you discover your post-education options, including which
certifications are helpful.

Researching Your Options

One of the most important factors when considering an education program is
accreditation. Not all programs are accredited, so it will require some extra
research to determine whether a program is accredited. Surprisingly, some
so-called organizations claim to offer accreditation to educational programs,
but they are not recognized by the U.S. Department of Education.

The DOE offers a useful tool to verify schools called the College Navigator:

```
http://nces.ed.gov/collegenavigator
```

Simply enter the name of the institution you want to check, click on the name
of the correct item in the list, and expand the Accreditation section.

The College Navigator is also helpful for a wide range of other information
that you'll want to look at. One of those items is graduation rates. Your choice

college should have a relatively high graduation rate. A high graduation rate indicates that students are engaged and pleased with the college's services and facilities and that the teaching staff is effective.

You should also contrast graduation rates with average salary for degreed persons. An institution with high numbers in both graduation rates and average salaries combined with reasonable tuition rates are the sweet spot you are seeking.

Another important aspect to investigate when selecting a program, aside from the curriculum, is how a school handles credits. The transferability of credits is directly associated with accreditation, as accreditation indicates an institutes ability to meet academic standards. As soon as a school tells you that you cannot transfer credits, you should find out why. It's either that your original school or the new school you are investigating lacks the appropriate accreditation.

Recovering from non-accreditation syndrome

It is unfortunate, but some of you may have to deal with the very real problem of having accrued credits in a school that isn't generally recognized as accredited by the appropriate authorities. It's not that your education lacked any form of validity, except in the eyes of the accreditation boards. You did learn, right? Of course you did, and that should count, but that is not always the case.

Fortunately, most schools offer a way of transferring credits from non-accredited institutions, but you won't always be thrilled with what is offered. Some schools require you to prove that you did, indeed, learn from your courses by maintaining a set GPA for a period of time (like a semester or two) and will then grant you some of your credits. Others have stricter requirements and limit the transfer to a small percentage, generally around 25 percent. Then there are the schools that evaluate your teachers

from the previous school and then base their decision on certain requirements. Even more look at your ACT or SAT scores. Some, but not all, will even charge a fee to test you for life experiences and grant you credit based on the results.

This process is not easy, and it can be terrible to find out that your old school wasn't up to the snuff expected by your new alma mater. Then again, there exists a vast array of accreditation bodies, and not all schools are accredited with everyone. Many schools are even accredited for portions of their programs and not the entire school.

So, make sure to take some time to verify your current school's accreditation status and match that up with the requirements for any schools you are considering a transfer to. You never know. It could save you a load of trouble.

Understanding the Cost of Post-Education Programs

Ah, the joys of school. You did, after all, complete high school, and now you're looking down the barrel of a college degree program. Yay. Don't get all melancholy, however. Relish this time. Being able to spend another four years in the warm embrace of an institution of higher learning will grant you experiences that are priceless. Unfortunately, this freedom doesn't come at a small price, especially in the post-recession economy.

There's also the elephant in the room that is college loan debt, which poses a huge problem for millions of young Americans. Getting a good education at a quality university will cost. The more renowned and exclusive the school, the higher the bill. Sure, you can find federal grants and loans, but by the time you get out of school, you'll have to work for years just to pay them off. It is a difficult and confounding conundrum American youths are faced with these days.

Sit down and work out the math of how such an education might work for you. Based on this information, you should be able to determine whether you are able to get it done or whether you'll have to pursue other routes.

I do, however, urge you not to give up the possibility of a college education easily. A number of high-quality programs won't necessarily cost you an arm and a leg.

Facing the Regional Dilemma

One of the issues with transferring into higher education is that not all schools are alike. Some have great IT programs, while others . . . do not. Having to relocate may pose a problem for you. In addition, almost all schools charge higher rates for out-of-state students, primarily to lessen the interest of non-natives to make room for more locals. Although charging higher rates isn't entirely fair, you must consider it.

According to the *U.S. News & World Report's* extensive database of higher education institutions, the top four schools, tying for top honors, in the United States for computer science programs are

✔ Philadelphia's Carnegie Mellon University (CMU)

✔ The Massachusetts Institute of Technology (MIT)

✔ Stanford University in California

✔ The University of California at Berkeley (UCB)

More schools in the top 20 (as compiled by *U.S. News & World Report* in an annual report include Cornell in Ithaca, NY, the University of Washington in Seattle, Princeton in New Jersey, the California Institute of Technology in Pasadena, and many of the other top-rated colleges in the United States.

It doesn't really matter if you live near one of these schools because the first thing you must do is get in. Without a foot in the door through qualifying grades and acceptance from your selected school, location won't matter.

After you get accepted, the first thing to nail down will be cost. You must know what it will cost you in order to attend one of these outstanding institutions.

Here's a sampler of some of the tuitions from the four top ranked computer science programs according to *U.S. News & World Report* as of 2013–2014:

The real cost of college

If you want to get a good idea what it's going to cost you to attend college, then you'll need to spend a lot of time getting friendly with your calculator. There are, of course, the fees for applying, which vary from school to school, and the tuition, but there's oh so much more. Are you taking a car? Then you'll need a parking pass and to consider costs for gas, upkeep, and insurance. No car? Then the cost of public transportation. How about a place to live? On campus, you'll have to get whatever the school offers, and off-campus can be a minefield of mostly unpleasant choices.

Then there's the money you'll need to spend on various fees for labs, your class materials (you can't forget those), various supplies, a student union membership, oh, and does your school charge for orientation? What about eating? Paying the rent? Maintaining phone service? Do you have enough money to pitch in for beer or a pizza?

It's a good idea to sit down and work out where the money will come from, what you can budget, and how you're going to keep money in your bank account in case of incidentals and emergencies. Needless to say, you may want to find work while attending school.

- Carnegie Mellon will cost you $48,786 per year.

- MIT will cost you $45,016 a year.

- Stanford will run you $44,757 each year.

- UC Berkeley is a bargain for in-state students at $13,844 and still not bad for out-of-state students at $25,064.

Even the cost of Berkeley can be high to most people, so you may prefer to consider a community college. Lots of excellent schools throughout the United States can give you the education you require. Unfortunately, *U.S. News & World Report* does not rank community colleges, so I'm just going to look at two that I know that are highly ranked, Pasadena City College in Pasadena, California, and Saddleback College in Mission Viejo, California.

The burden of a college education

A lot has been said about the rising cost of college and the debt that is incurred from the venture. Anecdotally, people have long expressed their dissatisfaction that they are still paying off their student loans many years after graduation. While I'm not keen on citing Wikipedia as a truly valid source, it has an excellent article regarding financial aid for U.S.-based colleges you'll want to look at http://en.wikipedia.org/wiki/ Student_financial_aid_in_the_ United_States.

I will cover a few points here. The FAFSA, or Free Application for Federal Student Aid (http://fafsa.ed.gov) serves as the basis by which the U.S. Department of Education's Federal Student Aid division determines which loans and grants applicants are eligible. It is generally considered one of the first things you fill out when you are accepted to a college, but that is not necessarily the case. Because the FAFSA papers are transferable to most colleges, you should start out finding what kind of aid you are eligible to receive. Financial aid can be critical when trying to determine the affordability of the schools you are considering.

If it's loans you are concerned about (and you should be), a number of schools have eliminated loans from their financial aid programs or have implemented loan caps depending on your family's income. This can and cannot be a plus, but it all comes down to the final price tag. Despite significant research, I have not been able to locate an exhaustive, up-to-date list of schools that have adopted the no-loan policy, but FinAid. org (www.finaid.org/questions/ noloansforlowincome.phtml) has a rather complete list and a great deal of additional information. It's worth a look.

One final item that the Wikipedia article briefly mentions, but fails to expound on, is the number of colleges that offer free tuition. Yes. Free, as in no cost for classes. It may seem strange in a time when tuitions appear to be rising out of control, but it's true. According to *U.S. News &*

(continued)

(Continued)

World Report, there are 11 such schools, many of which are military in nature, but FinAid.org lists 13. (Cooper Union recently cut its full-ride package in half.) Most of the schools require their students to work, while the military schools require service following graduation. Two of the more interesting options are California's Deep Springs College, which is only for men, lasts only two years, and covers everything, including room and board, but you must work on the ranch while attending. The second is New York's Webb Institute, which offers only one course of study, a dual bachelor's degree program in Naval Architecture and Marine Engineering.

If you aren't interested in college and everything that implies, you can check out the bevy of free online information that is now available from a range of colleges. There's MIT's OpenCourseWare (www.ocw.mit.edu) that started the whole craze, Carnegie Mellon's Open Learning Initiative (http://oli.web.cmu.edu/openlearning), and the Open Yale Courses program (www.oyc.yale.edu). You can find lots of free courses at the Open Courseware Consortium (http://ocwconsortium.org), and there's the Open Educations Resources Commons (www.oercommons.org). There's even Khan Academy (www.khanacademy.org), which is made up of thousands of really short lectures that explain all kinds of things.

Both are large schools on large campuses, and both have computer science courses and offer a much more reasonable rate for entry. For example, Pasadena City College (PCC) costs only $1,152 for in-state and $6,504 for out-of-state students. Saddleback is even more reasonable for Californians, costing only $762 for in-state and $4,694 for out-of-state students.

The cost of school, however, is just the starting point. You should also know how well the average jobs pay for graduates from these programs. Interestingly, the top four schools don't rank the same in post-graduation pay, according to PayScale.com. Here's how the top four schools rank when it comes to getting paid:

- ✔ UC Berkeley starts at $82,000 and mid-career pays $141,000.
- ✔ Stanford starts at $90,000, but mid-career falls to $120,000.
- ✔ MIT starts at $82,400, but mid-career drops to just $117,500.
- ✔ Carnegie Mellon starts at $81,300 and bottoms out at $111,000.

It becomes clear that school cost doesn't generally define your potential for success. CMU, despite being the most expensive of the top four CompSci schools, doesn't serve you well when it comes to paying off those student loans. Meanwhile, Stanford will get you a well-paying position to start, but you won't see a lot of growth over time. Berkeley, however, doesn't start as well, but really shines in mid-career advancement trends.

Of course, the elephant in the room here is location, location, location. Just because you are selected for a particular school doesn't mean it's in your state. Location has a significant impact on tuition. In many cases, the difference can make college a reality or just a dream. It is this fact of college life that makes location a rather critical issue when considering schools.

Isn't it rather convenient that you live in the age of the Internet, then?

Taking It to the Internet!

Do not, at this point, jump around and hoot with joy. Costs for taking classes entirely or partially online are not nearly as large a cost savings as you may hope. However, you can derive a number of benefits from taking all of your courses online:

- ✔ You have far more flexibility defining your schedule, making it easier to work while going to school.

- ✔ Instead of a flat tuition, you generally pay a fee per credit, allowing you to better control your expenditures.

- ✔ You don't have to pay additional fees for resources like transportation and parking, lodging and/or dorm fees, and whatnot.

- ✔ You don't have to get dressed to attend class.

That doesn't mean there aren't any downsides, of course. These benefits just mean that there are good reasons why considering an online course might be a good choice.

A large number of degree programs are available from almost every major university in the United States and Canada. Most of these institutions offer all degrees, including associate's, bachelor's, and graduate programs, in various combinations as well. According to the *U.S. News & World Report's* most recent and regularly updated rankings, the following is a list of the top five online bachelor's degree programs for information technology (this sample is taken from 2014):

- ✔ University of Southern California
- ✔ Boston University
- ✔ Virginia Tech
- ✔ North Carolina State University
- ✔ Syracuse University

Online courses from fully accredited universities charge per credit instead of a full tuition. On average, most students take on around 10 to 15 credits per semester. Some overachievers will take on as much as 20 credits, but I don't suggest you go that far.

Out of the top five programs, the University of Southern California cost per credit exceeds the others, which all cost $1,636. To take classes that will earn you 10 credits, you will spend $16,360, which is quite a bit less than USC's $48,280 tuition for regular attendance. These per-credit costs may not be inexpensive, but it is well worth the cost considering top scores for faculty credentials, student services, and engagement.

Contrary to most online programs, North Carolina State has different credit rates depending on in-state and out-of-state student status. This difference in rates will benefit anyone living in North Carolina, as NCS offers in-state students significantly better rates compared to any other program. At $352 per credit, 10 units will cost you a mere $3,520, versus the $726 per credit for out-of-state students, costing $7,260 for the same 10 units. Seeing as how NCS is #4, the cost is a value in comparison to the others.

In the rankings, Boston University charges $840 per credit, Virginia Tech charges $900 per credit, and Syracuse charges $1,294 per credit. The math to determine costs is rather simple, so it's easy to figure out what 10 credits will cost you.

To Cert or Not to Cert

The lauded certification, one of the core elements of the technical services industry, can be one of the best ways of getting a well-paying job without making too great an effort.

Now, don't go thinking that certifications, often called certs for short, are limited to technology. They aren't. Certifications exist for just about every type of job, but technology does represent an enormous percentage of certifications on offer.

You can earn certifications for various professional groups, software manufacturers, hardware producers, and others. You earn them from colleges, technical schools, and testing facilities.

Like universities, testing facilities that offer certification testing are accredited, so it's important to verify that you are looking at a good facility.

Getting a certification is quite a bit less expensive than continuing into higher education, so if you are eager to get working or just don't do well in traditional educational settings, it's an excellent alternative.

The problem with certifications

Certs do have some downsides, but they are more philosophical than practical. The most common problem some people have with certifications is that there is no practical way to determine whether someone is truly trained in a discipline or has just studied really hard to take the exam. Surprisingly enough, this issue frequently causes rifts among coworkers and newly hired employees.

What it comes down to is simple. Earning a certification does not mean you have learned what it means to be certified. Anyone can drop a few hundred bucks and take a test or two to become certified, but it doesn't mean that person has real, practical, in-the-field experience. Anyone who has worked with Microsoft technologies will tell you when it comes to managing Windows systems, there's the Microsoft Way, and then there's the Real Way.

Certification teaches you the Microsoft Way, but far too often there is another, more efficient and effective way of achieving the same solution. Ultimately, this just means that there is little better than real, actual hands-on experience.

Why certifications matter, anyway

Despite any issues some people or organizations may have with certifications, they are still important to employers and employees who work in the IT industry. Certifications illustrate a verifiable level of expertise in a given discipline, which can be helpful.

It's impossible to offer a clear number of how many certifications there are, but there are a lot. Almost every maker of technology that is used for enterprise purposes has some sort of certification associated with it. As a nerd, you've likely heard of certifications from the likes of Microsoft, Oracle, Red Hat, Cisco, and others.

The process of attaining a certificate establishing your expertise in a particular technology can be grueling. Of course, if you are an expert in the technology you are seeking certification for, you probably won't have too much trouble getting through the material. Knowing your stuff is, after all, what the certification is all about.

When the Microsoft way fails

One of my favorite stories is about Windows XP. One Microsoft guide stated that we needed to insert the Service Pack 3 update CD into the drive, but there was none. You couldn't even download one. It simply didn't exist. To make it work, we had to trick it.

We downloaded the Service Pack 3 software, which was embedded in an installer, but we couldn't get to the raw files, which the installation needed. We figured out that we needed to run the installer, leave it in the middle of the installation process, dig into the TEMP folder in the SYSTEM directory, and manually copy out the extracted files. Were we to quit the installer, it would have removed the extracted files. If we installed the service pack, it would have removed the files.

Once we had the SP3 files, we copied them to a thumb drive and labeled it. Then, when the installer insisted on getting the non-existent CD, we would insert the thumb drive instead, and it would work flawlessly. Had we followed Microsoft's instructions, we would never have discovered the workaround.

Because a number of certifications require being updated once every three to five years, keeping any certs you earn up to date will take a lot of regular effort. If, however, your primary credentials are certifications, then it will be worth your time and effort.

It's also important to note that the longer you have valid certifications, the more money you will be able to command when negotiating salary. That's a little hard to beat.

Helpful certifications to have

Sure, it's good to have an education, but it's not bad to have one or more certifications. The following, most of which are CompTIA certifications, are very helpful to have in your personal toolbox. Most any self-respecting professional nerd will be able to answer most, if not all, of the questions on these exams, but it never hurts to have a few extra letters after your name when applying for a new position.

✔ **A+:** CompTIA's A+ certification is one of those certs that have been around for a very long time. The A+ has been around for so long that the current requirements bear almost no resemblance to those of a decade ago. While the A+ is supposed to be for IT professionals who have 500 or more hours of experience, the exam can be studied for and is comprised of two parts, Essentials and Practical Application.

The A+ cert grants those who earn it credentials that indicate a wide-ranging awareness of both hardware and software concepts and practical applications of that knowledge in an entry-level IT setting.

✔ **NETWORK+:** CompTIA's Network+, or just Net+, is applied for those who can show competency in networking hardware and software. While it has a small amount of overlap from the concepts covered in A+, the Net+ cert is more specific to networking and associated concepts.

✔ **PROJECT+:** CompTIA's Project+ certification is earned through testing that shows that the test taker is familiar with the concepts and practical application of project management. This certification is not a complex one to earn, but it can be very helpful. While not entirely compatible with the blazingly hot Agile movement, all of the traditional concepts of project management are a huge help and can only improve your chances.

✔ **SERVER+:** Similar to the A+ certification, the SERVER+ certification program validates the recipient has demonstrated compensated competency in hardware, software, operating systems, and technological concepts that relate to server operations.

✔ **Microsoft Certified Professional (MCP):** Unlike the other individual certificates, the Microsoft Certified Professional is a group of certifications and an umbrella of support and services from Microsoft. Once you pass your first qualifying test (not all tests qualify, such as the Microsoft Technology Associate), you become a Certified Professional, but you are generally working toward building a portfolio of certifications for a specific discipline.

You can start with the Microsoft Technology Associate or move on directly to the Microsoft Certified Solutions Associate exams for Windows 7 and Windows 8. Take a look at Windows 8 as an example. In order to pass and become certified for Windows 8, you'll need Exam #687, Configuring Windows 8.1 and Exam #688, Supporting Windows 8.1.

Once you have an MCSA certification, you can more easily move on to a Microsoft Certified Solutions Expert, more commonly known as MCSE, and there are numerous paths in the MCSE to choose from.

Chapter 6

Feeding Your Inner Nerd

· ·

In This Chapter

▶ Getting a jumpstart on everyone else through personal growth methodologies

▶ Developing personal guides for expanding your knowledge base

▶ Fostering a greater understanding of the importance of cross-platform awareness

· ·

Getting an education is great, but unlike many other industries, IT technologies are constantly shifting, changing, and growing. In fact, the advances made in technology by the human race are accelerating over time. Since the advent of the home computer, computer technology has gotten smaller, faster, and more reliable.

This chapter is a guide to expanding your knowledge of things technical. Think of it as your go-to handbook of resources, tidbits, tools, and what-not that will come in handy for a range of things. I think that it's helpful to give you this guide so that you have a resource to look to when you have a question you need answered.

Exactly How Awesome Growth Can Be

Just what does that mean, though? Here's an example. If you are aware of NASA's Apollo missions to the moon, you will know that those spacecraft were mostly controlled by a guidance computer. What could be more power-ful than a computer that tells a space ship how to get from the earth to the moon? Well, an iPhone 4S, for one. The Apollo computer ran at 1MHz (that's megahertz) and weighed around 70 pounds. In contrast, the iPhone runs at 800MHz dual-core processor and weighs about 4.9 oz.

The Apollo program was about 50 years ago. The iPhone 4S came out back in 2013. The iPhone 6 Plus now uses 1.4GHz processor. Samsung's popular Galaxy S5 uses a 2.5GHz quad-core processor and even has a secondary GPU processor. Even the Samsung Gear S smart watch has a dual-core 1.0GHz processor, which is more than a thousand times faster than the Apollo's navigation computer.

Technological advances aren't just limited to computer processing speed. Software, connectivity, and networking advancements are being made all the time. Storage capacities continue to grow year after year. In 2007, the first 1.0 TB drive was released, in 2008 that jumped to 1.5 terabytes, then 2.0 TB in 2009, and 3.0 TB in 2010. By 2011, Seagate released the first 4.0 TB hard drive, expanding drive capacities four fold in just five years.

We've moved from USB 1.0 in 1996 to USB 2.0 in 2000 to USB 3.0 in 2008. That's three significant advances in a little over a decade. Display technology has taken off in the last decade as well, thanks to the explosion of HDTV through U.S. Federal requirements for the FCC. Mandates to move all broadcasting to the HDTV format have forced TV manufacturers to develop lower cost and higher quality displays to meet the needs of everyday consumers. Those technologies have bled into the PC market, lowering costs for higher resolution computer displays.

These and other advances are the foodstuffs of nerd life. We eat heartily from a grand, ever-changing buffet of technical specifications, product announcements, and the social lattice made up of sites like Reddit and Slashdot. Once consumed, we draw from these nuggets and our personal and work experiences to help guide others on the path to technological enlightenment. Because things change so fast, we must repeatedly return to the buffet to refill our plates.

Stay on Target for Growth!

Likely one of the least surprising aspects of nerd life is that nerds have an insatiable appetite for nerdy things. Like Luke Skywalker in the original *Star Wars* attacking the Death Star in his X-wing, nerds easily focus on technical subjects that interest them. Fortunately, some nerds before you created the Internet, the largest, most dynamic resource for communications ever created by humans. To help you stay on target, this section offers you a list of resources that are available on the Internet.

It's important to remember one thing, though. In order for you to have the best possible chance of consistently expanding your understanding of all things technological, you must create a program of learning that works for you. To that end, this chapter is not a methodology that you follow to expand yourself. It's a collection of information that helps you see the range of tools that are available to you.

One suggestion that I have is that you create a folder in your Bookmarks bar called Tech Library or something like it. Inside that folder, create subfolders for various items, like different operating systems and other categories like services, tools and utilities, resources, how-to's, and whatever else you can think of. Don't worry about getting it all right up front. You can add more subfolders as needed.

Now, whenever you come across something helpful, make a bookmark to it. Say that you need a guide to SysPrep syntax, a guide to installing DropBox as a service in Windows Server 2012 R2, a list of Mac OS X error codes, a link to a useful utility. You can save them all here. Over time, you will develop an entire library of resources for all manner of issues.

If that's a little old school for you, sign up for an Evernote or Wunderlist account. They are both free services that can save and organize all manner of information.

Online Resources

One place you can start that offers a great deal of resources is HDI, the Help Desk Institute, an organization for professionals working in the IT industry and whose focus is help desk services and operations. You can find HDI online at www.thinkhdi.com. HDI's resources are available only through subscription, but I believe it to be well worth the cost. As of 2014, these are some of the available subscription packages (all fees are annual dues):

- **Student** ($35): Gives you access to all of the same features as the Resources package, but at a dramatically reduced rate.

- **Local Chapter** ($75): The most basic package, offers access to the *SupportWorld* online magazine, peer forums, local meetings, and other features.

- **Resources** ($195): Offers access to all the features of the Student package, including all the Local Chapter package features and discounts to conferences.

- **Professional** ($495): Adds certification and training discounts and other features.

- **Professional Plus** ($795): Adds discounts on additional Professional accounts as well as one Professional account you can give to someone you believe would benefit from membership.

HDI is an interesting organization whose goals are specifically focused on the help desk, but HDI explains it better in this quote about what HDI is from its website:

> *"In 1989, HDI became the first membership association and certification body created for the technical service and support industry. Through the years, HDI has remained the source for professional development by offering resources that enhance the soft skills needed to provide exceptional service management and customer service. To put it simply, HDI helps the helpers."*

However, you'll also find other sources helpful. I have broken down the following list into categories so that you can quickly find what you're looking for.

Operating systems: Windows

Microsoft's Windows is the most commonly used operating system in the entire world and is used in both consumer and business settings by millions and millions of people.

- ✔ **TechNet.com** (`http://technet.microsoft.com`): The first place to look when requiring help with Windows in a business environment is Microsoft's own TechNet, a massive repository of IT information for all of its enterprise software and services. All the information is available free of charge, but there are no longer any TechNet subscriptions. Instead, Microsoft is moving all subscribers to Microsoft Developer Network (MSDN) subscriptions. TechNet still offers a range of free evaluation software, and the awesome TechNet Virtual Labs, which are free testing environments that save you from having to go through lengthy installation processes.

- ✔ **EventID.net** (`www.eventid.net`): When troubleshooting issues with Windows desktop and server systems, one of the most common tools help desk people use is Event Viewer. The problem is that it generates Event ID codes that don't mean anything to humans. EventID.net is a user-curated collection of information about specific event IDs and what people have done to solve the issues related to them. You may find it annoying that you cannot access all the helpful information without paying for an annual subscription, but take it from me, it is well worth every penny of the $29. That's a mere $2.42 a month for something that will save you time and time again. Corporate accounts that allow for multiple users in a single location cost a very reasonable $49 a year. Just do it. You won't regret it.

✔ **Superuser.com** (`www.superuser.com`): Superuser.com is a member of the StackExchange site network and is specifically designed to provide a user-curated Q&A system for power users and advanced users. The most common use of Superuser.com is to solve problems. People post new questions that describe their problem, and other users answer it. Even more, users then vote on the answers, pushing the most popular, and likely the most accurate, answers to the top. The site is organized using tags, so make sure to include enough information in your search string to find answers to the questions you need answered. Of course, you're free to ask questions that are not already accounted for. Superuser.com is entirely free.

✔ **Serverfault.com** (`hwww.serverfault.com`): Serverfault.com is another member of StackExchange, but it's focused on providing answers to questions about server systems and systems administration. It, too, is entirely free, as are all sites in the StackExchange network.

✔ **Petri.com** (`www.petri.com`): Petri.com is an interesting blend of community support forums and professionally penned editorial, how-to, and informational content aimed directly at the IT community. Since the site has been around for more than 15 years, you can find a massive amount of helpful information on almost all subjects related to Windows IT environments. It also offers a lot more information about related technologies, such as virtualization, networking, security, and cloud services, that are commonly used in conjunction with Microsoft server environments. There is no cost to use the site.

✔ **Experts-Exchange.com** (`/www.experts-exchange.com/OS/ Microsoft_Operating_Systems`): Experts Exchange is a commercial community assistance website that has a wide range of information and helpful articles about most systems in common use. It used to be a for-pay only site, but in recent years, Experts Exchange has adjusted its subscriber model to offer free accounts. Free access allows you to access its library of articles and select access to how-to's and video training. For access to all features and to eliminate advertising, you can upgrade to a Premium member account for $20 a month or $150 a year. A free 30-day trial is also available.

Operating systems: Mac OS X

Windows may still have far more installed users than Mac OS X, but Apple's OS has been growing at an astounding rate and is popular with many young companies and start-ups. Considering how common Mac OS X-based systems have become, it's all the more important that help desk personnel be familiar with both Windows and Mac OS X. The reality, however, is that very few Mac OS X servers are in use, and, as such, very few resources are available. On the other hand, Mac OS X Server isn't nearly as deep or complex as Microsoft server solutions, so there's less need for additional resources.

- ✔ **Apple Support** (`www.apple.com/support`): The first place you'll want to look is on Apple's own support site. You can find a great deal of information about all of Apple's systems and hardware, including guides for troubleshooting problems. Many individual users and companies invest in an AppleCare extended warranty for their hardware, but Apple doesn't make it easy to find the page where you can check warranty status. As a convenience, here's the link: `https://selfsolve.apple.com/agreementWarrantyDynamic.do`.

- ✔ **Mac OS X Server** (`www.apple.com/support/osxserver`): When you need help with Mac OS X Server, check out Apple's support subsite. It contains a lot of helpful setup, configuration, and troubleshooting information, and it's all neatly organized for easy navigation. You can also find downloads and access to online manuals. If you aren't using the latest version of Mac OS X Server for Mavericks, there are links to the Lion and Snow Leopard version pages as well. By the time this book is published, the Yosemite version may be available.

- ✔ **Experts-Exchange.com** (`www.experts-exchange.com/OS/Apple_Operating_Systems`): Experts Exchange is a commercial community assistance website that has a wide range of information and helpful articles about most systems in common use. It used to be a for-pay only site, but in recent years, it has adjusted its subscriber model to offer free accounts. Free access allows you access to its library of articles and select access to how-to's and video training. For access to all features and to eliminate advertising, you can upgrade to a Premium member account for $20 a month or $150 a year. A free 30-day trial is also available.

- ✔ **MacWindows.com** (`/www.macwindows.com`): MacWindows.com is one of the oldest and best maintained third-party sites for the unique relationship between Mac OS X systems and Windows server environments. The site has been running continuously since 1997, and most articles are written by just one person. Aside from the news and Windows integration-specific pieces regularly posted, you can find community forums and a large collection of tips and solutions. There is no cost to use the site.

- ✔ **The Unofficial Apple Weblog** (`www.tuaw.com`): Yes, it's mostly a news site, but it has a large collection of how-to articles that cover a wide range of subjects that users care about.

- ✔ **OSXDaily.com** (`hwww.osxdaily.com`): A website dedicated to Mac OS X, the Tips & Tricks section contains a number of helpful blog entries.

Systems administration and networking

The vast majority of businesses that have 20 or more employees have some form of server systems in place, growing exponentially depending on the size of the company. Because servers systems tend to be more complex, it helps to have access to resources. In addition, almost everything in the world is now networked. Computers, phones, tablets, watches, and even scales used to measure your weight all have some form of networking technology. Here are some helpful websites:

- ✓ **Tek-Tips.com** (www.tek-tips.com): Tek-Tips is among the longest running sites for systems administrators. All the content on the site is user-created, but it is detailed, and the community members are all very respectful and helpful. You can find a significant amount of information on a ridiculously large number of technologies. Besides, where else can you find forums that discuss Fortran and COBOL? The site is entirely free to use and has a lot of powerful features.

- ✓ **RedmondMag.com** (www.redmondmag.com): RedmondMag.com is the online element of *Redmond Magazine,* a publication dedicated to the Microsoft IT community. The site, like the print magazine, offers a lot of resources for all manner of systems administration subjects. The website is free to use, but you can also get a free subscription to the print version of a digital download.

- ✓ **WindowsNetworking.com** (www.windowsnetworking.com): If you've been around for a long time, you may recall ExchangeFAQ.com or MSExchange.org, which eventually became WindowsNetworking.com. The site is now one of the largest third-party resources on the Internet, and it offers a lot of information and resources. In addition to the regular information and other content, well-trafficked forums cover a wide range of helpful subjects. The site is entirely free to use.

Software as a Service (SaaS)

More and more people and businesses are using Software as a Service (SaaS) solutions for operations instead of monolithic applications and classic client/server applications. Following is a list of a range of popular services that provide a range of functions for businesses:

- ✓ **Google Apps for Work** (http://apps.google.com): Exchange is becoming less and less of an option for enterprise email as the Internet grows as a vehicle for applications, and Google's Apps for Work (GAW) has become one of the most popular options. Offering email, messaging, document storage, collaboration, calendaring, and many other features,

GAW can be easily integrated into most any company's operations. GAW works much like Gmail does, but eliminates ads and has comprehensive administration controls and domain integration capabilities. It costs $5 per month, per user, or $50 per user, per year.

✔ **Microsoft Office 365** (`http://products.office.com/en-us/ business/office`): Don't get the idea that Microsoft has been sitting on its thumbs while Google was establishing a foothold in its territory. Office 365 for Business is Microsoft's answer to GAW, but takes a different tack. Office 365 has three versions. The $5 per month version gives you access to online-only tools, email, online file storage, messaging, and conferencing. The $12.50 per month version offers everything from the $5 per month version and adds installation of Office applications and file editing on tablets and other compatible mobile devices. There is also an $8.25 per month version that offers only the desktop applications, online Office apps, and file storage. All accounts come with 1TB of online file storage.

✔ **Zendesk** (`www.zendesk.com`): Arguably one of the most popular SaaS help desk solutions is Zendesk. As companies grow, they need to develop a greater sense of accountability, track completion of tasks, establish pipelines for triage and solutions, and identify opportunities for improvement. One of the primary tools in this battle is the ticketing system. Zendesk offers all the features of a ticketing system, but online. That way, you don't have to support an installation of a monolithic application. Zendesk also has a very large number of integration tools for other services, and even has an API for integration into anything not already covered. Of course, I suggest that you have some developers to make that happen. Zendesk is priced to move. The Starter account is $12 a year per engineer if paid annually. Bump up to the Regular level, and it's $300 a year, but you get added features and a custom domain. The price goes up from there.

Antivirus resources

One of the least popular aspects of computing is the fact that a segment of society thrives on causing chaos and acting in a piratical fashion. In some regards, the Internet is akin to the Wild West. On occasion, you'll need to clean up after someone's mess, so BleepingComputer.com (`www.bleepingcomputer.com`) will come in handy.

Although BleepingComputer.com is a forum system that is aimed to help all manner of computer users learn how to use computers, it has an enormous repository of detailed information about how to identify and remove viruses and other malware. When I say enormous, I mean ENORMOUS. Just about every example of nasty virus that can infect systems is represented on the site, and the guides for removal are detailed and frequently include downloads for tools that facilitate removal of the most recalcitrant of malware. BleepingComputer.com is a free resource.

Software repositories

You can waste a great deal of time trying to find safe and useful software for use by users. Fortunately, a number of online resources provide lists of curated software that is organized for easy selection as well as one that can help you find alternatives to popular software:

- ✔ **SnapFiles.com** (`www.snapfiles.com`): One of the best sources for clean, safe software on the entire Internet is SnapFiles.com. Most of the software is oriented toward users and is freeware and shareware, but it has all been certified safe by SnapFiles staffers. The available applications are all organized into categories, and the search function works quite well. One of the nicer aspects of SnapFiles is the combination of staff and user reviews that help you identify the most popular and highest quality programs.

- ✔ **AlternativeTo.net** (`www.alternativeto.net`): It can be rather frustrating to try to track down alternative applications that can do the same thing as other applications. For example, if you need an application that can perform similar functions to Adobe's costly Acrobat, you just plug Adobe Acrobat into AlternativeTo.net's search field, and you'll get a list of applications that can also handle the creation and reading of PDF files. The site started out offering alternatives only to Windows software, but it now offers alternatives to an array of categories, including Mac OS X, Linux, online tools, mobile devices, and more. The service is free to use.

Use the Force, Luke!

Most people select a platform and stick with it. Nerds do this, too. It's not all that surprising. Taking the time and making the effort to learn an operating system inside and out takes a great deal of energy and doesn't generally allow for distractions.

Now, shake that concept out of your head. You are a nerd, a proud, powerful, capable nerd. You can take on just about any technological problem and whip it into shape in no time. You need to do that with the problem of expanding your reach when it comes to platforms, and the best way to do that is through exposure.

Love that Linux

Some people just seem to be born with the one gene that grants them powers over systems like Linux. I am not one of them, and yet today I am able to work with most any Linux distribution. How I did it is wholly unremarkable, but takes some time. I taught myself.

Linux is unique from Windows or Mac OS X because it is *open source.* That means nobody owns the code. Only the people of Earth own the code. When groups started to build versions of Linux to meet their own needs, they would then share them with others. Over time, these grew more mature, and were given names. Because they were distributed, the term *distributions* stuck, which is why we refer to each individual version as a Linux distribution.

Of course, I benefitted from a time when there was no Ubuntu. My first distribution was Caldera's OpenLinux back in the late '90s. Little did I know then that parent company SCO would go on to try to make the world pay it for the use of Linux, but that's another, longer story. Linux 15 years ago was not the preconfigured, friendly OS it is now. It started with a terminal session.

I learned rather quickly that if I wanted the nice things, I'd have to install them myself. That meant I needed to download the source code and compile it directly. There was no app store to point and click in. I had to compile Xfree86 and KDE to get a desktop environment. If I wanted a web browser, MP3 player, office applications, photo viewer, or anything else, I had to get the code and compile it.

The process teaches you about how Linux works and gives you a foothold into the basics of general operation. Sadly, that's a little complicated these days. Most Linux distributions are based on Ubuntu or Debian, both of which have developed and mature user environments. If you can be disciplined, however, you can give yourself an environment to learn in by downloading the Ubuntu Server edition.

The server version of Ubuntu's popular OS is vastly different from the desktop version. It does not come with X.org or Compiz or Unity, so you'll need to fetch the source, frequently called a tarball for the TAR extension, extract it, and run the MAKE tools against it. You could use the shortcut of APT-GET, but you won't learn as much about how Linux really works down in the core of the system.

You are free to grab just about any Linux distribution you like, so don't limit yourself to Ubuntu. Here are some links to popular distributions:

- ✔ **Ubuntu** (www.ubuntu.com): The official release of Ubuntu Linux, regularly updated and maintained.

- ✔ **Xubuntu** (www.xubuntu.org): An official version of Ubuntu that uses XFce as the window manager than Canonical's Unity desktop environment. Xubuntu is perfect for older systems as it uses fewer resources, but it still offers a lot of golly gee whiz features.

- ✔ **Lubuntu** (www.lubuntu.net): Another official derivative of Ubuntu, Lubuntu uses LXDE instead of Unity and uses even less resources than XFce, so it's an even better choice for older systems.

- ✔ **Debian** (www.debian.org): If you'd rather get your hands on the Linux distribution that Ubuntu was derived from, then check out Debian.

- ✔ **DistroWatch** (www.distrowatch.com): While not an actual Linux distribution, DistroWatch is a fantastic site that tracks all of the available iterations of Linux. As you'll note from the Page Hit Ranking list on the right side of the page, Mint is the most popular distro available, at least at the time of this writing. Another distro you may be interested in for very old systems is Puppy Linux, which is surprisingly small.

Just for hoots, you may even want to look into installing Linux into a virtual machine. This installation allows you to create a number of different machines that you can investigate whenever you like without requiring a lot of other computers. Then again, every nerd enjoys setting up several machines, so I wouldn't tell you not to.

Don't be an OS hater

For many, many years, Windows and Mac OS X users have had a loose rivalry. In fact, the rivalry has been around since Windows 3.1/95 and Mac OS 6/7 days and still rages obliviously on. There's no rhyme nor reason to this schism, but it is what it is. I believe in a different ideal, however. Use whatever you like and whatever meets your needs.

To that end, I have a little treat for you. The following sections help fans of one operating system understand how to quickly start using the other operating system. The reason why is simple. If you can understand the small differences between the two operating systems, then you are far more likely to stop disliking that system. Fortunately, only a few things are different when using Windows versus Mac OS X and vice versa.

These differences in operation are presented in list format for easy consumption. After all, these lists aren't meant to be a comprehensive guide, but are merely highlights of those aspects that are different enough to cause confusion or frustrate users when switching. The one interface element that is common between the two operating systems is the mouse with its clicking and icons and such.

Mac OS X for Windows users

The Mac is a powerful computer, but it's still a computer, and Apple has long had its own ideas about user interfaces.

- **Start menu:** Unlike Windows, Mac OS X does not have a Start menu. There is an Apple menu in the top left corner of the main display, but it offers access only to system preferences, system information, and a few other items. Instead of the Start menu, Mac OS X has the Dock, a bar that holds icons. You can use the Dock to start applications and switch among them. The Launchpad appears in addition to the Dock. The Launchpad can hold several pages of additional application icons.

- **Windows key:** In Windows 8.1, the Windows key is used to activate the Start panel and perform various actions. Mac OS X has no similar key, though the Command key does act in much the same way with various keyboard shortcuts.

- **Control key:** In Windows, you use the Control key to perform various actions, such as cutting, copying, and pasting text. In Mac OS X, you use the Command key, even though a Control key does appear on the Mac keyboard.

- **ALT + Tab:** In Windows, you can quickly switch applications by holding the ALT key and pressing Tab until the application you want is selected and then letting go. This same function is performed on a Mac using the Command and Tab keys.

- **Control panel:** The Windows Control panel is a huge mess of stuff to control how your computer operates, what it looks like, and how it does things. The Mac OS X version of the Control panel is called System Preferences and is located in the Apple menu.

Windows for Mac OS X users

Windows may be the single most used operating system on Earth, but it's still a computer, and its user interface can challenge anyone.

- **Dock and Launchpad:** The Windows taskbar may appear to be similar to the Dock, but there are some significant differences. Active applications have boxes around the icon. When clicking an application that has several windows open, a picker appears above the icon instead of just switching to the program and showing all windows.

✔ **Applications menus:** The Mac OS shows all menus in the menu bar at the top of the display. In Windows, each application window has its own menu bar.

✔ **System Preferences:** In Mac OS X, all preferences are shown in a single panel. In Windows, many Control panel elements are in a large list of different properties boxes. You can open the Control panel to show the entire list of available controls, or you can open each item individually.

✔ **Windows 7 Start menu:** In the previous version of Windows, which is still widely used around the world, the Start menu is the focal point of most operations in Windows. From there, you can start programs, search for items, access various settings and the Control panel, open the Windows Explorer to various user folders, and perform power operations like restart and sleep.

✔ **Windows 8 Start panel:** With Windows 8, Microsoft made a significant shift in how the Start menu works, much to the chagrin of most Windows users. Clicking the Start button takes you to a panel with rows of tiles that can launch applications. If you have a keyboard, you can start typing anywhere on the Start panel to activate the search function. For quick access to the Control panel, File Explorer, and other functions considered nerdy, right-click the Start button. Alternatively, you can press Windows + X.

✔ **Windows 10 Start menu:** In the upcoming release of Windows, it has been revealed that, due to popular demand, the Start menu will return. It will become a combination of the Windows 7 style with a side panel to hold tiles. No, you aren't going mad. Microsoft is skipping Windows 9 and going straight to 10.

Upward Mobility

Another critical area to become familiar with is the mobile space. Developing knowledge and awareness in the various mobile platforms of today can be somewhat difficult as it requires having access to a range of devices, and the cost of such acquisitions can be prohibitive. Unfortunately, I don't have any tricks or tips to get around spending money to learn other mobile platforms, but I can help you understand the core differences.

Android

Google's Android OS powers most mobile phones or smartphones in the world, at least as of this writing. Google's aggressive marketing and subsidy programs have made powerful Android handsets affordable, while Apple's prices have remained relatively high. You can commonly find large, powerful models available for less than $100.

Android is based on Linux, but looks and operates nothing like the desktop versions of Linux. Google specifically developed Android to run on mobile devices and to compete with Apple's iPhone. As such, the most common form of Android device is the touchscreen candybar. There are versions of Android for tablets, but Android tablets can't hold a candle to Apple's iPad market share.

The term *candybar* is a reference to the general shape of a device. Back when there were still flip phones and the idea of a smartphone was a BlackBerry, the candybar was just a rectangular phone that didn't flip open. Smartphones of today are a lot wider, but the name has somewhat stuck.

The standard user interface design of Android is focused around panels with widgets. After you unlock the device, a panel with program widgets appears. You can swipe left and right to show other panels that you can customize to your needs. From the bottom controls, you can access the lists of install apps and the preferences panels to change settings on the device.

Each interface from the major manufacturers are slightly different, and Android comes in many different versions, which has created division among devotees who believe the Android market is too fragmented.

iOS

When Apple introduced the iPhone in 2007, it was a bombshell on the stagnant mobile phone market awash with cheap, derivative devices. Nobody had done anything like Apple, and it had an astonishing effect on the entire mobile device industry. Seven years later, and the vast majority of phones being sold are smartphones that are based on the general concepts the iPhone brought to the table.

While Apple did hold the title of No. 1 smartphone, Google's aggressive pricing has pushed Android devices into No. 1 spot. Apple has responded slowly, but with the release of the iPhone 6 and 6 Plus models and the retention of the iPhone 5C/5S models, Apple now offers models for free to premium with all price points in between. The one thing that Apple can do that Android still cannot, however, is have people line up outside of Apple stores to be the first to buy a new iPhone.

In the tablet market, Apple has everyone beat, hands down. Unlike the iPhone's disruptive influence, everyone was perfectly clear that users just did not want tablets. Apple proved the industry wrong again with the iPad. The first version sold well, but the iPad 2 exploded in dramatic fashion, and Apple seemed to be sealing the fate of competing Android tablets to play second fiddle. To this day, Apple has held an impressive lead in tablet sales, and with the release of their new iPad Air 2 and iPad Mini 3 and retention of older products, they now have an impressively broad lineup of price points.

Apple's iOS interface is based around the Springboard, which is nothing more than a number of rows of icons arranged in a grid. You can organize the icons in any order you like, drag apps on top of each other to create folders, and create more pages. Each icon is an app, and even the settings is an icon. While multiple apps can run at one time, Apple employs a unique freezing function that limits the amount of CPU cycles apps use when they are not being used. The iPad version of iOS is almost identical to the iPhone version, but offers some concessions to the larger screen format and also lacks phone functions.

The general argument Android fans offer for why they don't like iOS is its lack of customizability and that Apple locks you into their ecosystem. I believe this argument to be a fair point, but it doesn't stop millions of people from investing in that ecosystem.

BlackBerry

According to Statista, as of 2012, 15.8 million people were actively using BlackBerry devices. That's not a huge number when compared to the markets commanded by Android and iOS devices, but it does outstrip the roughly 8 million users of Windows Phone devices by almost double. RIM's market has been steadily declining since the introduction of the iPhone and later Android devices, but the Canadian company has not been resting on its former laurels.

RIM recently introduced its new Passport device, a large format BlackBerry 10 device with a large $1,440 \times 1,440$ display and physical keyboard. The device has been surprisingly popular, and the first production run sold out, much to the delight of RIM CEO John Chen. More Passports have been built and shipped to eager customers. To highlight that success, the BlackBerry Classic was released before the end of 2014 and also sold out quickly. The Classic looks and works a lot like BlackBerry's older devices, many millions of which are still in use today, and offer a clear upgrade path for those old school holdouts. While I don't know the numbers at the time of publication, this is good news for RIM and for fans of BlackBerry.

If that weren't enough good news, the BlackBerry Messenger service (BBM), which has recently been opened to all other mobile platforms, now has a reported 170 million registered users and more than 88 million active users. Aside from the Passport and extraordinary growth of BBM. There are good indications that RIM could be positioning itself for a return to profitability in the coming years.

RIM has chosen to develop two different OS tracks for its devices, BBOS 7, which is the most recent version of its classic system, and BBOS 10, a next generation OS for new BlackBerry devices.

BBOS 7 is the evolution of the classic BlackBerry OS and has a wide range of very mature features. The Notifications feed is where you see all your incoming messages, phone call log, social network items, and more.

BBOS 10 is an entirely new OS built around QNX, a closed source OS RIM purchased in 2010. BBOS 7 applications cannot run on BBOS 10, but a number of applications are available for the new OS, and it has an included Android runtime that expands the number of available applications significantly. In the latest release of BBOS 10, version 10.3, the Amazon App Store is included by default on all compatible devices. The interface features the BlackBerry Hub, which is similar in function to the Notifications feed in BBOS 7.

There are no real complaints against BlackBerry, but RIM has been under fire for some time for poor management decisions. Until the recent installation of CEO John Chen, RIM had been losing money and market share.

Windows Phone

Windows Phone is the most recent effort of Microsoft to get at least a small portion of the massive mobile phone market. This effort has been going on since 2002. Twelve years is a long time to try to make a dent in a market without making any real headway, but Microsoft has proven that it is a tenacious organization.

The most recent version of Windows Phone is 8.1, which is available on a range of new handsets. Earlier in 2014, Microsoft acquired Nokia. Between the lauds Windows Phone 8.1 has received and the fact that it now owns a phone maker, Microsoft may finally start making that dent.

Windows Phone 8.1 and Windows 8.1 for desktop and tablet systems were designed to have similar operational features. The idea is to extend a familiar user experience across all devices a person may use. The Start screen of a Windows Phone device is comprised of a single vertically scrolling field of user configurable tiles, each of which represent a program or function of a program.

Windows Phone can run only applications designed specifically for Windows Phone. Microsoft recently released an updated software developers kit (SDK) that allows programmers to create applications that work on both Windows and Windows Phone, but not all applications that are currently available have been updated to support the new format.

The biggest problem with Windows Phone is the significant lack of apps on the App Store. Microsoft's own development teams have created versions of a number of popular apps for Windows Phone, including Facebook and YouTube.

BYOD

BYOD, or Bring Your Own Device, is an operational allowance many companies practice to varying degrees where employees can use devices they own on the corporate network. One of the most common examples of BYOD is the use of an employee's smartphone for both work and personal purposes. The concept is simple enough. Instead of providing a phone for each employee, requiring them to carry two phones in many cases, policy allows users to use their own phone.

The process requires a shift in operations to accommodate the different platforms in order to work. For BYOD to work, you must support the platforms that people bring in. That means you have to train your help desk staff to handle the platforms you are willing to accept. In general, the more devices you plan to support, the more training you require for your help desk team, and that takes time and money. Fortunately, most nerds are rather well versed in one or more of the common device platforms.

If more than phones are going to be supported, however, things can start to get complicated. For Macs and now that Yosemite is out, three or four major OS revisions are in common use: Lion, Mountain Lion, Mavericks, and the latest. Fortunately, for Windows systems, there's pretty much just Windows 7 and possibly a smattering of Windows 8. Then there are the tablets running iOS, Android, and Windows or Windows RT, a version of Windows that only runs Modern apps.

If that's not bad enough, there are all of the versions of Android with 4.0 Ice Cream Sandwich, 4.1, 4.2, and 4.3 versions of Jelly Bean, 4.4 KitKat, and the new 5.0 Lollipop. Then there are the different launchers and bundled apps to deal with from LG, HTC, Samsung, Motorola, and tons of other manufacturers. The only so-called pure Android that is commonly available is Google's own Nexus line.

Part III
Finding the Right Position for You

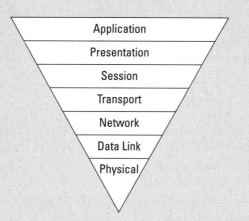

Find out which form of help desk engineering is right for you in the article "How to Find the Right IT Help Desk Job for You" at www.dummies.com/extras/ gettinganithelpdeskjob.

In this part . . .

- ✔ Find out what a consultant does and whether that position fits your personality.

- ✔ Discover the pros and cons of being hired by a company to decide whether to sign on as an employee.

- ✔ Get the inside scoop on what it's like to solve IT woes remotely.

- ✔ Find out which form of help desk engineering is right for you in the article "How to Find the Right IT Help Desk Job for You" at www.dummies.com/extras/gettinganithelp deskjob.

Chapter 7

The Consulting Nerd

This chapter reveals the life of a nerd for hire. Many IT help desk candidates have previously worked in some form of consultative capacity, from helping friends and family to working for a local computer consultancy. These experiences are foundational in developing the basic skills of the IT help desk engineer.

Traditional Versus Managed Services

Consulting is an old game that's been around for ages. In ancient times, elders were consulted on a wide range of topics based on expertise and knowledge gained from a lifetime of experiences. As the technological age took hold, consultants became a field in which experts could work to assist others with their technical needs. In the beginning, it was computer experts helping those who were not experts. These were simply known as *consultants*. As time passed, new technologies were introduced that reduced the amount of time consultants had to spend on site fixing broken systems. These new technologies collectively became called *managed services*.

As the personal computer market began to take shape in the late '70s and early '80s, it became necessary for companies to form that offered help designing and maintaining computer networks for other companies, small and large. The scope of services provided by these consultancies varies wildly from simple break/fix to advanced, high-dollar network architecture development.

Over the years, while consultancies matured, so did various technologies that were designed to offer consultants powerful tools to help manage client networks. These tools are known as *managed services,* and consultancies who offer them are called *managed service providers,* or MSPs. The concept behind managed services is based on bringing corporate-style management to consultancies.

The amazing thing about managed services is that it works, but it requires that consultancies change certain processes and convince clients that changes must be made in their operations. It's not an easy process. The typical small company is accustomed to making its own decisions about technology based on its needs at any given time. After all, the people running the business built it with their own blood, sweat, and tears.

The problem with this ethic is that business owners who don't have a company in the technology market generally don't understand technology as deep as those who consult. Choices are made based on immediate need. If the owner hires a new employee and that employee needs a computer, someone is sent to Best Buy, Costco, or the like to buy one off the shelf. System selection isn't based on the technologies required, but far more frequently on a budget. Consultants frequently hit a wall when the problem a user has is with a Home edition of Windows.

In an enterprise setting, the IT department has a greater level of control over what hardware and software is used by the company, and those systems, primarily servers, are monitored for stability and whatnot. Managed services systems are designed to level the playing field in the often chaotic small business market, allowing engineers to remotely manage all manner of systems.

In a typical managed services deployment, an on-site server or servers that is managed by the consultancy, and small agents are installed on client machines. These agents collect information and allow for a range of remote access functions. Some systems allow only remote desktop access, while others offer instant messaging, remote console, and remote desktop. Most systems allow for unattended access, which is generally used for servers, but can also be used for user machines.

On the server side, the managed services system can be configured to collect and act on data when certain values are met. A common example is hard disk capacity, such as one or more users who have problems managing how much space they are consuming. In these cases, you may send a message to the engineer who is assigned to the client. If no particular individual works for the client, you can create a service ticket, and the first available engineer will be automatically assigned. Engineers can be alerted to various issues in countless different ways, leading to a more proactive stance when managing client systems.

In a traditional consultancy, which has little to no monitoring, the standard practice is to deal with problems after they start to have an effect on client operations. This is the break/fix model. Engineers are constantly scrambling to fix error after error. Attempts to prevent problems from becoming significant requires many engineer hours manually managing systems. This can represent a significant operational cost burden, which is one reason why many traditional firms have opted to move to managed services.

With a managed services system in place at a client's location, those endless hours of manual monitoring melt away. Now the time available for engineers to work on meaningful projects is significantly expanded, and costs can be controlled at a much more atomic level. Reliability of systems at client sites is increased as well because many common issues can be detected early and dealt with in short order.

There is a fallacy that exists in managed services, and it's commonly used in marketing speak. When an MSP courts a new client, it frequently claims that one of the best features of managed services is that problems can be predicted and handled before they cause problems. This is simply not true, but the concept is almost entirely false. Sure, a problem with hard drive capacity running out can be predicted, but that's more of a sales opportunity. Real problems, like component failure, cannot be predicted, and this is the marketing promise of managed services that is claimed. In my estimation, it's far better to be honest than to make a promise you can't make good on.

The real challenge when implementing managed services, however, isn't the configuration. The real problem to deal with is the clients. Most small businesses prefer to make their own choices, so it's that ideal that must be countered. An MSP must offer an alternative to clients that replaces their need to control their own destiny or risk having to work with whatever systems the client chooses to purchase. The more inappropriate purchases the client makes, the more time the MSP must spend making it work with existing systems, and that adds to the time engineers spend on unplanned client work.

As such, a delicate balance must be struck between the values of enterprise IT methodologies of homogeneity with the loss of buying power that enterprise generally has. Large corporations can make deals on hardware and software that save them millions of dollars. Small businesses cannot, but a network of small companies whose purchases are made through an MSP can. This kind of community cooperation, however, is another complication in the process. It's difficult to convince small companies to put money into a fund that purchases hardware in bulk, much less be constricted to a limited selection of products to choose from.

There are ways to make things more attractive from a cost stance, though. Most MSPs offer services at a flat monthly rate, with prices set for desktops, servers, software, and various other pieces of equipment that a client might expect services. Don't be surprised when clients balk because most potential customers will compare their incidental, break/fix costs with the new flat rate. It's not uncommon for managed service costs to be higher than traditional break/fix, and that will drive some clients away, even if they know it's better for their business.

Ultimately, there are a number of very good reasons to migrate a traditional consultancy to managed services. There are also a large number of solutions to implement managed services. In fact, a few of them are entirely free.

One free tool that is very popular is SpiceWorks (/www.spiceworks.com). SpiceWorks is supported by its advertisers, but offers monitoring of all manner of Windows hardware and software, networks, inventory, and more. It even offers a help desk and knowledgebase.

For a price, take a look at Kaseya (www.kaseya.com), a managed services platform that offers more advanced versions of the features of SpiceWorks, but isn't inexpensive.

There Is a You in Teamwork

Working as an engineer in a consultancy is a job that requires wearing all manner of hats and changing those hats quickly. Because consultancies work with a number of different clients, engineers encounter a wide range of personalities and installations of technology. As engineers perform their various tasks, they are asked to do them alone or with teams or call on others when the need arises. As such, you work with some different personalities in your consultancy as well.

Part of developing an understanding of working as a roving engineer is getting a clear sense of what work is like in a consultancy. In this section, I examine the work types you will encounter and how they interact. In addition, I help you gain a respect for the all-important team work that makes IT operations work like a well-oiled machine.

Working alone

There is no way to give you a sense of how often you will work alone, but it will happen frequently enough. When performing tasks for clients alone, you are entirely responsible for all work. As you go about your days, you will handle any planned projects and deal with issues that arise while you are on site. In this role, you would generally be considered the designated engineer for the client.

On occasion, you may take the place of another engineer at a site that you are not deeply familiar with. In these situations, you will count on both your personal experience with technology in general and the client's technical documentation (covered in detail in the section "Documentation: The Lifeblood of Consulting," later in this chapter). When taking another's shift, your responsibilities are no less important. In fact, your diligence is even more critical. If your efforts aren't above reproach, that will reflect poorly on the usual engineer and your consultancy.

When stationed at your own clients, your time must be filled with project work, fixing systems with issues, performing upgrades and installations, and checking in with all employees to make sure all is well. Depending on the size of each client, you may visit more than one a week. Of course, that also depends on the contracts signed with the clients. Some companies prefer to have someone on hand a few days a week, which may lead to engineers not having a lot of tasks to perform. If the client is fine with this, knowing that you may not always be busy, then you'd have to be on call at all times.

There will be times, however, when one person just isn't enough to get something done.

Working with a team

When project work is more complex and must be completed in a short period of time in order to transfer or restore services, teamwork makes it all come together. Imagine trying to install half a dozen new servers and a new battery backup system, configure all server software and networking, install server software specific to the client, get everything patched up, and then work on every single client system to install any necessary software to enable access to the new services all by yourself. Such an enormous project may take you three or more days to complete to the client's satisfaction.

Now, apply the efforts of a team to the problem. With three or four engineers working together to complete the work, the solution ends up taking a day with a second day set aside for verification and documentation updates.

Unsurprisingly, teamwork requires coordination and cooperation in order to be successful. Working with other people involves engaging with various different personalities, trusting your teammates, and regularly reporting achievements and roadblocks to whomever is designated project lead.

If the designated project lead just happens to be you, you will need to understand your team members' abilities and assign them appropriate tasks in order to ensure project success. In addition, it's helpful to know your team's debits so that you can avoid putting people into a position to fail. Failure also adds to the time required for project completion and can damage relations with the client.

Even more important than completing advanced projects within the scope contracted with the client, regular day-to-day operations must continue uninterrupted. It may seem like extra busy work, but it is key that you perform your daily tasks while engaging in project work. Maintaining a positive relationship with clients is tantamount to most everything else, and that necessitates fulfilling all responsibilities.

Leveraging your resources

Regardless of whether you are working alone or with a team, it is important to feel confident that you have access to resources whenever you need them. These resources are dependent on the fact that the entirety of the consultancy you work for acknowledges that they will, indeed, act as resources when the need is clear. Sadly, not all engineers are necessarily willing to share their experience and expertise with others.

Groups of engineers are frequently fertile grounds for a wide range of personalities. Some people are introverts, while others are extroverts. Some work well with others. Some don't. Despite all the possible iterations of personality traits, however, most engineers share technology in common. In order to establish the best possible relationships with the other people you work with, focus on those things you have in common and don't dwell on differences.

One thing to keep in mind that can be helpful is that you don't need to be friends with someone in order to work well with them. It is quite common for people to work together in a professional capacity and never form anything more than an acquaintance-level relationship. There is nothing wrong with this. There isn't a job on this planet that doesn't involve working with people you either don't like or find difficult to create a positive bond with.

If at all possible, do everything within your power to make as many equitable relationships as you can, even making friends. Negative relationships can have a deleterious effect on your job performance and your position within the consultancy. It's best to avoid this situation.

No engineer is an island

Much in the same way no one person knows everything, there are no engineers who know everything about technology. Engineers must, at some point, rely on others to deal with unfamiliar issues by asking others, looking them up online, or calling the support division of the company that makes the product.

Calling on those who can assist you when necessary should never be viewed as an indicator that you are lacking in any way, shape, or form. This is why IT has so many different roles. There are those who understand networking completely, but aren't skilled at systems administration. There are others who know everything about how Mac OS X or Windows works, but know only basic networking concepts. The fact that you don't know something, but know others, doesn't make you any less a nerd.

It's a terrible thing to be made to feel stupid, and it's hurtful to make others feel that way. As such, it's important to foster within yourself the ideal that no question is a stupid question. As engineers work out problems with each other, it's helpful to work through all possible iterations of said issue. Some of the proffered solutions may not work, but all ideas may suggest other potential solutions that weren't previously considered. This process is just a version of the scientific method, and science is able to achieve things, so it must work.

When working alone, it's easy to get lost in the problem and feeling like you need to solve it. There's nothing wrong with you. This happens to engineers all the time, but if you get too lost in the process of finding a fix, you are more likely to waste more time that necessary. To avoid this, I suggest a rule. If you cannot determine a possible fix or direction for research within 15 minutes, reach out to your resources. It's just possible that someone else has had previous experience with the problem or something similar.

Documentation: The Lifeblood of Consulting

Truth be told, documentation is critical to all forms of information technology, not just consulting. Suffice it to say, it remains one of the most important tools engineers can leverage when providing support to clients. A well-documented client can provide any incoming engineer with all of the information he needs to provide support, which goes a long way to maintaining excellent relations with all clients.

Keeping track of madness

Any company you might provide services for will likely have a sizable number of technologies in use. There are computers like laptops and desktops, printers, mobile devices, scanners, servers, backup devices, not to mention the software they run, licenses that are consumed, and whatnot. There are all manner of usernames and passwords, IP addresses for all systems and devices, and other information like serial numbers and support IDs, such as the ones used by Dell to identify support contracts.

Collecting this data can be time consuming when first taking on a new client, but it's well worth it. If the company had a previous consultant, make sure to get any documentation that was created by them. Just keep in mind that if the company left them to contract you, it's likely that documentation was one of the areas the former provider was deficient in.

The process of documentation should always be an ongoing one. Every time you sit down to work on something, you should log it so that you can report on your work in detail. You don't need to be overly detailed, but it's important to record all salient data because much of it will be indicated as part of the client's monthly bill. You wouldn't be satisfied to get a bill from some service without understanding why you are being charged the way you are.

Standardize or suffer

Documentation formatting is just as important as having documentation in the first place. The best possible course of action is to develop a series of forms that perform three functions:

- ✔ The forms allow you to collect all important data in a consistent manner.
- ✔ The forms give you a guide you can use to make sure you've collected everything that needs to be collected, something like a documentation checklist.
- ✔ All documentation developed with these assets will conform to a single style, making it easier to navigate.

 Consistency really is the watchword when dealing with client technical documentation. It's a terrible thing to have to deal with all kinds of different documentation created by different people with different ideas of what is necessary and what is not. I have worked with one consultancy that did not believe documentation was necessary, that memorization was key to being a quality service provider. Sadly, that was a fallacy, and the consultancy was unable to continue without making significant changes.

Documentation is super helpful whenever an engineer is faced with managing unfamiliar systems. Of course, because technical documentation also contains sensitive information like administrator passwords and software licenses, it's important to both provide clients with assurances that their information is safe from theft and that you actually do secure the data. There is nothing less effective than a client that will not allow you to maintain the information you need to support them.

Finishing School for the Well-Rounded Consultant

A few more things are specific to the roving consultant. I include these additional, smaller tidbits of helpful guidance in hopes that you enter into your work life with a fully loaded toolkit.

Managing service vendors

One thing you will frequently encounter is the request from clients to manage interactions with service providers. This request generally happens when there is an outage, so you'll find yourself calling the ISP's technical support line whenever things are slow or have simply failed to connect. One of the most powerful tools at your disposal is a kind of trick when dealing with other support people.

The trick is two-fold. There is a small element of making yourself appear somewhat less familiar with the systems and technologies, while making them the expert. The second part is simple. Be nice. There's an old saying, "You attract more flies with honey than vinegar." Be friendly, but not overly so. It also helps to be patient. Take your time, make notes, and keep track of everything.

If you experience difficulties when working with a vendor, maintain your cool and collect data. You'd be surprised how well it works when you reference failed attempts at a solution and leverage them into what you want, all without getting upset. Do not confuse being calm with being soft, however. Firmness and confidence can be powerful allies when dealing with vendors.

Serving as the Convincer in Chief

One of the roles you will develop with clients is that of Trusted Advisor. In essence, if you do your job right, you will be the go-to person for just about everyone on almost any subject that is even vaguely technical in nature. You'll be something like the Shell Answer Man (or woman. I didn't create the advertising series).

Being the well-dressed consultant

As a consultant, you can't get away with dressing like a slob. A few consultancies will have an easygoing wardrobe of branded golf shirts, but most prefer the traditional business casual format, which involves dress shirts, ties, khakis, and dress or walking shoes. There will be no jeans, sweat clothes, or t-shirts.

Dressing nicely also reflects well on you as an upstanding person who cares about how they look. People feel more confident working with people who look confident in themselves. This may seem superficial, but the sad truth is that people do judge others on their appearance. Take advantage of that predilection to judge others without knowing the person underneath to make a good first impression.

Building your bag-o-tricks

Every engineer worth their salt carries around with them the tools and accessories they will need when in a pinch. The following is a list of items to keep in your bag that will save you when the chips are down and you need to prove yourself:

- An Ethernet cable, preferably 5' in length, and make it CAT-5e, just to be compatible
- One Parallel ATA to USB adapter because you never know
- One SATA to USB adapter because these are most common
- One microdriver set, both Philips and Hex
- One Serial to USB adapter for managing switches
- One LED flashlight for dark corners
- One USB wireless mouse because they are handy to have

✔ A few AA and AAA batteries

✔ Some blank CD and DVD discs

✔ Some pens, small notepads, and sticky notes

✔ One small pair of pliers

✔ One roll of electrical tape, preferably the kind that comes in a tin

✔ A USB cable extender of around 3 inches

✔ A small penknife

You may find some additional little tidbits helpful, but these items cover a lot and don't take up a lot of space.

Accounting for travel

It's extremely rare these days that a company will provide you with a vehicle. It's far more likely that you'll have to use your own car.

Make sure that your car is in good operating condition and keep close track of your mileage so that you can claim it for work and collect any additional funds your company may provide in compensation.

Tax time: Pay your own way

A small percentage of companies will hire you as an actual employee, but most will hire you on a 1099, a subcontractor. When working as a subcontractor under a 1099, you are responsible for paying your own taxes at the end of the fiscal year.

Make sure to keep track of all work-related expenditures so that you can account for them and keep your tax returns clean. It's a pain in the rumpus, but it is what it is.

Chapter 8

Working for a Company

In This Chapter

▶ Understanding the corporate hierarchy and your place on the inside

▶ Getting a handle on Agile

▶ Deflecting or leveraging difficult situations to work for you

*T*his chapter, which is really part one of two chapters, covers working for a company. The next chapter discusses IT help desk people who do not see their clients, which is diametrically opposite of performing help desk functions in a company.

When working inside of a company, you directly interact with your charges, an environment that has its own, unique atmosphere.

Welcome to the Jungle

Working as an engineer to provide technical support for a company is different from a consultancy. When consulting, you are an external service provider, which shields you from most office politics. You provide expertise as a trusted advisor and perform tasks that are requested of you, but you aren't a part of your client's organization.

When working for a company, you are an employee, and, as such, you are a member of the hierarchy of that organization. You are fully exposed to the ins and outs of the company and whatever office politics are at play. Unless you are a senior employee, you will not likely be considered a trusted advisor, but you may have opportunities to prove your worth.

In this section, I talk about how organizations commonly arrange their operations, the kinds of tasks you may perform, and ways to make yourself an asset. While I can't make any guarantees, you should do well by using these instructions as a guide.

The typical IT department structure

The standard arrangement for almost any business is a hierarchical one. At the top is the executive staff, made up of the decision-makers and labeled by the specialty they bring to bear for the company. A chief executive officer, or CEO, is the head of the company. The role of a CEO is to rally his team of fellow executives to manage the company and produce revenues, preferably in the positive.

Under the CEO are the rest of the executives, including the Chief Information Officer (CIO) or Chief Technology Officer (CTO). One or both of these two roles generally form the top of the hierarchy that make up the Information Technology organizational structure. The size and scope of an IT organization is dependent on a number of factors, but mostly the number of employees in the company. Smaller companies require less complex organizations, while large companies can have a deeply layered organization.

The top-down format is very common throughout the business world, and near the bottom of that chain fall the entry-level positions. It is among the entry-level positions that you will take your first steps into the world of IT via the help desk. Junior roles are one or two steps above unpaid and paid interns. Above the junior roles are standard, senior, team leader, manager, section head, division head, and other roles, all with increasing levels of expertise and responsibilities. As is typical of hierarchical organizations, lower roles are designated a report-to role, a manager that individuals report to.

The so-called flat model

You may note the touch of sarcasm in the heading for this section. I don't mean to be entirely snarky, but it's critical to understand that many smaller companies and startups employ what is termed the *flat model* of business organization. You may then be surprised to discover that companies using the flat model still have a traditional business structure, complete with executives, section heads, managers, team leads, and other employees. It may seem odd that a company may claim to have an employee-friendly flat model when it doesn't, but it appears to be common.

In some cases, however, some companies do use something akin to a flat model. These companies may have executive staff and managers, but the bulk of employees are hired to fill roles and work together in teams, sharing responsibilities, solving problems, and making advances as one. The executive team typically works closely with all aspects of the company as well and tend to make themselves available to anyone for any reason. Most people know this as an *open door policy*.

The real difference between the two can be determined through how that open door policy is actually implemented. After acclimating yourself to your position and working with your team, you should have a decent understanding of the personalities of the people you work with. Knowing personalities helps you determine how others will react to suggestions and how they deal with their teammates.

Another method used to determine the receptiveness of those you don't work with frequently, such as the executive staff, is to casually drop a non-critical suggestion. For example, your company uses an old drip coffee machine, and you've heard complaints from other employees that the coffee is terrible. You might, at some moment when you casually meet the CEO or CFO in the break room, suggest looking into investing in a Keurig machine, as a number of models are made specifically for business use. They may casually dismiss your casual idea, but they may also be intrigued.

Just don't try this method that often. You don't want to make anyone think that you believe the company is chock full of faults. You may also give people the impression that you know better than everyone else. That's bad. It's far better to allow others to make suggestions and follow their lead. The application of a fair balance of making suggestions and following instructions can help establish that you are a solid team player.

A rundown of common, everyday tasks

When working on a help desk for a company, you may be called on to perform any number of tasks. Unlike an external-facing help desk, a corporate help desk doesn't deal with customers, but only with employees. The following is a list of things you may do, in no particular order:

- ✔ Install a desktop or laptop
- ✔ Install a printer
- ✔ Upgrade an application for one or more users
- ✔ Update a user's password
- ✔ Replace a printer's ink or toner cartridges
- ✔ Update documentation
- ✔ Develop user guides for internal software or processes
- ✔ Run deduplication software on archival data
- ✔ Troubleshoot a problem someone is experiencing
- ✔ Order software or hardware for new employees

- ✔ Create, work on, and close service tickets

- ✔ Make rounds to see how employees are doing

- ✔ Collect inventory data

- ✔ Verify success or failure of backup jobs

- ✔ Rotate backup media

- ✔ Create virtual machines to test software patches for general deployment

- ✔ Install new typefaces for use in creative work

- ✔ Migrate data from a user's hard drive to a new, larger drive, install, and test

- ✔ Upgrade RAM in desktop and laptop systems

- ✔ Install new networking equipment

- ✔ Configure new rules for firewall access

- ✔ Image new computers and create account for use by new users

- ✔ Implement virtual servers for use by various departments

- ✔ Advise users on implementing better ergonomics to prevent repetitive stress injuries

- ✔ Test software for potential deployment within the organization

- ✔ Recover lost files from a backup

- ✔ Remotely disable a lost mobile device

- ✔ Research products for a hardware upgrade

- ✔ Review web server logs for signs of possible incursion

- ✔ Assist users in the field with connecting to mobile networks

- ✔ Configure accounts for VPN access

You'll find that, once you start working, this list is incomplete. All companies have their own needs, wants, and problems, and every team deals with them in their own, unique way. It's common to find that your experiences with one company may not serve you at another. There are, however, enough similarities that you will benefit from regular, hands-on work with various systems. Over time, you will establish a greater understanding of a wider range of technologies, all of which can help expand your curriculum vitae.

Projects that may give you a leg up

Not all IT ops do everything the same, so you may just be helping yourself if you bring a new process that will improve things for your new employer. Saving time and money are important to corporations, and there is real value in being the one to deliver that savings through project work.

The following projects may help you, but also look beyond the specifics here and develop creative alternatives that best fit your circumstances.

- ✔ **Virtualizing servers:** One of the great things about virtualization is that it can significantly reduce the number of physical servers that are installed, while maintaining a larger number of virtual servers. There are additional benefits as well. You can move virtual servers from one physical machine to another physical machine with a few clicks. Fewer physical servers means smaller electricity usage, which, in turn, lowers electric service bills. Savings spread out over a year can be rather sizable.

- ✔ **Replacing old, slow tape-based backup libraries with fast, reliable SAN devices:** Tapes are slow, and with system capacities the way they are these days, those tape drives are likely no longer enough. SAN and NAS devices are a lot faster, but also a lot more expensive. However, several vendors are out there that can give you a deal, especially on a smaller unit for testing. The drawback, sadly, is that you have to convince bean counters to part with more beans than they may like, even for some testing. Take a look at Drobo (www.drobo.com) for testing a deployment because it's extremely reliable and quick to set up. Just keep in mind that unless your company has no plans to grow, you may want to look at another vendor for large-scale deployments if testing is successful.

- ✔ **Upgrading older, less effective uninterruptable power supplies:** It's not uncommon for smaller companies to have purchased a battery backup system at some point and then just forgotten about it. About the only time they do pay attention is when it's screaming because it needs new batteries. That could be a possible cue to push (lightly) for an upgrade to newer, longer lasting, more effective, and frequently much lower cost replacement devices. One of the benefits of such a project is that it can illustrate a number of different skills you have, making you an even more valuable asset. It's best, however, to show how you are *saving* them money, instead of just spending it.

Understanding the Concepts of Agile

One of the more intriguing advances in project management in the last 15 years is *Agile*. Agile was originally designed as a process methodology for software development, but in recent years, Agile has been adapted to a range of projects. The term Agile comes from what was dubbed the Agile Manifesto, conceived on a skiing trip back in 2001. You can find out more at the website `http://agilemanifesto.org`.

Agile was not created out of whole cloth. It took many years and many different methodologies developed by groups like Extreme Programming, DSDM, Pragmatic Programming, and others to achieve a result that all participants could agree on.

Agile has 12 principles:

- ✔ Our highest priority is to satisfy the customer through early and continuous delivery of valuable software.
- ✔ Welcome changing requirements, even late in development. Agile processes harness change for the customer's competitive advantage.
- ✔ Deliver working software frequently, from a couple of weeks to a couple of months, with a preference to the shorter timescale.
- ✔ Business people and developers must work together daily throughout the project.
- ✔ Build projects around motivated individuals. Give them the environment and support they need and trust them to get the job done.
- ✔ The most efficient and effective method of conveying information to and within a development team is face-to-face conversation.
- ✔ Working software is the primary measure of progress.
- ✔ Agile processes promote sustainable development. The sponsors, developers, and users should be able to maintain a constant pace indefinitely.
- ✔ Continuous attention to technical excellence and good design enhances agility.
- ✔ Simplicity — the art of maximizing the amount of work not done — is essential.
- ✔ The best architectures, requirements, and designs emerge from self-organizing teams.
- ✔ At regular intervals, the team reflects on how to become more effective, then tunes and adjusts its behavior accordingly.

Most of these principles can be modified easily to be compatible with almost any process, and software development firms do frequently integrate Agile into other aspects of their operations. Agile itself, however, is just a set of ideals, a kind of mission statement in 12 parts.

Why Agile is so popular

Interestingly enough, it isn't just the principles of Agile that make it popular, but the methodological frameworks that have been developed around it. The term Agile, in this context, is now used as an umbrella term for all Agile-derived methodologies. A number of different forms of Agile are used, but only a few are popular, such as SCRUM, Lean, and Kanban.

SCRUM

SCRUM, named after the formation in rugby and not an acronym, is a methodology that uses scheduled periods called a *Sprint* during which all project work is done. Sprints run from two to four weeks and run a specific schedule. This means that each team member makes a commitment to complete various *User Stories* from the Backlog, and all commitments are confirmed by the Sprint's designated Scrum Master.

The hallmark of SCRUM is that each team is self-organizing. This means that all team members are responsible for the success of that team. The team prioritizes its backlog based on the needs of the overall project as indicated by the Product Owner. The Backlog is made up of what are called User Stories. Each User Story is formatted like so:

As a <INSERT USER TYPE>, I want <INSERT REQUIREMENT> so that <INSERT DESIRED RESULT>.

Problems and goals are broken down into small chunks that represent some level of progress when complete, but do not require time greater than the Sprint timeframe to finish. For example a user story may be as follows:

As a remote user, I want fewer steps to login to remote access so that the process is less complicated. The format is nice and tidy, conveys the need for a change, and is clear about what will satisfy that need.

User Stories are the smallest element of what is termed an *Epic.* Inside of Epics are *Themes* of related User Stories. Epics are very large (for example, Email client), Themes represent distinctive elements within an Epic (for example, Email client inbox), and User Stories are details within the theme (for example, fetch IMAP inbox content list). In IT, you may have an Epic for Upgrading servers, a Theme of Installing servers, and a User Story of Install server rails in a rack.

Not all User Stories, however, need to use this format, especially in IT-style implementations of Agile. It's not always necessary to employ the entire theme in order to convey the need and sometimes the task just doesn't fit the format. Some examples may be

- ✔ Replace paper roll in large-format printer on fifth floor
- ✔ Test server OS patches for November
- ✔ Upgrade Ethernet cables to CAT-6e in Graphics Lab

Lean

Lean, or more specifically Lean Production, is a concept of manufacturing that is derived from the Toyota Production System. The idea is that anything produced should be only to the benefit of the customer, and that all other costs are waste.

Lean may have been developed for manufacturing, but it has been adapted to project management. A significant element of Lean is Kanban, which was the design basis for SCRUM's backlog system (see preceding section).

Kanban

Kanban uses a simplified process of three bins: To Do, Doing, and Done. Kanban boards are traditionally areas where actual cards, or sticky notes, are posted in one of three bins. Any cards at the top have the highest priority. Any cards in the Doing bin must be actively worked on in the given period of time. Any cards in the Done bin must be verified complete by management.

Putting it all together

Agile, in these instances, is implemented as a way to reduce wasted time in development, organization based on immediate need and available resources, and integrate better progress reporting tools into the development process. Implementations for IT work in much the same way. Some differences are made to Agile to accommodate IT projects to reduce wasted time in project implementation as opposed to development, but the remainder of the ideals of Agile generally remain unchanged.

Companies benefit from the implementation of Agile because its processes help refocus efforts within the company. Customer satisfaction has been recognized as a means to engender growth in the customer base, therefore increasing profit margins. Agile is also helpful at adding productivity metrics where there are few. Individuals are gauged on their performance based on these metrics as opposed to less accurate management-guided employee evaluations.

Using Agile in IT

The use of Agile in IT departments is rather simple and can range in complexity from straightforward Kanban organization to full-featured Agile SCRUM with multi-board implementations, Sprints, burndown charts, daily standups, or any mix of the elements that can make up Agile. Like development forms of Agile, projects are broken down into user stories. It's not uncommon to see a greater number of Epics in IT, as there are a lot more diverse, large-scale projects that benefit from being compartmentalized for easier planning.

In an effective environment, everyone has their own Kanban board and pull backlog items from the team board. If the Sprint format is used, then at the beginning of each Sprint each team member makes a commits to working on a number of items from the backlog. During the Sprint, the team meets every day to talk about progress, and identify Roadblocks so that they can be removed. One engineer's board may look like this:

To Do	*Doing*	*Done*
As an engineer, I would like to standardize administrative access credentials to speed up work.	As a user, I need to be able to access all printers on the third floor.	Order HP LaserJet 4M toner carts for HR.
Deploy patches for latest version of FileMaker 13.		Verify documentation on new installs for master inventory.
Install new gigabit switch in third floor network closet.		
As a technical support engineer, I need a guide to migrate from Windows 7 to Windows 8.1 for existing users to standardize the process.		

When working like this, you keep only the items in the Doing bin that you are actively working on at any given time. It's also helpful to complete the tasks in their entirety before moving on to the next one. This method helps you focus on the goal in case issues crop up, and you need help.

One of the elements that makes Agile seem inappropriate for IT is that random problems crop up more frequently than in software development. There is an easy way to integrate it, however. One way is to set up an additional backlog for incidentals. Another way is to set up a whiteboard in the technical support office for physical sticky notes and bins for all users. Yet another way is to use integration tools to connect your ticketing system with your backlog tool or just leave all break/fix issues in the ticketing system.

Dealing with Agile and developers when you handle the company website

Yes, it's a long title for a simple problem. It often crops up when a company develops its own website and uses a framework like WordPress or Drupal. There are two general camps when it comes to using Content Management Systems (CMS). One states that it's just code, so why not treat it as a development project? The other states that it's already a working system, so why not treat it like an IT administration project? In essence, both are right, but there will likely be some bad blood between departments if it isn't managed correctly in the first place.

Because Agile development frequently uses the Sprint model, project periods often last anywhere from two to four weeks, and the work isn't deployed until the end of the Sprint. This presents a problem with IT people who are accustomed to deploying changes as soon as they are ready. IT people, after all, don't have to compile code or refactor anything. In addition, CMS are designed to make it easier to make changes, add content, and manage media without constant tending by programmers.

If the development team does have control over the website for your company, and Agile is in use, you'll have to deal with Sprints. If Sprints run on a two-week schedule, then it's not as hard to deal with, but if they run every four weeks, it can be a real problem. It's too much of a burden to wait a month to install a new plugin or modify a banner to reflect a new partnership.

Ultimately, the best way to manage the relationship is through collaboration with whomever is managing the website, clearly documenting everything, and detailing all the problems that are created via the delays in deployment. You also need a well-developed sense of patience. Use that patience when working with the development and management teams to get a new working model in place to accommodate the more immediate changes the website needs to be more agile. It's rather ironic, when you think about it.

Grin and Bear It: A Pocket Guide to Workplace Personalities

There's nothing more fun than working in a company where hostile personalities and corporate politics abound. When I say fun, I really mean annoying, but I think you get the point. Dealing with people can be frustrating, but this is part of how life operates, so I suggest you get used to it.

 One of the ways to manage these potentials is to be familiar with some of them. It helps to be prepared, and those who are forewarned are those who are forearmed.

Things you may have to put up with

I've put this in list format so that it's easier to read through:

- One or more users who constantly call up or email with all manner of small issues that you can never track down
- A fellow engineer who is frequently condescending and only helps begrudgingly
- An executive who insists on maintaining an outdated system that has long been surpassed with newer versions merely because it would represent a large, single cost
- A manager who is either completely incompetent or prone to overcommitting the resources of his team

Things that may make it easier

On the other end of the spectrum, some things make having a job quite nice, especially if it's a startup:

- A real coffee bar with a cappuccino machine
- Fully paid benefits and low copays
- Travel to work-related shows, conferences, and programs
- Lots of bits and whatnot from companies courting your executives to make an investment in their solution

✔ Various discounts and services offered by partners

✔ Discounts on service fees from your wireless carrier

✔ Free food from a well-stocked kitchen or breakroom

✔ Outings with fellow workers for lunch, dinners, and holiday parties

✔ Paid vacations

✔ Trips to interesting places for company retreats or rewards

There's always something rewarding you get from working just about anywhere. Not every workplace is a carnival or horrors. Just buckle down and find the silver lining in your company. They all have at least one.

Chapter 9

The Remote Nerd

In This Chapter

▶ Acclimating yourself to cubicle life

▶ Clarifying the differences between remote support and other types of support service

▶ Detailing the different ways customers communicate with companies

*W*orking as a technical support engineer for a company that provides a product to customers is fundamentally different than working as a consultant or an internal help desk. Your primary role is to connect with users and provide them support for one or more software or hardware products. You don't have direct access to them, but they need your help, and it's a difficult enough thing when you can work with people face to face.

Another factor of working for an external help desk is that you don't generally work directly with other engineers, but alone in a cubicle. You get a computer, a phone, a headset, and access to a range of tools to help you provide service to customers. Some work is done entirely in email, while other work is performed over the phone, through instant messaging, or using remote access tools.

The different forms of communication are used in different ways in order to facilitate the delivery of solutions for the range of different skill levels of customers. Issues can scale from simple questions to extraordinarily complex problems. Customers who are familiar with the technologies can often make due with an answer to a simple question, while others require more of a hands-on approach.

The Disruptor Called Social Networking

If any one thing has had an enormous effect on interactions between customers and the companies who need them, it's social networking. The simple idea that anyone on the Internet can tweet an unpleasant experience or post to Facebook about a product disaster and have it seen by tens of thousands of people within the hour is horrifying to marketing teams worldwide. In a period of 24 hours, a company's stellar reputation can crumble to dust if these issues aren't managed in a timely and public fashion, and the corporate world knows this well. Okay, corporations *almost* know this well.

Before the Internet took hold of life (and now limb via smartwatches and sports bands), the only way people could complain about being mistreated by a company was to take it to the Better Business Bureau, or BBB. The BBB was, and still is, responsible for helping industry maintain positive relations with their customers and neighbors. Someone would purchase a product, discover it had a problem, take it to the manufacturer for resolution, and hit a wall. This is where the consumer could get the BBB involved as a facilitator to discussion of a mutual solution.

Back in the '70s and '80s, that involved writing a letter and mailing it in. Now, anyone with a Twitter or Facebook account can publish an angry screed in seconds or contact any number of popular blogs who smell blood in the water to be angry. Most everyone knows now that anything posted to the Internet is forever. It gets scanned, spidered, indexed, screencapped, notated, cached, curated, and/or aggregated in seconds. I haven't run PDA Handyman in many years, but head over to Archive.org and search for "pda-handyman.com" in the WayBack Machine, and you can read most of what I wrote back in the early 2000s.

Remember this rule: Nothing leaves the Internet.

The Internet is like an anti-Las Vegas. Anything that happens on the Internet ends up staining the rug, and no amount of elbow grease will get it out. In fact, those who try to get something removed from the Internet incur the exact opposite and shine a bright, unflinching light on whatever it was they were trying to conceal. Marketing people know this, and many companies have created teams of customer service and technical support people to keep tabs on movements in the social part of cyberspace.

Social networking isn't all scary. Social networks like Twitter, Facebook, Google+, and the new Ello can be excellent resources for understanding the mood of your customers. Gauging the temperature of your customers can come in handy for a range of reasons, such as determining priorities and identifying opportunities for documentation and knowledgebase expansion, passing on helpful data to development teams for issue resolution, rewarding loyal customers, and much more.

The help desk tier model

While not a requirement, the vast majority of customer-facing help desks are configured using a Tier system. The concept is simple enough. Tier-I engineers are the first line of support and are frequently not trained in technical matters. If you've ever called into a service desk for your local cable provider, you will likely have encountered Tier-I personnel. Their task is to reduce the amount of time higher grade engineers spend solving simple, common problems. Tier-I staff generally follow scripts and walk those in need through a planned process to troubleshoot the issue. Of course, the technical ability of Tier-I engineers is determined by the requirements of the products supported.

Tiers work as you might expect. Customers are first directed to Tier-I, which tries all standard troubleshooting methods to achieve a solution. If that fails, the customer is connected to a Tier-II engineer who is generally more knowledgeable and can perform more complex troubleshooting methods. If even Tier-II efforts fail, then customers are routed to a Tier-III engineer. In some cases, the Tier-III staff are developers and are rarely called from their coding duties to perform help desk work. When the technical support group is supporting consumer users, it's rare that there even is a Tier-III team. Tier-I is what is used for primary support, and Tier-II is made up of managers.

In the late '90s, I was employed as a Tier-I support technician by IBM in Northern Vermont, and it was my job to take calls from engineers who were experiencing issues with ChipBench, a CPU design application. I would listen to their problem and then decide which ChipBench developer was best placed to answer the question. I was never an electrical engineer nor had I any experience with ChipBench, but I was able to perform my duties with just a little mentoring and the right tools. I even managed to learn quite a bit about how CPUs work and better understand computer architecture.

In the mid-2000s, I was the service manager for a consultancy in Southern California where I managed a team of engineers. Our job was to provide support for our clients through our Kaseya managed services system. Users from various different client sites would call or email to request help, plan a project, or just ask for some advice. The person who took the call or email would be responsible for completing the service call and, if they needed help, would talk to me. My team was made up of the same people who worked on-site, so there was no need to escalate most tickets.

These are just two examples of possible help desk deployments. There are countless others, and they take shape based on the needs of customers and the resources a company has available.

When working for a cloud service startup a few years ago as a technical writer, I watched as it built its 14-hour a day help desk service into a 24-hour service over a period of a year by setting up teams in the United States and in Europe. Customers could call, email, or chat at any time, which is a really good way to fend off frustration when customers frequently burn the midnight oil.

Random monitoring: The gaze of Sauron!

One aspect of external technical support that you may need to get used to is being monitored without knowing it. Well, you'll know that you're being reviewed, but you won't know exactly when. Managers use random monitoring because they believe it gives them a pure, unadulterated snapshot of the performance of subordinates. They listen to your work and review your behavior, something like a coach reviewing tapes of previous sporting events in order to offer personally tailored critiques to team members.

It's not easy to work in a place where you are spied on and then have to endure others telling you how to talk and behave. Then add the element of pressure from external forces like difficult customers, frustrating problems that defy solutions, or you just having a bad day, and it can be a difficult job. Then again, a well-organized, open minded, and progressive organization can offer rewards and potential for advancement that makes the initial unpleasantness well worth the effort.

Unfortunately, I've found that most people behave out of fear as opposed to the need to perform well or serve others. It is unsurprising that management types do not generally agree with this assessment, but I do have an alternative method of monitoring that eliminates the element of fear or sense of being spied upon. Instead of randomly connecting to employees, sit with them and share their experiences. This approach has the dual benefit of fostering a sense of mentoring while allowing each engineer to receive tutoring on points that can bear improvement per call.

Sadly, not all companies handle their support operations in this progressive manner. This doesn't mean that those who are not progressive are bad or unethical. It just means that you'll have to bear in mind what you will face when working for such a corporation.

Remotely, kind engineer

When seeking assistance from technical support, customers use three primary forms of communication. Sure, websites full of static information and forums offer sporadic, so-called community support. There are even forums that are staffed by employees, but all of these forms of communications tend to be less than consistent in providing results and are difficult to search. If forum posts are to be believed, then staffers don't always show up when asked, either.

The following sections describe the most reliable methods of contacting support.

Phone

Being placed on hold to wait for dozens of minutes is not exactly the high-light of anyone's day, but the simple phone call is, arguably, the most common method customers use to contact technical support. Voice communications is a very efficient form of conveying ideas, and people feel comfortable relaying information about their problems over the phone. Most systems do not directly connect customers with support staff, instead employing some form of speech recognition or dial tone menu tree to route callers to the appropriate support group.

If you commonly have unpleasant interactions with phone support from various companies, imagine how your customers feel when they call for help. As such, you can do a number of things to make their experience pleasant:

✔ Be friendly.

✔ Don't react to emotional bait.

✔ Try not to make your customers wait on hold too long.

✔ Don't promise, or even suggest, anything you can't deliver.

✔ Keep the microphone of your headset away and to the side of your mouth to improve voice quality.

✔ Limit personal discussions as much as possible, but don't be rude.

✔ Try not to sound like a robot, but just be yourself, even when reading from a script.

✔ Don't try to force customers to walk through processes they say they have already completed; instead move on to other possible solutions.

Email

While I'm sure email is the second most used form of contacting technical support, I wouldn't be surprised to discover that instant messaging is closing in. Regardless, email is great because it allows customers to send detailed messages for help.

This abundance of information isn't always the case, though. On occasion, you will receive a request for help that contains little to no useful information.

In these cases, you will need to coax more information from the users and possibly direct them to another form of communication to solve the problem.

Despite how it can be used, email is not an instant form of communication. It's important that you respond to each and every question asked or point made so that the customer feels that you are paying attention. Email should be governed by the same ethical rules as phone support.

Chat

Chat, also called instant messaging, is a common form of communication used by many companies as one way to serve their customers. Chat isn't limited to technical support, as it is frequently used for sales as well.

Customers have grown accustomed to seeing a chat function. People who have used it like chat because it alleviates the need to wait on hold for an indefinite period of time with a phone pressed to the ear. When I need to use the phone to contact technical support, I bust out my headset, but I always look for chat first.

Chat is an excellent tool for engineers as well. Chat is interactive like a phone call, but adds the ability to send links and even act as a conduit to starting remote control sessions. In addition, engineers can work on two or more chat sessions at one time, whereas people can generally function only on a single phone call at a time. In chat, customers don't expect to constantly hear from the engineer every second they are connected.

As with email, you should apply the same rules of conduct for phone conversations to your chat sessions.

Remote management tools

One of the best and most powerful systems administration tools ever created is remote access. It's been around for a very long time. Old UNIX mainframes were almost always accessed remotely through their connected network, but that was limited to text-based terminal sessions. Current remote access technologies, of which there are quite a few, allow engineers to control remote systems visually.

Here's a breakdown of popular remote access tools:

✔ **Microsoft Remote Desktop Connection (RDC):** This is Microsoft's very own tool, and it's been around for a long time. Both the client and server are included in all installations of Windows, but the server is disabled by default to prevent any unauthorized access. There's even a version of the client for Mac OS X systems, but it hasn't been updated since 2011. There are also additional third-party clients for various platforms, including mobile devices like smartphones and tablets.

✔ **Apple Remote Desktop (ARD):** Apple also offers its own remote access tool, but it's designed more for administrators than just regular users. While the server is included in all versions of Mac OS X, the client is not. You can purchase the client for $80, but it's designed to do a lot more than Microsoft's RDC client. Not only can you manage and track several systems at one time, you can also distribute software and program Automator scripts.

✔ **VNC:** Originally developed by engineers at the AT&T Labs in Cambridge and then pushed into the Open Source software space, VNC has almost become the go-to remote access client/server for almost any platform. VNC is a simple Remote Frame Buffer system that incorporates remote mouse and keyboard input elements, as well as a few other helpful cross desktop tools. The original programmers formed RealVNC after AT&T Labs were closed in 2002 and have built a successful business from their efforts.

Because VNC is open source, a number of other VNC-based packages, including TightVNC and UltraVNC, are available. Those two are Windows-specific, however. RealVNC offers installations for Windows, Mac OS X, and Linux, and there are viewer apps for iOS, Android, and even Google's Chrome.

The key requirement for use of VNC, however, is that you'll need to secure connections through your firewall as the free version does not include integrated security features. There are paid personal and enterprise versions, however, that do include integrated security functionality.

✔ **LogMeIn:** LogMeIn is a commercial remote access system that works on Windows and Mac OS X and offers a number of different ways to remotely control those systems. There are two different versions of LogMeIn: Pro for desktop users and Rescue for technical support teams. While LogMeIn is not free, it is very secure and well supported.

✔ **TeamViewer:** TeamViewer is another commercial product that offers its own take on remote access. TeamViewer enjoys broad platform support for Windows, Mac OS X, Linux, iOS, Android, Windows Phone, and even BlackBerry. It is even free for personal use, and it's remote screen buffer technology is very fast.

You can purchase commercial licenses under its unique Lifetime License plans, but be prepared for some sticker shock. The Business license is $750, the Premium license is $1,500, and the Corporate license is $3,570. This may seem overly costly, but these are Lifetime licenses, so you will get updates as long as they release them, and you can install as many customer modules as you need.

Remote access tools are plentiful and can go a long way toward reducing the amount of hands-on time you spend directly handing systems that just need to be checked in on. You will quickly find that remote access is one of the most critical tools you will have in your toolbox.

Getting to Know Your Products

Developing a complete understanding of all the products you support is important in all forms of technical support, but none more than remote support. The grim reality is that people simply won't tolerate waiting on hold so that you can research a problem. Customers expect swift and decisive assistance the moment they need it and will feel abandoned the second you duck off to figure out how to fix their issue. As a remote support engineer, it is critical that you get to work immediately memorizing everything you can about all of the products you support.

There are a number of different methods to improve memorization, but everyone has his or her own way. If you already have a way to learn new things and commit them for quick recall, then do so. If you need some help, however, I've included some information on a few methods in the following sections.

The first thing, however, is to collect as much information as you can about the products.

Collecting materials

Gathering details and documenting them is one of the best ways to start establishing an internal database of products and how to work with them. To collect that data, you need a centrally located, organized format to store the information. I know of two ways that work very well and require almost no effort.

The first method is to use bookmarks in your favorite web browser. I use Google's Chrome, but any browser will suffice. Using the Bookmarks Bar, I create a base folder that I call Tech Library, but you can name it anything you like. Inside of that folder, create additional folders. Just get the ones you can think of, as you can add more later. When you come across or locate anything that is helpful, sort it into the appropriate folder.

The second method that I use is a service called Wunderlist, but there are others. The most popular of these services is Evernote. Both are freemium

ou can get a few additional features for a mere $5 per month.
items manually or add them using a browser plugin. Adding
allows you to upload PDF, Word, and other nonwebpage files
ater.

ng information

the old standby of rote memorization, but you can expand
t repeating content so many times and drilling it into your
that you did this with your multiplication tables. That
, right? You can't really drill actions in that way, so you
peated usage. If there is any way that you can personally
u support, then by all means, do so.

Another form of memorization technique that is commonly employed is *mnemonics*. According to Dr. Dennis Congos of the University of Central Florida, nine fundamental types of mnemonic devices can help you forge better memories and tools to recall them. I personally use a couple of them already, but you may find the others to be a better fit for you.

Mnemonics is a way of learning to recall complex information that is commonly structured. Mnemonics uses your ability to recall smaller things as leverage to store more detailed information. There are no real rules to mnemonics, and you can use your imagination to develop anything that will help, but I'm going to look at the nine that Dr. Congos discusses.

Names

I'll start with names because one of the most common mnemonics uses names. You'll recognize it immediately. Probably. It's the following:

ROY G. BIV

This is the mnemonic for the colors of the spectrum, Red, Orange, Yellow, Green, Blue, Indigo, and Violet.

Music

Music is often used as a form of recognition. I have this odd ability. I can't recall song lyrics until the song is actually playing, and then I can sing along with confidence.

Kids learn their ABCs or the States in the Union by singing songs. The lyrical, musical, and repeating aspects of the music helps seat those memories, and when you start singing, it comes out.

Words and expressions

Popular mnemonics often form phrases into words or create nonsense phrases to collate the recollection. For example, look at the order of operations in math:

PEMDAS = Parentheses, Exponents, Multiply, Divide, Add, Subtract

Now look at an expression that may help you remember the order of planets from the Sun outward:

Mercurial Venus eats marshmallow jello snacks under nearby planets

Mercury, Venus, Earth, Mars, Jupiter, Saturn, Uranus, Neptune, Pluto

Model

A model gives you a visual cue to a process. It helps order your memories for concepts like processes and methodologies, which are often difficult to describe in single words or simple phrases. A common model in IT is the OSI model of networking, shown in Figure 9-1.

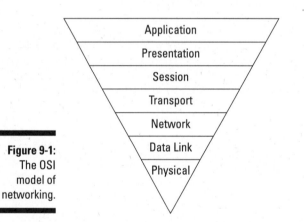

Figure 9-1:
The OSI model of networking.

The form of the pyramid leads from the smallest element of the data, the bit, to the largest representation of that data, which are the Session, Presentation, and Application layers. Figure 9-1 alone gives you a pictorial representation of what the information looks like, helping you recall even more information.

Ode of Rhyme

While I was never good at recalling this old saw, my sisters were:

> 30 days have September, April, June, and November
>
> All the rest have 31
>
> Except February my dear son
>
> It has 28 and that is fine
>
> But in the Leap Year it has 29

Everyone I know remembers "In Fourteen Hundred and Ninety Two, Columbus Sailed The Ocean Blue."

Then there's the English rules for the letter certain letter sounds.

> I before E except after C
>
> or when sounding like A
>
> as in Neighbor or Weigh

These are structures developed to help you recall practical information that you may not use frequently. After all, how many times do you need to figure out how many days there are in a month.

Note organization

There are a number of ways people use notes to organize their thoughts. One of the more common ways is using notecards. Concepts are broken down into smaller parts. You place the idea or problem on the front of the card and the details or solution on the back, like a more complex form of flashcard. You then study each card and try to recall what's on the back. If you cannot, you look and then move on. Over time, you start to associate the detail with the idea and make the connection.

Another common form is using outlines. This is how I organize my thoughts and how I push out detail when I write. It works just like a book is organized. You have sections and then chapters, and those chapters have headings and subheadings, all drilling down from an overall idea to its component parts. The great thing about outlines is that you don't have to get everything in the first time. Just start where it works for you and start building outward. If you get stuck, move on. When it hits you, go back to insert it. Then look things over and move them around as needed.

Then there's the Cornell System. It's very similar to the notecard concept, but uses a single sheet of paper with a vertical line positioned 3 inches from the left. The ideas go to the left, and the details go to the right.

Images

Yet another form of mnemonic is the image. These images are not pictures you take necessarily, but sketches or thought pictures. Apparently, the sillier an image, the easier it is to recall. One example suggested by Dr. Congos is that of a man named John Horsely whom you meet at a party. To recall his name, you envision a horse on a toilet.

Connections

Connections are the single most common form of mnemonic used with computers, and people often don't realize they're doing it. The Graphical User Interface, or GUI, came out of the idea that people have visual memories, and Windows and Mac OS X use a lot of visual cues to help guide users.

The very first mnemonic that you learn is that whatever the mouse pointer is over, clicking will affect it. You also use a form of muscle memory to see things on the screen. When you press the Start button on the keyboard, you look to the lower left for the menu to appear in Windows.

Icons are also an important aspect of connecting visual cues to results. The next time you go launch a program, consciously pay attention to whether or not you check the icon text to make sure you're starting the right program. In fact, in Windows 7, the taskbar doesn't show the name of the application, just the icon. When you walk through menus, you are using another form of connection. This is why it is important for developers to use consistent and established forms of basic application design. Otherwise, users would be confused.

Spelling

Many people use this last one. When I come across the rare word that gives me trouble, I give it a mnemonic. Then, every time I have to spell that word, I get the mnemonic and not the word.

A long, long time ago in a lifetime far, far away, I used to have problems with Wednesday. To this very day, I still say this in my head:

WED NES DAY

I lived in New Mexico for a few years and had to be able to spell the city's name:

AL BOO KWEER KWEE (Albuquerque)

There are state names as well:

T E N N E S S E E

M ISS ISS IPP I

Familiarity breeds . . . expertise!

I can't help but use one of the most oft used tools of education: repetition. As I said before, work with what you support. That's the best way you can offer others help. You've been using Windows or Mac OS X for years. Where is the Control Panel? How do you get to it in Windows 2000? What about in XP? How do you manually update drivers for a wireless adapter? How do you import fonts into Mac OS X? What if they're using Mac OS X 10.4 on a PowerPC-based machine? Does it still work the same as on Mavericks?

Quiz yourself. Ask yourself questions and then work through the solutions. Look through the ticket system's logs and find the questions that are most frequently asked and answered and learn those first. Grow organically from there and spiral out until you know as much as you think you can.

Then learn more.

Technical support is a neverending process. To feed that beast, you must constantly be on the lookout for new prey, stalk it, and study it until you really, really know it. Inside out. Don't worry. You can do it.

I have faith in you.

Part IV
Landing the Job

March 12, 2014 *(the date of your interview)*

Mrs. Johnson: *(the colon is used in formal correspondence)*

Thank you for affording me the time to meet with you today. As discussed, my three years of consulting experience for small businesses meshes well with the needs of your internal help desk. I also wanted to highlight my experience with technical documentation, which would be a great fit for your company.

Please let Mr. Addison know that I was very pleased to meet him and his team and appreciated the time he spent with me.

Should you have any questions, please don't hesitate to contact me at 999-123-4567 or email me at jobseeker@awesome-

Joe Awesome

Discover the steps you need to take to get hired in the article "How to Use LinkedIn to Land the IT Help Desk Job You Want" online at www.dummies.com/extras/gettinganithelpdeskjob.

In this part . . .

- ✔ Brand yourself the right way to land the job.

- ✔ Impress interviewers with a killer resume and cover letter.

- ✔ Stand out from other candidates during the interview process.

- ✔ Make all the right moves after the interview to guarantee a job offer.

- ✔ Discover the steps you need to take to get hired in the article "How to Use LinkedIn to Land the IT Help Desk Job You Want" online at `www.dummies.com/extras/gettinganit helpdeskjob`.

Chapter 10

Branding Yourself

· ·

In This Chapter

▶ Gaining mastery over the branding tools the Internet offers you

▶ Developing a presence for yourself that others will be drawn to

▶ Establishing a verifiable level of credibility through action and word

· ·

*I*n this chapter, I illustrate the various methods you can use to brand yourself as an IT expert. It's not quite enough to just have a Twitter or Facebook account. You must also express your expertise in various public outlets or, even better, publish a blog with helpful information. I also cover the benefits of using LinkedIn and various other services to get your name in cyberspace.

Developing Who You Are Online

The Internet is no longer some kind of fad. It hasn't been for a number of years now. The Internet has become a critical component to daily communicating, media consuming, and shopping, researching, and entertaining.

Setting up a blog

For some reason that is unclear, people like to set up blogs and express themselves on the Internet. I'm not trying to suggest that setting up a blog isn't a good thing; it's just an interesting phenomenon. It's likely due to the fact that, before the Internet, most people didn't have a public voice. So, it's not that the reasons are unclear, but more to the point, manifold. Some people like to complain about stuff, others prefer to share their talents or with fellow practitioners of their profession, and the reasons beyond that are unlimited.

Your reasons, however, will be to establish both an online presence and yourself as an expert in your various disciplines. You can establish your expertise online in a number of different ways, but the most common outlets are some form of hosting service. Technically, all services providing you remote access to their tool is hosting that tool for you so that you don't have to. There are, however, different kinds of hosting services, and while some are outstanding, others . . . not so much.

The most common online blogging platforms in use these days are Automattic's WordPress.com, Google's Blogger, SayMedia's TypePad, and Yahoo!'s Tumblr, which is actually a microblogging service. The idea is that you can go sign up for an account, and the blogging platforms generate one or more blogs for you. You can customize it, add some features, and don't have to be bothered with managing all the junk in the background.

There's blogging and then there's microblogging. WordPress, Blogger, and TypePad are essentially blogging services/platforms. Tumblr is considered a microblogging platform because it doesn't have the extensive rich-media control and formatting that are central to the other platforms. Typically, you think of Twitter for microblogging, but that's the most "micro" of them. From there, you get Facebook and then Tumblr at the top. Some people use Tumblr as their blogging platform, while others use it to augment their reach to a wider audience.

Call me biased, but I think most people would agree that WordPress.com has become one of, if not the most, popular blogging services there is. According to people who know, that being W3Techs.com, 61 percent of all sites using a known Content Management System (CMS) are using WordPress. That works out to 23.2 percent of all websites on the Internet.

WordPress has attained such high usage due to a few factors. One, WordPress is solid, easy to use, stable, and secure. Two, it's very easy to extend and customize. Three, it's free. Four, there's an enormous developer community out there who can provide paid services.

The benefits of a personal domain name

While I'm sure it's fine to have a web address that looks like the following to most people, it's not really quite professional looking:

```
http://blogname.bloggingservice.com
```

After all, if you work in technology, shouldn't setting up a website to use a custom domain name be easy for you? You know it's easy. Heck, you've probably done it a number of times already. It's also well documented, so why not get your own domain and set up your website so that it looks like this:

```
http://www.blogname.com
```

The benefits aren't just applied to your website, though. You can focus all your communications around that name. Your email won't be a generic Gmail or Outlook.com or Yahoo.com or Aol.com email address, but a professional-looking custom domain address. I'd bet you can guess my own personal domain and find me rather quickly. Give it a try and see what you find.

You'll want to work it out as best as possible to work with all your social networks as well. I detail it in the social network sections later in this chapter, but the idea is to get as many of them configured for the same name across all platforms. It's going to take some effort, but it's well worth it if you want to brand yourself as a positive resource. Some networks don't let you do what you want, though, so you'll just have to make do with what you have available to you. (I'm not naming names, Google+.)

Webmastering on a budget

One of the things you don't want to do when getting your Internet presence all set up is have to spend a lot of money to maintain it. You can, if you're not careful, but this section is where I give you tips on how to get the most out of free and very cheap, all without sacrificing quality.

Utterly free

If you want to go the completely free route, you can. You'll miss a few features, but you won't have to spend a dime. Here's the breakdown:

- ✔ **Website:** Tumblr, Blogger, or WordPress.com
- ✔ **Email:** Gmail or Outlook.com
- ✔ **Social networks:** Twitter, Facebook, Google+, and LinkedIn

Almost utterly free

If you're willing to spend a little money, you can start making things look quite professional:

- ✔ **Website:** Tumblr
- ✔ **Email:** Google Apps For Work ($5 per month per account)
- ✔ **Domains:** Name.com ($8.99 per .com per year)
- ✔ **Social networks:** Twitter, Facebook, Google+, and LinkedIn

In this arrangement, you get your domain from Name.com, which is the most reliable and lowest priced registrar I've ever used and highly recommend. You can then configure DNS to point to Tumblr for website traffic and Google Apps for Work for everything that service offers (email, calendar, contacts, Drive, and more). That's about $70 a year, which isn't bad.

Crank it up a notch

If you want to really kick it into the stratosphere without breaking the bank, you can do it:

- **Website:** BlueHost.com (as low as $6 per month pre-paid for 36 months)
- **Email:** Google Apps for Work ($5 per month per account)
- **Domains:** BlueHost.com (the master domain is only $5 per year)
- **Social networks:** Twitter, Facebook, Google+, and LinkedIn

BlueHost's Starter account will run you about $90 a year, which is generally a great deal better than you can get from other hosting sites and includes the first domain. (BlueHost, in this case, is your registrar.) BlueHost offers email accounts, but if you want to take advantage of what Google Apps for Work has to offer, spend the extra $5 per month. At the very least, you get some of the best spam filtering in the business.

If you have some disposable income, check out BlueHost's multiyear discounts. You can get the Starter account for three years for just $215. If you want to move up to the mostly-unlimited-in-all-aspects Plus account, you'll spend $144 for one year and $360 for three years, which breaks down to $10 a month. One of the nice things that BlueHost offers is unlimited bandwidth, which means you don't have to fear getting turned off when you start having some solid traffic rolling in.

There are other hosting solutions that are popular and provide quality service, though. There's iPage.com, which claims that its datacenter is 100 percent wind powered. I have no real reason to disbelieve this claim, but I do know that datacenters require a lot of power. Then there's HostGator.com, which has been around since 2002, the same as BlueHost. There's also 1&1.com and JustHost.com, both which offer about the same as the others.

As for WordPress.com and Tumblr, you can pay various fees to add services, but they both start free. The only thing you can pay for on Tumblr is premium themes. Quite a few are very nice, and you only have to pay once, but if you run a few blogs and want to use the same theme, you'll have to pay for each site individually. WordPress.com Premium accounts will cost you $99 a year to get a custom domain, advanced customization, and no ads, but you are limited to 13GBs of space. The Business edition will run you $299 a year, but gives you unlimited storage, live chat support, ecommerce, and a sizeable gaggle of premium themes, as well as the knowledge that the people behind it really know their WordPress.

Then there's TypePad. You can get their Plus plan for $9 a month, but for real expandability, you'll want to look at their Unlimited plan for $15 a month. All plans get unlimited storage and the ability to apply custom domains to blogs, but Unlimited allows you to fully customize the sites and have as many as you like. It's actually a rather good plan, and the company is very stable. TypePad was started in 2003 by Six Apart and based on the company's popular Movable Type blogging platform. It is used by some media heavyweights like ABC, the CBC, the BBC, and Sky News.

Just keep in mind that the kind of hosting BlueHost offers is called *shared web hosting*. This means that you are assigned a partition on a box that will have other user accounts on it. They are segregated, so nobody can just cruise through your files, but you don't get your own server. I ask that you think about what it might cost to run a datacenter before complaining that their rates are too high. They aren't.

Your very own email

When it comes to communicating with people, one of the most common formats is email. While it's not as much a stigma as it used to be, emailing with a potential employer from an AOL.com email address likely won't win you any kudos. Gmail, and to an ever-growing extent Outlook.com, is generally considered acceptable, but email addresses that end in yahoo.com or Hotmail.com just won't cut it. You don't need it, but it helps to have the power of a personalized domain behind the @ sign.

The vast majority of hosting providers offer a few to a load of email accounts with their plans, but spam filtering is often a paid add-on. If you're going to pay for it, you may as well get the best in the business, Google Apps for Work (GAFW). At $50 a year or $5 a month per account, it's a steal considering what you get. Like Gmail on steroids, you get Gmail, Hangouts, Calendar, Google+, Drive, and Docs, but you also get access to a complete management console.

You can associate one primary domain and either add domains as add-ons or aliases. (Covering that process in detail is a bit much here, but if you choose to go this route, you'll learn about the details.) In a way, it's sort of like Microsoft's Active Directory, just sugar free. I won't say it's dumbed down, but it simplifies a lot of the domain administration tasks that can be complex in AD environments. One final point that you'll really like is that instead of the 15GBs of free space you get with Gmail, each GAFW account comes with 30GBs. You can upgrade to unlimited for just $10 a month per user, but if you have less than five users, you'll each get 1TB. Regardless, it's a seriously good deal.

LinkedIn

When it comes to networking, LinkedIn is the king. It's rather ironic that the world's largest professional networking website is on the world's largest network, the Internet, but that's beside the point. LinkedIn.com is a must-have for professionals of most any stripe. If you are unfamiliar with it, think of it like a complete, Internet-based replacement for business cards and your curriculum vitae. When you create your free account, you are asked to input all of your work history and a wide range of other work-related information. This information builds your profile.

You can then share that profile with people you work with or just meet. Just email then an invite to join your network and, if they accept, you are linked. Unless you've been living under a rock, you'll immediately notice the resemblance to the Six Degrees of Kevin Bacon. Say that you work with Bob and Sally. You link up with Bob, but haven't linked with Sally yet. Bob will become a #1 link for you, and Sally will be a #2 link because she's connected to Bob. If there's a Jimmy who knows Sally, but not Bob, he'll become a #3, and so on. LinkedIn gives you the ability to contact people you are directly connected to you to moderate introductions to people they know.

As you add more and more people to your network, you will start to have more and more contacts, and you can illustrate how you know people. One of the more interesting aspects of certain job listing websites is integration with LinkedIn, so you can see who you may know that is working somewhere you want to get a job, or at least get an introduction to someone through the people you do know. To see this networking in action, just head over to the site (assuming that you've already setup your profile and network), find someone you're interested in, and look down the right side of the page. You'll see a listing of how you are connected to them through people you know.

LinkedIn is free, but the service has some limitations to unless you pay, and it's not cheap. I strongly suggest that you don't consider a Premium account as an annual cost unless you have a good amount of disposable cash. At $30 a month, you can't categorize it as an impulse buy. LinkedIn does offer 30 days free pretty much all the time, though, so if you need a hand up for a month, it's a good idea to take it up on its offer. Even if you have to spend $30 to $60 for Premium for a bit, it can really help. Just remember to cancel before you get charged when you can least afford it.

Twitter

I'd like to think everyone knows Twitter, but you never know. Twitter is the lowest common denominator in microblogging. The idea originally sprang from a brainstorming session where the concept of distributing an SMS (Short Message Service) to a group of people was floated. Because SMS are limited to 140 characters, tweets were limited to the same number of characters so that there wouldn't be any issues with compatibility. When Twitter was unleashed on the public in 2006, a lot of people didn't understand what it was for, but that has changed over the years.

Twitter is now one of the Internet's largest information networks and processes hundreds of millions of tweets and well over a billion search requests every day. This extraordinary level of information sharing has enabled a wide range of statistical magic, including alerting people to impending earthquake activity and breaking news. If you can build a following, you will have a network of people who, at least in part, will help spread your words to their followers. It's something like dropping a stone into a calm pond. The larger the stone, the larger and longer the ripples that will be caused on the surface.

User accounts are generated in the form of the @ sign followed by a user name, like so:

@tylerregas

When you create your Twitter username, you may face issues with names that are already used. You may be surprised, but another person on this planet has my exact name. I met them on Facebook and became friends with them. I don't know them personally, but we frequently joke about our shared name. Before meeting my counterpart, I thought I was fortunate enough to have a unique name, but I would periodically find it difficult to use my preferred username on certain services.

After meeting myself, I learned why. Take this lesson for yourself. It will help you determine as consistent a username as you can across all networks.

Facebook

If you didn't know about Twitter, you probably know about Facebook. It seems like everyone does. Formed in 2004 from a college project at Harvard University by Mark Zuckerberg, his roommates, and some other students, Facebook now has over 1.6 billion active users worldwide. Facebook is second to Google in overall, daily Internet traffic. Facebook is a wide range of things, including a microblogging service where users can post their statuses, pages, images, and photos they are interested in and to share with their friends.

Facebook is arranged in a few forms. The most common form is a user profile, which is designed for use by a single person. The second form is a Page, which is a kind of profile that is designed to be used by an organization or group. Pages can have multiple managers assigned to them, making them suitable for use by companies for promotion and community sharing.

As an individual, you can also create a Page, essentially using it to brand yourself. Creating a Page allows you to not only have your own personal profile that you can keep private for friends and family, but also a Page that promotes yourself on the Internet alongside your website, Twitter, and other services. To that end, Facebook allows you to create a custom URL for your Pages. In order to best leverage your name, try to create a Page URL that matches up with your other service accounts.

Google+

After MySpace began its decline in 2008 (Justin Timberlake and Specific Media Group purchased MySpace from News Corp. in 2011 and completely redesigned the site, but it still hasn't made a significant impact) and failing to offset Facebook's growth, it seemed as if nothing was going to take over the mantle or offering an alternative social network. It took a few years, but Google finally stepped into the race with Plus, Google's own form of Facebook.

Truth be told, Google+ isn't all that different than Facebook. It has user profiles. It has Pages for group and company promotion. It's has +1s that are similar to Likes. You can share images, links, videos, and text. It all ends up in a stream, it just looks different — more Google-like.

There are some differences, though. For one, Google+ offers Hangouts On Air that links with YouTube allowing users to broadcast live shows, which then become recordings that can be played back at any time on the associated YouTube channel. It takes a little bit of setup, but if you prefer to help people with videos, there are few better resources.

Google doesn't really publish numbers on its services, but Google+ did have 540 million users by late 2013, which is a very large number, and it's likely grown since then. That's still only a third of what Facebook has, but it's nothing to sniff at.

Creating a Page is an easier process than on Facebook, but there is one snag. Google, for reasons not entirely realistic, chooses to force you to add extra characters to your custom URL. For example, when I wanted to create a custom URL based on my name, I had to add more characters to it, so it could no longer be just tylerregas. It's annoying, but that's the way things are.

You may want to start with Google+ when creating your global usernames.

Don't Forget to Post

Once you get started with establishing your presence online, you don't want to let it sit. It will take determination to forge regular posting into a habit, but it will come. You just need to work hard at it. At least at first.

What to post

This one's simple. Post what you know. You don't have to plan things or have a schedule. You aren't a publishing house. You can post tutorials about all manner of things, from the most basic to very advanced. You can post guides to how you solved a problem or creative solutions to complex issues. You can post opinion pieces about various different things from products to the quality of documentation.

Don't limit yourself to just technology, though. You can also post things that interest you. I love animation, so I post stuff on my WordPress blog about animation all the time, including videos from YouTube and Vimeo. I write reviews of products and guides to using applications to help people out. Some of my most popular posts are about Amazon's FireTV and how to hack it (legally, of course) to add functionality.

When to post

When you post will have to be based on when you have time. That cannot be helped. The best thing to do is to establish a schedule for yourself. One way that I do it is to spend at least one part of everyday reading the news outlets in my newsreader. (I use Nextgen Reader for Windows 8 combined with Feedly to manage RSS feeds.) Because I look at headlines and read stories from all manner of sites that interest me, I am regularly inspired with items I want to share or get ideas for things I want to research.

You don't have to post every day, but you should post at least once every week. This helps keep your website active and keeps it moving up in the search ranks.

Making sure you propagate

Now it's time to make sure everything comes together. There's nothing more inconvenient then having to repost everything to all your social networks, but fortunately there are tools that help you do that automatically. Okay, at least mostly. Nothing is ever perfect, and the weak link in this chain is Google+, but I'll get back to that in a moment.

You'll want to start with WordPress (unless you've chosen another CMS, and then I can't help). If you follow my instructions, you've looked into WordPress and have connected it to Automattic's JetPack service through WordPress.com. Among dozens of other features, JetPack adds Publicize, a tool that automatically posts to your social networks when you publish new stories on your site.

Fortunately, Publicize has got you covered. Not only does it support sharing to Twitter and Facebook, but also LinkedIn, Tumblr, Google+, and even Path. All you need to do is go to your Publicize settings page in WordPress Admin and authenticate all the networks you use. Due to Automattic's efforts, it's an easy process that shouldn't take you very long. Once it's all set up, each time you click on the Publish button in a post, those networks will be updated.

Why Do You Need This?

You need to brand yourself because companies and headhunters from hiring firms do research candidates on the Internet. It's a very common practice, even though it's not exactly appealing. The following sections outline some other reasons, though.

Establishing a presence

Creating a presence for yourself on the Internet gives you, well . . . a presence. It gets your name into the search engines. It gets your published posts something to connect to and be related with. Because you have a little digital army on the Internet doing your bidding, people will be able to find you on most any popular network, no matter what they use. That's priceless. When someone goes to find you, they will pull up all manner of stuff.

 Don't just limit yourself to your own outlets, though. Make sure to get out there. Participate in the community culture that thrives on the Internet. Be active on forums answering questions or helping sort out issues with research. Be friendly and approachable, as if the people you are rubbing elbows with are the same ones you are supporting in your company.

Giving your words weight

As you put yourself out there, you are creating a map of who you are that others can follow. If you are successful, then others can get a better sense of who you are and what you like. More than that, though, you can lend yourself some gravitas through the process of being clear, concise, and accurate with your words.

When you speak on the Internet, it's akin to talking to people in person. They will derive from your posts how you are as a person. When you talk about high-level programming on Linux all the time, they won't have any feelings about your skills at working with Mac OS X or Windows and may not consider you for a position in those areas. Show people who you are as a whole, not just one small part. It all carries weight.

The giving soul

Some of that gravitas you are generating can come from giving from yourself selflessly. When you write about how to deal with common issues or how to move from Windows XP to Windows 8, you are creating a sense of giving that others will pick up on. If you are willing to take the time to pen a guide to cleaning up Windows or effectively removing applications from Mac OS X on your website, you are telegraphing to others that you are helpful and generous. These are positive values to have and reflect well on you.

Lessons for your future past

If, on the other hand, you are posting selfies from your latest frat party experience where you hammered a beer bong or decorated someone who passed out with a permanent marker and beer bottles, you are sending a very different message. This is the kind of message you do not want to send, and it will be seen. Don't trust that Facebook's security settings will protect you. They likely won't, and the timing will probably not be opportune.

Be kind to yourself and others and don't post unpleasant or ludicrous things about your debauchery or drunken conquests, illegal deeds, or anything that may reflect badly on you as a person. I'm not suggesting that you stop having any kind of fun. I'm just suggesting that you don't let everyone on the Internet know about it.

The reconnoitering recruiter

People everywhere are researching you on the Internet when you come up as a viable candidate for a position. The last thing you want to give them is ammunition that will harm your chances. Instead, give them ammunition consisting of love, compassion, skill, and a sense of fair play. Even though it's not exactly a fair estimation of a person as a whole, recruiters still base their initial impressions of you on your Internet presence.

Make it count.

Chapter 11

Creating a Winning Resume and Cover Letter

In This Chapter

▶ Discovering the importance of a resume

▶ Finding out about the importance of a cover letter

▶ Integrating tips and tricks to give yourself the best chance at success

*I*n this chapter, I walk you through of a resume format that leverages the information hiring people are looking for, help you understand why your resume is important, and even reveal what people look at and how long they give your resume to decide whether you'll get looked at or binned. Preparation, focus, consistency, attention to detail, and sheer doggedness are all critical when it comes to preparing the documents that could very well land you a job. Think of working on these documents as a personal test for the job you are going to get. You will need to prepare a version for every job you submit your documents for, and they must be tuned for each position.

I'm not saying that you should pad, also known as falsifying, your resume, of course. That would be wrong, but you do need to shift the focus onto the skills that the particular position requires. You will find that, over time, you will be able to reuse major portions of certain versions for similar positions at different companies. Just make sure that you don't leave traces of another potential employer!

The Dreaded Resume

If there's one thing people don't like doing when they are looking for a job, it has to be the preparation of the resume, or Curriculum Vitae (colloquially known as the CV). However, one misconception about what a resume is commonly overlooked. The resume is your sales brochure for employment. It is not a simple listing of your work history.

Think of the resume as the difference between a catalog of all kinds of different products, all laid out with SKU, simple description, prices, options, weight, and other boring stuff versus a slick, clean, targeted presentation giving the buyer the one thing they want. Which one do you think will interest the interviewer more? It's not actually a question, really, because you know that the latter is what will draw the eye. Nobody is interested in dry and boring.

When creating your resume, you need to keep it simple, put the stuff that you believe the HR people or recruiters need to see, and don't add anything that won't help you. One addition, however, that will help is the cover letter. The idea of a cover letter is simple. You must include a resume, but cover letters allow you to break everything crucial down into a single page that can be scanned quickly.

It is the cover letter, nine times out of ten, that gets you at least a phone conference. That kind of power cannot be ignored.

Why the resume is important

You know that a resume is you, just on paper (or at the very least, a digital file). You are illustrating who you are and what you are capable of on one or two sheets of paper. That's a lot to ask of paper, and so little of it.

The value of your resume doesn't come from a comprehensive, exhaustive, breathtakingly detailed review of your skills, however, but from your ability to tune it to the audience.

For example, a few years ago, my wife found an ad for a technical writer position at a local video game company known for its popular MMORPG game and urged me to apply.

I read through the requirements and found that I was a perfect match for everything the company was asking for. One requirement caught my eye, though. The company wanted to know what my favorite video game was and why. In the end, it wanted a cover letter, a short essay on my gaming habits, and my resume. It was certainly a creative way to suss out people.

In the end, I never got any more than an email apologizing that I was not going to be included in the interview rounds. I don't know why, and my requests for additional details on the company's decision went unanswered. It could have been that I just didn't tailor my materials enough to interest it, but I suspect it may have had something to do with my essay. The company's popular online game wasn't my favorite, but a game from another publisher.

In this instance, I felt it would be important to be honest. The company's game was known to me. Heck, I had played it for a year before giving up, but my gamer's heart belonged to another game, and that game is completely different. I took the risk that bearing the brightest light in my video game soul would stir it to, at least, ask me in for an interview. I was wrong.

This will happen, but you can't let that stop you. My cover letter was one page. My essay was one page. My resume was one page. Even though my effort didn't get me the job, my work met all the requirements for a good submission. I made sure my cover letter clearly indicated my strengths were the ones the company was looking for. I supplied the short essay. I even made sure that my resume had all the keywords from the job advertisement.

So, just to be clear, here's why your resume is important:

✔ It sells who you are for that particular job.

✔ It shows that you can follow instructions (so make sure you do).

✔ It shows that you are aware of the very tedious job the HR people have combing through stacks of similar documents.

✔ It gives them everything they need to make the initial decision.

✔ It gives them everything they need to contact you the way they want to contact you, even if that means they want to ignore you.

✔ If the HR people decide to give your resume a second or third look, it won't take them long to get everything they need from the document.

✔ A good resume won't waste anyone's time with useless information.

It helps to step into the shoes of anyone who reads your resume. You want to make sure that all your grammar is correct, all words are spelled correctly, all sentences are complete and not run-on, and all information salient to the job is included, and nothing more.

In other words, if you want the job, you'll work hard to make your CV show them you want the job.

What recruiters look at

If you cannot imagine it, then I'll make this clear. Due to the state of the job market these days, a lot more people are applying to the same jobs you are looking at than back in 2008 before the recession got rolling. It shouldn't be surprising, then, that hiring people are looking at a lot more applicants than in the past, and you need to catch their interest in as little as six seconds.

That's right. Six seconds.

A study commissioned by The Ladders back in 2012 used eye-tracking technology to see what recruiters were looking at when they reviewed a candidate's resume. The results were astonishing, to say the least. A number of interesting things were derived from the study, including the fact that professionally rewritten resumes scored much higher with the test subjects, specifically in the area of usability. In short, the recrafted resumes were easier to read.

What's more revealing, however, is what the subjects were looking at. The study showed that 80 percent of their time was spent looking at the following, in this order:

✔ Your name

✔ Your current position and title

✔ Your previous position and title

✔ Your previous position's start and end dates

✔ Your current position's start and end dates

✔ Your educational background

Following these points, the test subjects quickly scanned the remaining information for keywords associated with the position they were looking to fill.

What, then, does this tell you? Simply put, you need to give them what they want as quickly as possible so that they can spend the precious additional seconds finding those all-important keywords. Any leg up you can give the HR people can give you the edge you need to make it to the next stage, so formatting is very, very important. Whether you build your own resume or part out the work, you need to make sure that it has a strong focus on what the study calls *strong visual hierarchy,* meaning you need to put the most important information right up front.

Some people are also prone to believe that online profiles are helpful. This is not exactly the case. This poses a conundrum. Do you work to make your online profiles more readable, or do you just put everything in and count on the strong likelihood that it will rarely get looked at? I lean toward the latter. The Ladders study showed that, when subjects were reviewing LinkedIn profiles, they spent 19 percent of their time looking at your profile pictures. The study also made it clear that the additional clutter presented in online profiles made it more difficult to find the information that could help you get a job.

Ultimately, you'll have to decide which is better for you. Just keep in mind that the more profiles you have online, the more you will have to keep track of and make sure they are up to date. After all, you don't want HR people looking at information that is out of date on that one site you didn't get around to and potentially losing you that job.

The Ultimate Template

Well, here it is, folks. The Ultimate Template. That's right. Based on the research done and the common information provided by the people who hire other people everywhere, I have created a template that gives HR people what they want, fast. Combine this template with the customized cover letter, and you have a really good chance of making at least some impact.

Why do I say some? Simple. You will not get an interview out of every application. It just doesn't happen. You can only do you best, and combining this resume template with my cover letter template should give you a better chance than most.

The template I provide is in Microsoft Word's .docx format. While you can edit it using the online Word editor, I don't suggest it. You can use any version of Word from 2007 to the latest without expecting any issues. I don't use any of the more advanced features of Word specifically to avoid such problems. Figure 11-1 shows what the Ultimate Template looks like.

As you can see in Figure 11-1, the document is laid out in columns. The columns are controlled using simple tables. The document has one table with two columns per block. In order to make the document look neat and clean, I have turned off the table borders. If you want to control their appearance, click any text to activate the table control, which appears at the top left corner of the table.

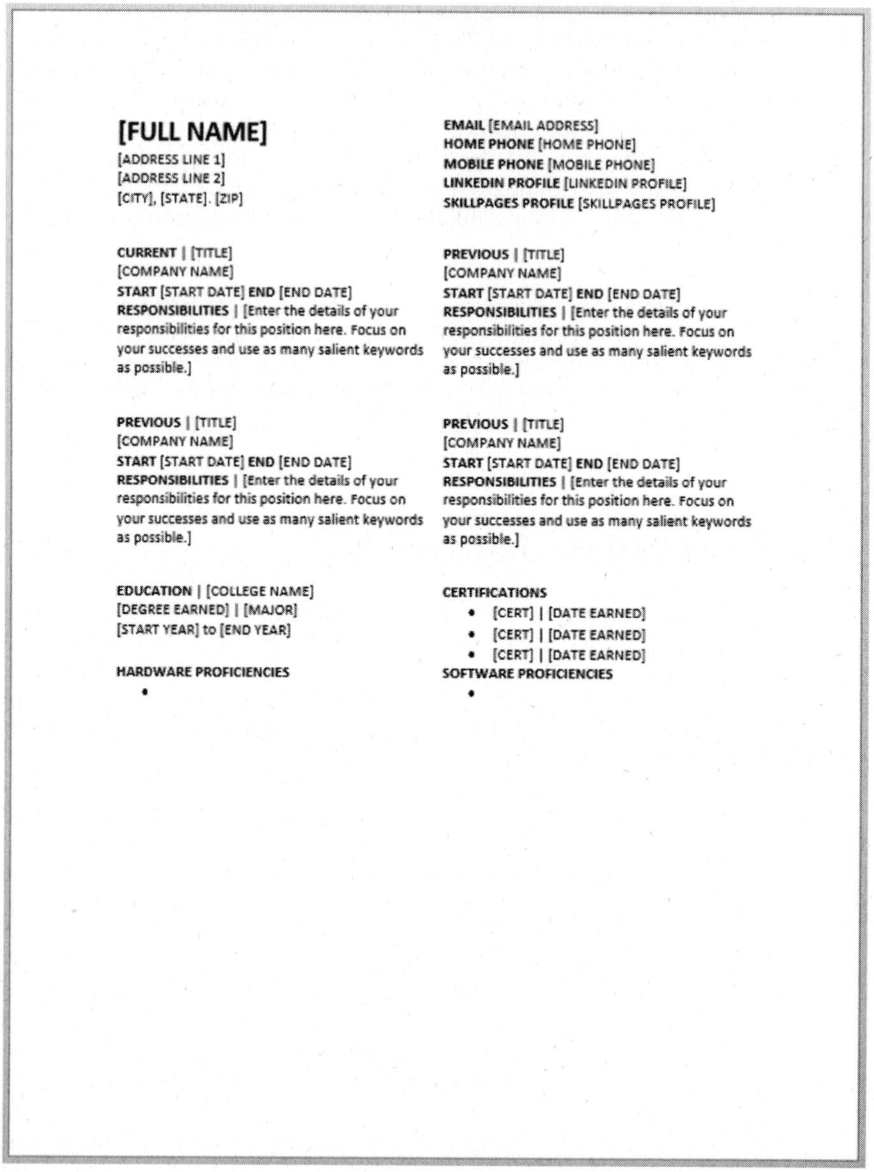

[FULL NAME]
[ADDRESS LINE 1]
[ADDRESS LINE 2]
[CITY], [STATE]. [ZIP]

EMAIL [EMAIL ADDRESS]
HOME PHONE [HOME PHONE]
MOBILE PHONE [MOBILE PHONE]
LINKEDIN PROFILE [LINKEDIN PROFILE]
SKILLPAGES PROFILE [SKILLPAGES PROFILE]

CURRENT | [TITLE]
[COMPANY NAME]
START [START DATE] END [END DATE]
RESPONSIBILITIES | [Enter the details of your
responsibilities for this position here. Focus on
your successes and use as many salient keywords
as possible.]

PREVIOUS | [TITLE]
[COMPANY NAME]
START [START DATE] END [END DATE]
RESPONSIBILITIES | [Enter the details of your
responsibilities for this position here. Focus on
your successes and use as many salient keywords
as possible.]

PREVIOUS | [TITLE]
[COMPANY NAME]
START [START DATE] END [END DATE]
RESPONSIBILITIES | [Enter the details of your
responsibilities for this position here. Focus on
your successes and use as many salient keywords
as possible.]

PREVIOUS | [TITLE]
[COMPANY NAME]
START [START DATE] END [END DATE]
RESPONSIBILITIES | [Enter the details of your
responsibilities for this position here. Focus on
your successes and use as many salient keywords
as possible.]

EDUCATION | [COLLEGE NAME]
[DEGREE EARNED] | [MAJOR]
[START YEAR] to [END YEAR]

CERTIFICATIONS
- [CERT] | [DATE EARNED]
- [CERT] | [DATE EARNED]
- [CERT] | [DATE EARNED]

HARDWARE PROFICIENCIES
-

SOFTWARE PROFICIENCIES
-

Figure 11-1:
The Ultimate
Template.

Replace any text within brackets, like this [TEXT], with your information.
I have labeled each field so that you can quickly tell what I expect you to
insert. Because this document is meant to be a template, you'll want to keep
copies of the versions you create for each position you apply for. Your end

product should be limited to a single page. More than one page is generally considered too much to fiddle with. Don't tempt fate.

One final note. Don't feel constrained by the format I supply. This is a baseline, and you are free to modify it any way you like. Just keep in mind that I designed the template this way to maximize the information that someone reviewing it will receive. You should also feel free to modify the sections to match your needs. If you don't have any certifications, you'll likely want to put something else there because leaving it blank would stand out like a sore thumb. If you worked with any nonprofit organizations, earned any awards, or completed any notable freelance projects, you can note them here instead.

The Even More Dreaded Cover Letter

Despite the name, a cover letter is not a letter. You aren't addressing anyone, primarily because you don't know exactly who you are addressing. There aren't exactly rules for preparing a CV, but there are some very important rules for writing a cover letter:

- ✔ Keep it short and to the point; try not to go over half a page, but do not go into two.
- ✔ Don't just copy from your resume.
- ✔ Definitely don't copy from the job ad.
- ✔ Don't start with telling them your name and what job you are applying for, as they already know.
- ✔ Open with an anecdote or relate some historical information that will paint you as the candidate that is interested, knowledgeable, and eager.
- ✔ Follow that with a very brief, conversational summary of your experience.
- ✔ Follow that with examples of your qualifications, making sure to include job-specific keywords.
- ✔ Close by clearly stating when and how you will follow up; just don't be too firm.

That should do it. You have the rules, but you need to create the cover letters.

Don't be lazy

If you want a job, you will apply to a lot of jobs. That means you will be pumping out a lot of cover letters. You cannot slack off. You must create a cover letter for each job, even the ones that don't seem likely or fall into the lower end of the pay scale. This customization shows both that you are diligent and interested, both solid traits.

If you skip one or more cover letters, you may just be skipping out on opportunities, and that won't do. Your aim is to get a job, and you need to make every effort possible to make that happen. If that means you will be working a job without pay in order to get a job that does pay, then you must make every effort to do so.

Why the cover letter matters

Unlike the CV, the cover letter is important because it can provide a foot in the door for your CV. If you craft your cover letter just right and catch the eyes you want to catch, then it's likely they may spend a little more than six seconds looking at your CV. Even if they spend just ten more seconds looking at your CV, that can increase your chances of getting an interview immeasurably. That has to be worth some time preparing the cover letters in the first place.

This is why it is critical that you make every effort to help yourself at every stage along the way. This point is the culmination of all your work before it ends up in the hands of someone else to decide your fate. You need to put that intensity, energy, and enthusiasm into every cover letter you create so that the eyeballs on the other end feel it emanating from you like the warm rays of the sun.

Creating a template

When you are at the point where you are ready to create your cover letters, you can create a template. I provide a few for you, but you may choose to create your own. Using the rules provided in the section "The Even More Dreaded Cover Letter," you should be able to create a template that just needs to be tweaked for each new potential.

The only real way to create a template is using Microsoft Word. With Word, you can create a document and save it as a Template format. When you open that template file, it creates a fresh, unsaved copy of the template that you can modify. Unfortunately, you can't use Google Docs to create templates unless you have a Google Apps for Work account, but it's not a good idea to use Docs because it converts only to Word formats.

When you're done creating your customized cover letters, however, you want to save a copy as a PDF, which you can then send along with your CV and other required materials. PDFs are universal and can load directly in most web browsers, allowing those coveted eyes to see them all the more quickly.

Customizing your cover letter for each mark

Take particular care to make sure that you customize each cover letter for your intended target. Read it once, twice, and a third time, just to be sure. Don't leave anything from the template unchanged or risk being noticed. There's nothing less helpful than something that looks like a template. This is why it is critical that you go over your work a few times before committing the final save.

I'm not kidding. Check it again. Now.

The Cover Letter

Take a quick look at the template, shown in Figure 11-2.

Modifying the cover letter is different than the resume because much of the language doesn't change from version to version. It is, however, key that you read through any new version a few times. You will need to make sure that you've updated everything that needs to be changed for the new mark. If the reviewer sees anything that references someone else, they'll know, without question, that it is a template.

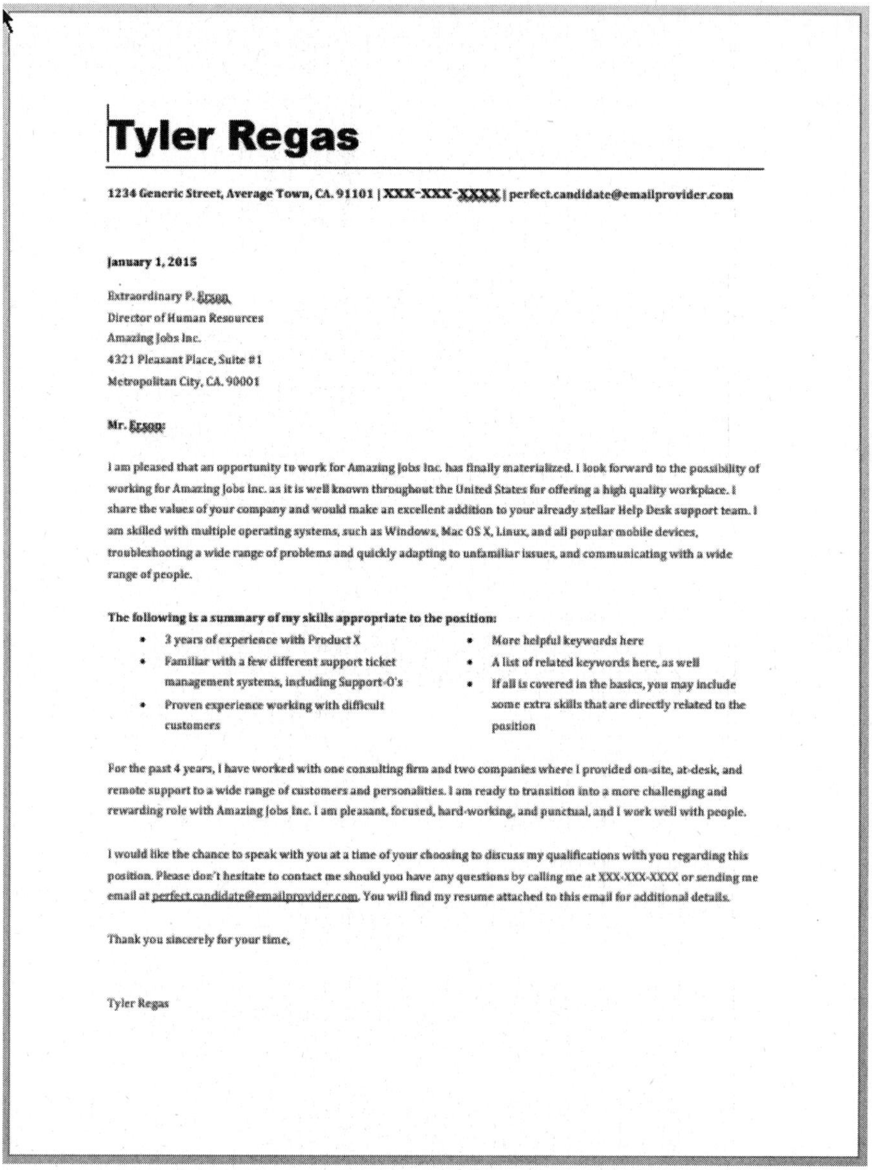

Tyler Regas

1234 Generic Street, Average Town, CA. 91101 | XXX-XXX-XXXX | perfect.candidate@emailprovider.com

January 1, 2015

Extraordinary P. Erson
Director of Human Resources
Amazing Jobs Inc.
4321 Pleasant Place, Suite #1
Metropolitan City, CA. 90001

Mr. Erson:

I am pleased that an opportunity to work for Amazing Jobs Inc. has finally materialized. I look forward to the possibility of working for Amazing Jobs Inc. as it is well known throughout the United States for offering a high quality workplace. I share the values of your company and would make an excellent addition to your already stellar Help Desk support team. I am skilled with multiple operating systems, such as Windows, Mac OS X, Linux, and all popular mobile devices, troubleshooting a wide range of problems and quickly adapting to unfamiliar issues, and communicating with a wide range of people.

The following is a summary of my skills appropriate to the position:

- 3 years of experience with Product X
- Familiar with a few different support ticket management systems, including Support-O's
- Proven experience working with difficult customers

- More helpful keywords here
- A list of related keywords here, as well
- If all is covered in the basics, you may include some extra skills that are directly related to the position

For the past 4 years, I have worked with one consulting firm and two companies where I provided on-site, at-desk, and remote support to a wide range of customers and personalities. I am ready to transition into a more challenging and rewarding role with Amazing Jobs Inc. I am pleasant, focused, hard-working, and punctual, and I work well with people.

I would like the chance to speak with you at a time of your choosing to discuss my qualifications with you regarding this position. Please don't hesitate to contact me should you have any questions by calling me at XXX-XXX-XXXX or sending me email at perfect.candidate@emailprovider.com. You will find my resume attached to this email for additional details.

Thank you sincerely for your time.

Tyler Regas

Figure 11-2:
The cover
letter
template.

Why You Should Keep Everything

In the process of finding work, you will start to amass a rather large collection of files. It will take some work to organize them, but if you start right, it will be easy over time.

First, you need to standardize a method of naming your files. I use the following:

- ✔ For cover letters, I use company-position-CL-YYYYMMDD.docx.
- ✔ For CVs, I use company-position-CV-YYYYMMDD.docx.

For example, if I am applying for a job at Google, my files might look like this:

google-helpdesk-CL-20150115.docx

google-helpdesk-CV-20150115.docx

Now, at a glance, you know that you are looking at a cover letter and CV for a help desk position at Google and what date you prepared them.

You will also want to sort your CV's folder by date modified so that all your new stuff appears at the top. Then the last thing is you don't want to lose them.

Google Drive

If you have a Google account, set up Google Drive, download the desktop client, and create a Resumes folder. Store all your files related to getting work in that folder. Also get the mobile version of the client for your smartphone so that you can retrieve them and email them anytime you need. You never know when being instantly responsive can help you get a job.

Microsoft OneDrive

If you have a Microsoft ID, you can instead use OneDrive, which works just like Google Drive. Download the client for Windows 7 and 8.0 (Windows 8.1 has it baked in) and create your Resumes folder. Store all your files there. Get the smartphone client for your Windows Phone, BlackBerry, iPhone, or Android device in case you need to have immediate access as well. Always be prepared.

Other online storage services

There are a number of services, but stick to the big ones because they are reliable, backed by large companies, and are more likely to have mobile clients.

If you don't use Google Drive or Microsoft OneDrive, you can use OneBox or Box.com and get roughly the same results. Just be sure to hold onto your old stuff. You never know when it will come in handy, and you can modify previous work that is close to positions you have already applied to, saving you more time.

Just make sure to read it again. That's right. Now.

Chapter 12

Surviving the Interview

n this chapter, I help you reader prepare for and survive the interview process and include helpful information from various industry sources, all of whom I know personally and will collect original content from.

The Big Day Has Arrived

Now you've gone and done it! You've gotten a job interview, and in person, no less. Good work, but your job isn't anywhere near complete. Getting an interview is one thing. Getting through the interview is another thing entirely. There are those of you who will have had experience with interviews, but most of you will not feel confident. Interviews, after all, are writhing pits of self-doubt and anguish over answering difficult questions the "right" way. Interviews are not an easy thing to get through, at least most of the time.

There are benefits to being nervous, however. For one, it keeps you alert. Nervousness also amps up your attention. At the same time, however, it can make you overthink everything, and, if your mind is racing, you won't be able to focus on your interviewer.

What to do when you wake up

Ah, the morning of your interview has arrived. With any hope, you went to bed early enough the night before to get a complete and restful sleep. You should be able to spring from bed and prepare for your big day. For the morning, just focus on making sure that you get everything taken care of that needs caring for and arrive early at your interview.

Have a good, but not large, breakfast. Shower yourself. Brush your hair and teeth. Be sure to perform any other regular grooming tasks so that you appear neat and clean. Put on comfortable clothes so that you don't do anything unpleasant to your interviewing clothes before you get there. Sweat stains are not attractive, nor are food, blood, or any other kind of stain. If you wear a scent, don't use too much as that can be off-putting. If at all, don't wear any.

For clothing, prepare something neat and plain that fits well without being baggy or tight and is not brightly colored or has logos. Conservative clothing is the best. You also don't need to get all gussied up. An interview is not a formal affair. The so-called business casual is the accepted norm for interview-wear.

Business casual is generally considered the following for women:

- ✔ **Don't be flashy.** I'm told (ahem, I'm a guy) that basic colors that don't clash with your "season" are best.

- ✔ **Be discreet all over.** Nothing overly revealing is the smart direction.

- ✔ **Be classic.** The classics are the best (whatever those are, but I'll assume you know), so nothing from the current year's fashion rack.

- ✔ **Dress for an interview.** It doesn't have to be a pant suit, but it can't hurt, either. I cannot advise you on details, just don't dress for the club or a BBQ.

And for men:

- ✔ **Like women, wear nothing flashy.** Stick with the basic dark and colorless look that guys seem to be good at. Personally, I wear all black, all the time.

- ✔ **Practice discretion.** Discretion is the better part of valor. If you have pecs, an interview is no place to showcase them, nor your six-pack, glutes, or biceps.

- ✔ **Stick with the classics, such as pressed dress slacks or cotton dress trousers in black or navy.** Up top, nothing beats the classic elegance of a long-sleeve oxford in blue. Wear the sleeves down and secured, or you're missing the point.

- ✔ **Wear a belt and dress socks.** At the very least, wear plain black walking shoes.

- ✔ **Wear a tie.** Go with Windsor, zip-up, or clip-on, but just no bow-ties.

All genders should avoid sweat (or glow) stains. Also make your hair neat and clean and tend to those things that are appropriate to you and what society expects of you.

Your pre-interview checklist

Louis Pasteur, the famous French chemist and inventor of the pasteurization process, once said, "Chance favors only the prepared mind." In essence, this means that people who make the effort to prepare themselves will have an increased potential for recognizing opportunity when it presents itself.

This is where carpe diem, Latin for seize the day, comes in. Just to make sure that you have the opportunity to seize the day, make sure that you've got everything ready to go:

✔ **You have prepared your outfit the day before, and it's clean and pressed and looks really, really good both on and off you.** Always dress nicely (don't go overboard), even if they wear shorts and t-shirts in the workplace. You'll have plenty of time to fit in if you get the job. For the interview, you need to look like you respect the importance of the position.

✔ **You have prepared all documents and/or files that the interviewer requested you bring along.** You should also bring along a few copies of your CV and any references that you supplied to the HR department. Put them next to your interviewing clothes. I also suggest you bring a small notepad and pen to take notes. Jot down things that you want to address again so that you don't have to interrupt your interviewer.

✔ **You have your ID and another form of identification, typically your Social Security card.** If you don't have the latter, you should at least know the number and have a photocopy of the original. At some point, however, you will have to produce the original.

✔ **Print out a route map to the address you were given.** At the very least, print out the address so that you can enter it into your GPS when you get on the road. While you are doing that, you might as well add the name of the interviewer and the phone number to the front office in case you get turned around.

✔ **Make a list of everything that you might ask questions about and memorize them.** Just be prepared to have all your questions answered before you ask them because most interviewers generally cover everything that may be asked anyway. It never hurts to be prepared.

✔ **Research the company you are interviewing for so that there are no surprises.** Go through everything on the company's website and read its Wikipedia entry if it has one. Check into any rounds of layoffs, acquisitions, or funding the company may have gone through.

✔ **Don't forget to get everything in this list dealt with early so that when you're done, you can relax and get your mind off things.** The last thing you need to deal with when heading out to the interview is pre-interview stress.

Getting there early to arrive on time

The first of the last things you want to do is to be late to your interview. Nothing shows a lack of interest or import more than being tardy. Even if you are typically late to most things, you must make a concerted effort to avoid being late to your interview (and if you get the job, then that as well).

Make sure to either have a map printed out from your favorite map service (for example, Google Maps, Bing Maps, and so on) or use the GPS feature in your car or on your phone. Whichever form you choose, make sure that you are fully prepared once you start moving, or you'll get lost and may show up late. That's why you need to leave early. Give yourself a buffer of extra time so that even if you do get lost, you can still get there early.

There are two kinds of people in the world: those who eat directions for breakfast, and those who can hardly tell when they're facing forward. If you are among the latter, don't worry. It's not your fault. It's just the way you're wired. Some people are good with directions, and others aren't. It's the people that aren't good with directions that I'm worried about.

For those of you whom maps are gobbledygook, I strongly suggest that you use GPS. If you don't already know about GPS, there are a few ways that you can get it rather easily. In fact, you likely already have it. If you have an iPhone, Android, Windows Phone, or BlackBerry smartphone, you likely already have it. Just go to your maps app and look for Directions. A lot of feature phones offer GPS as an add-on from your carrier as well.

If all else fails, either borrow a GPS unit from a friend or buy one. It's a good investment, and they aren't all that expensive anymore.

How to greet your interviewer

While much of the information in this list should be common sense, it's a good idea to go over these points just to make sure:

✔ Be friendly.

✔ Look the interviewer in the eye, but don't stare.

✔ Offer a mildly firm handshake, regardless of gender.

✔ Smile, but don't make your face tired.

✔ Speak clearly and concisely.

How not to greet your interviewer

There are things you can do to be a good interviewee, but you should avoid some things:

✔ Don't scowl, grimace, or sneer. It's unbecoming.

✔ Don't chew gum or chewing tobacco.

✔ Don't smoke before your interview. The smell can remain on you for a few hours — even longer if you smoke a lot. Better yet, quit.

✔ Avoid making loud noises or laughter. If you find something funny, a light chuckle will do.

✔ Don't illustrate the strength in your hand to your interviewer.

✔ Don't slouch. Just sit up as straight as you can.

✔ Don't make jokes, no matter how funny you think they are. They don't break the ice.

The Least Comfortable Chair in the World

After you are sitting (not slouching) in the least comfortable chair in the world at the moment, you are ready to begin your interview. You will have already passed around introductions and pleasantries regarding the weather, and it's time to get down to business.

The most common questions asked in interviews

It's rather annoying, but a number of questions are regularly asked in interviews that aren't exactly easy to answer. I'll break them down:

✔ **Tell me something about yourself.** This question is likely the most open-ended question you will be asked. Don't chatter on about yourself, but about how you work, your interests in the field that you have applied for, and what you like about work. Keep it short and to the point and illustrate your interest in the position.

✔ **What are your greatest strengths?** Focus on your skills that are beneficial to the position you are interviewing for. Don't try to go into detail. Just hit a few points like punctuality, communication skills, organization, teamwork, and the like.

✔ **What are your greatest weaknesses?** Your best defense here is a good offense. Turn this question around on them and illustrate one or more weaknesses that you were able to convert into a strength.

✔ **Tell me about an achievement you are most proud of.** Outline a project that worked out for you and how you achieved it, but keep it simple and short. If you have not yet completed any projects at a job, discuss how you succeeded on a school project.

✔ **Do you prefer to work alone or on a team?** This one is easy. You are happy working with a team as much as alone and leverage all your resources as needed. For a unique spin, talk about how working alone can also be considered working as a part of a team because it takes everyone working together to make the department the capable resource that it is.

✔ **How do you handle stress?** Don't talk about stressful situations you have experienced, but instead talk about how you relieve stress through hard work and expanding your knowledge. You can also talk a bit about real recreational activities, such as video games or sports.

✔ **Where do you see yourself in five years?** This is one of my least favorite questions, but interviewers ask it anyway. Talk about how this position fulfills this stage of your long-term goals and how advancing in the company is in line with your future outlook.

✔ **Why did you leave your last position?** This can be a loaded question, and interviewers know it. Honesty is the best policy, however, as it's easy for them to find out what really happened. If you were fired or laid off or quit, just let them know. Don't sugarcoat it. If you are looking for a better paying job, just say so. If this is your first job, tell them.

✔ **Why are you interested in this job?** If you actually are interested in the position, then you should be able to easily answer this question. Just make sure to hit on all the points that the position describes. If you are not actually interested in the position, but are just looking for a job, make sure to hit on all the points that the position describes. In other words, act interested.

✔ **Why should we hire you?** Have you ever heard the term elevator pitch? An *elevator pitch* is a term used in the entertainment industry to describe a pitch that can be made to a movie mogul you happen to run into during a short ride on an elevator. This question is when you give your elevator pitch. Your pitch shouldn't take any more than 30 to

45 seconds and should get right to the point. You can say something like, "I meet all the requirements for this position, enjoy this kind of work, enjoy expanding my horizons, and feel that I can be a real asset to this company." Of course, tailor your pitch to yourself and don't just copy this one.

✔ **What are your salary expectations?** If the interviewers ask this question, it's generally a good sign that they are interested in you. Unfortunately, this is the one question that puts butterflies into most everyone's stomach. The fear rises the very moment you are asked to give a number. They want to know what you think you should be paid for your work. If you've done your research, you have determined the average salary for such a position. It's even better if the company listed an expected pay range in the job advertisement. In either case, start by indicating that you are relatively open-ended on this and are willing to negotiate for a salary that meets both your needs. Then, unless they didn't specifically ask for a number, you'll have to give one. If you have to work from an estimate, give them the average range. If they gave you the range, then tell them that. It's a crapshoot, but if you are clear and confident, then you are giving yourself your best possible chance.

✔ **Do you have any questions?** This question generally indicates that the interview is winding down and that the interviewers have completed their planned presentation and question and answer sessions. If you did as I asked and took little notes during the interview, you may have some questions. At the very least, the interviewer should have gone over the position expectations and responsibilities, dress code, perks, scheduling, team hierarchy, benefits programs, training compensation, workplace culture, and whatever else they think is important to pass on. If there's anything you think they missed, you can ask about those items. If, however, they did not bring up salary, don't ask about that. While it's rare, it can sometimes indicate that they are not interested in you for the position. In these cases, you'll just have to be patient. It's difficult to predict what might happen, even if you think the interview didn't go well, so just sit tight and keep moving forward.

How to answers questions you never expected

Unfortunately, there's no easy answers to the unexpected questions. Because they are uncommon or oddball questions that arise on occasion, you can't prepare for them. Just hang in there and answer them with respect, clarity, and diplomacy.

Glassdoor.com, a popular career community that compiles information from employees and employers, published a list of the 25 oddest interview questions that had been reported. Here's a selection of some of them:

- How many cows are there in Canada?
- A penguin walks through that door right now wearing a sombrero. What does he say, and why is he here?
- What do you think about when you are alone in your car?
- If we came to your house for dinner, what would you prepare for us?
- How do you make a tuna sandwich?
- Estimate how many windows are in New York.
- What's your favorite song? Perform it for us now.
- Have you ever stolen a pen from work?
- On a scale from one to ten, rate me as an interviewer.
- If you could be anyone else, who would it be?

As you can see, these questions may be strange, but they have meaning behind them. There are more questions like these, and they are all designed to test some aspect of you as an analyst or problem-solver. The interviewers want to see how you operate when put into an awkward or unexpected position.

It's not always about getting the exact answer to the strange question, either. In the case of how many windows are in New York, it's likely more about the process. Are they asking about the city or the state? City Hall has records on all buildings in a given city so that you can collect that information there. How would you collect and then collate the data? What would be the purpose of collecting such information?

Just be aware that you may be asked a strange question.

Remain calm and remember your training

The last thing you want to do in an interview situation is to get excited or upset or frustrated. You don't want to illustrate any negative emotions, either verbally or through your body language, to your interviewer. If you can't get through an interview for an hour without getting emotional, how are you going to handle a job for eight hours, five days a week? How about a bunch of different people with different personalities instead of just one or two interviewers?

Stay calm. Don't get excited. Don't get mad. Don't roll your eyes. Don't use bad language. Don't talk about religion, sports, or politics. Don't criticize anything. Don't make fun of anything. Just focus on the interview and answering questions. Oh, and be nice, engaging, and personable.

Why you don't offer information you aren't asked for

Anytime you start to offer up details about things you weren't asked about is an invitation to additional judgment on the part of the interviewer. Don't do this. Just answer the questions you are asked. Think of it as a courtroom, and you are the one on trial.

Your skills and worthiness are on trial

Don't be fooled. The moment you walk into that interview every aspect of who you are is on trial. It starts with your looks and goes from there. I know it's superficial and that shouldn't be right, but that's the way it is. You are instantly judged by your cover, just like a book. The interviewers will transpose their own beliefs and values onto you and compare your looks and behavior to them. Yes, it's illegal, but it's sadly common.

You cannot know what the person or persons across from you think or feel, so you need to make the best possible effort to demonstrate who you are, what you believe in, and how you can be a part of their team, all from the perspective of your potential employment. You cannot know what you will face inside the interview room, either, so you need to prepare as much as humanly possible.

In the end, you just need to be you. Be confident in who you are and what you know and do your best to project that confidence in your interview. There's no guarantee that it will work every time, but there is no surefire method for ensuring success.

Ending the Interview

Interviews wind down at their own pace, but you can generally tell when it's coming when you are asked if you have any questions for the interviewer. At some point, someone will say something like, "Well, that's about everything then," signaling the end of the interview. You will have to use your own perception to determine whether there are any additional potentials you can exploit at the end of the interview, but remember to continue to follow the rules.

Aside from being able to tell when it's over, you must also leave with something. Business cards are good. If you were taking notes, then you should have the names of anyone you met jotted down. Remember LinkedIn? You can search for these people when you get home and see whether they have any connection with your LinkedIn connections. You never know who may be able to help you get your foot further in the door.

What not to ask when you're done

"So, when do I start?"

Yes. This is as aggressive sounding as you think it is. It's too aggressive. While some people suggest that this question can benefit certain people at the end of an interview, I am not one of them. You are selling yourself for the job, and taking that kind of tone is both jarring and disrespectful and is very likely counter to the personality you have projected during the interview. There is a lack of balance to conducting a positive and mild interview only to leave it with such a bold question.

Your best bet is to aim for a consistent and predictable performance throughout, interspersed with memorable moments and a delightful and information-rich closing.

What to tell the interviewer as you leave

Before things are all wrapped up and there are no more opportunities to bend the ear of the interviewer, you'll want to slip in some additional elevator pitch talk. You want to leave the interviewer with something memorable. What movies do you remember for the Oscars? Are you thinking about the movies that were released early in the year? Of course not. You may not even recall any of them. You are thinking about the movies that came near the end of the year, those that are closer to your recollection.

You want to do something similar for your interview. By that I mean leave them with something memorable. It doesn't have to be Oscar-worthy, but it helps if it's distinct. It helps significantly if the interviewer says anything about a possible follow-up interview. Second interviews are often very good signs that you are, at the very least, in the running for the position. What you need to shoot for now, however, is a sense of timing and reinforcing your suitability for the job. You might say something like:

> *"I really enjoyed meeting with you and believe that we were able to make a connection. I am looking forward to the opportunity to prove that I am the best fit for this position. I'd like to be prepared to set aside time in case you need me for anything else. How soon do you think that might be?"*

You will want to personalize this ending narrative. Tailor it to the job and add some items about how your skills mesh with the requirements. If the interviewer already indicated a timeframe, make sure to repeat that instead of asking when. If you forget, you will appear forgetful. That's not good.

How to thank the interviewer

After that you're done reinforcing your chances of being selected for the next round, it's time to say your goodbyes. This part is simple. Thank them for their time, shake their hand in a respectful manner, and smile. Make sure to use their name. If they lead you out to the lobby, try to find some aspect of the offices to compliment.

If it's modern and clean and sterile, find something to speak well of. Maybe the parking is convenient, or there is a deli or coffee shop in the lobby. At the very least, you may be able to indicate that commuting is easy. If the offices are modern and rustic (with exposed pipes and girders or brightly painted concrete or even just a lot of glass), you can indicate that you like it or that it feels like a creative space.

How to leave (yes, there is a way to do this)

It may seem odd, but it's a thing. The best way to leave an interview once all of the pleasantries are finished is to just go. Don't hang around. Don't use the bathroom. Once the interviewers have indicated that they are done and project the body language of a people who want to get on with things, it's time to go. They may even tell you that they have another appointment or even another interview.

You leave a better final impression if you just leave. Just don't forget to leave smiling and thanking them.

Some Possible Tips and Tricks

I have suggested that I am sad that there are no surefire tricks to getting a job. There are, however, some things that may work in your favor.

Getting a tour

Certain workplaces just beg to be learned about, and getting a tour can be an opportunity to express further enthusiasm for the company. This won't work in all cases, but there are places where it can.

I have a number of experiences in my own work history where it worked quite well. Two of them were consulting gigs where I provided services for clients. The first was an industrial flooring wholesaler that had a large warehouse behind its offices. The third time I was onsite alone to perform some work and had started to develop a bond with the assistant manager of operations, I asked for a tour. He was only too glad to show me around, and I learned a lot about industrial flooring. It helped me bond even more with him, and I was able to get his support for a number of larger projects I may not have been able to get approval for without his backing.

The second was a short-term consulting gig with an agency providing installation support to a major cement manufacturer in the United States. I was the manager of the installation team, scheduling and supervising engineers at various sites for the three-month project and coordinating with the in-house IT team in another state. When we got to the company's mine, I arranged a tour for the entire team, and we were lead around for two hours learning about how concrete is made. We even got to view a detonation. Not only did we all learn something we didn't know, but I was able to forge a better relationship with my team. We finished two weeks early, and there were bonuses all around.

The other two instances were on job interviews. The first was an interview for an adult products company. The job was purely in IT for the offices of this major company, but I was given a tour of the facilities. I was quite surprised to find that the company had a very large warehouse attached to the back of its modern glass office building with row upon row of products on high, metal shelving. We talked about the products and how much the company shipped. Due to the nature of the goods, I didn't express a significant amount of appreciation, which may have cost me the job. It was an eye-opener, though.

The second was for a company that repacks and liquidates overstock and returns for major retailers. The interview went quite well. I met with several people on the executive staff, and after two hours, we were about to wrap up. Just before things got weird, I asked whether I might get a tour of the warehouse floor and was happily granted one. Because many of the products the company dealt with were consumer electronics, I was very interested. We ended up looking around and discussing issues for over an hour. Two days later, I was contacted by the HR person with an offer. Sadly, I had to turn that one down because the company was unable to get anywhere near my salary requirements, but I believe the tour was what pushed me over the edge.

If you can swing a tour, it can help you.

Glomming onto an interviewer's obvious interests and running with them

Depending on where you end up for an interview, you may be in the interviewer's office. The offices of long-term employees are often festooned with personal items that suggest interests. Chances are, however, that you'll end up in some nondescript conference room. Regardless, you can get clues about the interviewer's interests. All you need to do is pay close attention.

It can be tricky, but with care and the luck of good timing, redirect the course of the conversation from you to the interviewer, at least for a little while. You do not, however, want to appear to be expressing interest in the interviewer for the sole purpose of advancing your chances for the job. It must seem natural and come with the flow of the interview. It has to seem as if the subject just sprung up naturally. Of course, it goes without saying that should have your own interest in whatever interests your interviewer has. At least have a healthy and real curiosity about the subject.

Just don't drag it out too long. In fact, if you get more than four or five minutes into a conversation about something exciting, start looking for a way to transition the conversation back to the interview before the interviewer does. It's not that hard. If you are discussing something technical, then you can easily switch back to the interview by connecting it to how you might integrate an aspect of that interest in your job.

Chapter 13

Post-Interview Etiquette

In This Chapter

▶ Discovering the ins and outs of the post-interview period

▶ Gaining powerful insight into managing the emotions of recruiters, head hunters, and placement agents

▶ Getting the edge on your competition through powerful thank you notes and careful gifting

*I*n this chapter, I reveal the secrets of how to really deal with the post-interview period. There are things you can and cannot do, and I help you understand why something you may think sounds reasonable just might be a huge mistake.

Managing HR Departments

Human Resources, or HR, departments are organizations within or contracted by companies that manage the people who make up those companies. HR doesn't manage projects or define product specifications. HR manages employees — hiring, firing, payroll, benefits, and whatnot. HR departments may handle people, but they are also made up of people, and these people know HR.

That's the thing, isn't it? They know HR, but HR departments are expected to hire for all manner of other departments, which introduces an unfortunate irony. HR departments know HR, but they are often handling the position description composition, selection of candidates, interviewing, and, if the winds are favorable, the hiring of you.

That's not always the case, though. Many forward thinking companies use HR to handle the overall process, but use departmental managers to be a part of the selection, interviewing, and hiring processes. This is a more reasonable approach to the entire hullabaloo, as it puts the people who know what they need in the mix. You need to pay attention to the people involved, understand their role in the process, and work with the correct people at each stage.

Be nice

The one key rule that stands in all instances is to be nice. Being unpleasant won't get you anything you want, much less a job, so it behooves you to be patient and friendly. Being nice is even more important if the other end is unpleasant with you. You want to take the high road. It will only help you in the long run.

You should also keep in mind an added element to the quality of being nice. If you are on the phone with someone unpleasant or difficult to handle and you retain your cool head and clear process, people will remember that. Conversely, they will remember if you fly off the handle or use bad language.

Don't send gifts

If there's ever a bad idea, it has to be the concept that sending a gift to HR will get you a job. This is simply not the case. The idea that a gift is a suitable replacement for actual feelings of friendship or loyalty because it represents the physical manifestation of hard-earned money spent in the recipients honor is just silly. Gift giving, after all, is a capitalist trend and should not be considered a valid form for illustrating thanks.

In fact, gift giving is bad precisely because it represents the physical manifestation of hard-earned money spent. At best, your gift will be ignored or be dismissed as a contributing factor to your selection. At worst, it will be considered a bribe, and your application will be discarded. The last thing you want to do is suggest that anyone in any HR department can be bought by trinkets and baubles.

When is "too soon" to send a thank you note?

There is something you can do, and it has the added benefit of being accepted in the hiring industry.

You can send a thank you card. Sending a thank you card, however, introduces yet another element of angst and concern into your hiring process; when. It almost seems inevitable. You have to send your resume to every suitable job, customized for each employer to highlight your strengths in relation to the position. You have to prepare a personalized cover letter for each job, which makes you worry over its content. You have to prepare for a possible interview, which is riddled with nervousness. You have to go to the interview, which is emotionally difficult. You have to answer difficult questions, worried that you'll say the one word that will ruin your chances. Now you have to figure out the best possible time to send a thank you card.

Looking for a job is bad enough without the additional fretting brought on by thanking the interviewer for their time! Yet, it is done because any extra effort on your part can go a long way toward getting you the best job possible. The thank you can be that one element, that last point you make, the last word that cannot be countered, that will keep that opportunity alive, and you should take it. Every time you interview, no exceptions.

Thank you notes have several benefits. The show that you are

- ✔ Organized and thoughtful
- ✔ Skilled at working with people
- ✔ Serious about getting a job
- ✔ Willing to go out of your way to be nice

Not only does sending a thank you note make a real impression on the people who make decisions, they will especially remember you if you were the only one to send in a thank you note. In today's job climate, it's important to stand out and make a positive impact.

There are two general forms of thank you letter: the classic and the handwritten. The classic should be used most of the time, especially with people you don't know well, such as your interviewer(s). The classic looks something like what you see in Figure 13-1.

As you can see, Figure 13-1 shows a very standard, clear, simple letter that quickly and neatly gets to the point. Also note how the example is signed (very badly, but it's just for illustration), so make sure to leave enough room between the complimentary closing and your printed name for your physical signature. Once done, print your note, sign it with a real pen, neatly fold it into an envelope, place a stamp on it, and mail that thing.

March 12, 2014 *(the date of your interview)*

Mrs. Johnson: *(the colon is used in formal correspondence)*

Thank you for affording me the time to meet with you today. As discussed, my three years of consulting experience for small businesses meshes well with the needs of your internal help desk. I also wanted to highlight my experience with technical documentation, which would be a great fit for your company.

Please let Mr. Addison know that I was very pleased to meet him and his team and appreciated the time he spent with me.

Should you have any questions, please don't hesitate to contact me at 999-123-4567 or email me at jobseeker@awesome-

Joe Awesome

Figure 13-1:
The classic thank you note.

Here are some notes regarding formatting:

✔ When starting a letter, end your salutation with a comma (,) for personal messages and a colon (:) for formal letters.

✔ Don't use Dear to open a formal letter. It's more than a little overly familiar.

✔ Always physically sign your letters with a real pen. Inserting it digitally makes it look mass produced. Sure, you created the letter on a computer, but the In Real Life signature gives it just enough personal touch to indicate that you took the time to put this together.

As for timing, I'll save you any need for angst. Prepare it the night of the interview. You can use your notes from the interview itself to help you recall any details that are helpful, like if your interviewer or any key figures are women, whether or not they are married (Miss or Ms. is unmarried and Misses or Mrs. is married). Once you're done, drop it in the mail. It will get postmarked at your local post office the day after the interview, and that will be noticed when it arrives a few days later.

The other type of thank you note is the handwritten note. A handwritten letter is nice, but it's too informal for use with anyone you don't already know and (this "and" is crucial) you aren't talking about business in your letter. In other words, you can use an informal handwritten letter if you know the person beyond mere acquaintance-level "know" and the subject matter is informal, like a simple thank you note to a friend who helped you with your search. Otherwise, don't use it for HR people.

So, why don't you simply email a thank you note? Simple. It's too impersonal, lacks character, illustrates an unwillingness to work hard to attain a goal, reveals a need to take shortcuts, and just isn't done. If you're going to send a thank you note, do it right. If not, don't do it at all, or you'll just hurt your own chances.

Managing Recruiters and Placement Agencies

Unlike HR departments at companies, the recruiters and placement agencies of the world are separate companies whose sole purpose is to provide people for other companies. That's how they make their money, and they are typically not a part of the company that takes on an employee from one of these agencies. Their business is the business of others businesses, and as such, you treat them differently.

What's the difference?

- A *recruiter* is a company that seeks individuals to fill specific roles for other companies. The slang term frequently used is head hunter. A recruiter will place ads for positions, take resumes, interview people, and submit them to the company for consideration. Recruiters sometimes act like moderators and will suggest specific candidates based on positive previous results.

- A *placement* or *staffing agency* is a company that supplies workers to fill various roles, frequently temporary ones, hence the colloquial temp agency. A placement agency will take resumes and build out lists of people who have various skills. When jobs come up that require those skills, calls are made, and whoever gets in first typically takes the work.

Essentially, the core difference between placement agencies and recruiters is that they are at different levels in the hierarchy. Placement agencies handle mostly entry-level positions, while recruiters work with mid-level and executive candidates. Both types, however, are paid by other companies to provide bodies for jobs. Some do it well, while others do not.

In fact, money is the key element to the relationship between these agencies and the companies who use them.

Be nice, but firm

Unlike HR departments, recruiters and placement agencies don't have any sense of loyalty beyond the money, so you can treat them somewhat differently. This is not license to be disrespectful to these people. They work hard in an often thankless job with few rewards, so it behooves you to be nice to them. On the other hand, these people are handling possibly hundreds of different people for countless positions. It may not be great, but they don't have time for you.

It's your job to get yourself a job, though, so you have to get out there and get one, not leave all the work to others. They have no reason to work hard for you, so you need to be vigilant and firm. You might ask yourself how someone can possibly be firm and nice at the same time!? A fair question.

Always be respectful, but you can push the envelope.

A typical scenario

You've called XYZ Agency, a head hunter specializing in technology positions for major companies and have spoken to Dana about getting work. Dana asks you to send in your CV and to come into the office to fill out some forms and whatnot. You can tell Dana is busy because Dana talks quickly and gets you off the phone in five short minutes. You feel as if you were just railroaded. This is common.

You head into the office at the specified time and you end up waiting for 20 minutes longer than you expected. Dana finally rushes in and drags you into a conference room. You speak for a while, talk about your past experience, what you're looking for now, and what Dana needs to help you find something. You exchange contact information and promise to send over the materials requested. Dana says you will hear from their office in a few days.

A week passes, and you've heard nothing. What do you do? Do you give Dana time, or do you step in and ask for a status update? Actually, you don't wait a week. First, you need to pin Dana down to a particular time for contact. If Dana does not contact you by that day, you contact Dana the following day. Remind Dana that you need work and would like to be apprised of anything suitable so that you can make a decision quickly. Set another date.

Again, if you haven't heard from Dana by the next date, call in to the office that same day, but near the close of business (typically 5 p.m., but verify with the receptionist). Remember to always be nice, but consistently remind Dana that you are eager to work. That timely communications is the key to success. When done, thank Dana for the time she is spending on finding you work.

Gifts aren't necessary

While it's not beneficial to give gifts to placement agencies, it can come in handy with recruiters, especially when the target salary is $25 an hour or better. Depending on the quality of the position, you may want to consider giving a small gift of chocolates or a Starbucks gift card for $20 or go all the way up to a nice bouquet of flowers or a nice lunch.

There is, however, some question as to whether you give gifts to prompt the recruiter to work harder or hold off until the recruiter finds you a position. You can go both ways, if you have the resources. Get the recruiter chocolates to help him remember you and take him to lunch when you get the job. The issue comes down to how much money the recruiter makes when getting you a position. Depending on the recruiter, he can make anywhere from 15 to 25 percent of your first annual salary.

Recruiters, however, won't tell you what they make. You can do the math, though. Just run the numbers based on the numbers in your offers, and you'll get an idea of what your Dana will make if you take the position. You find that they make pretty decent money, so don't go overboard on gifts, and don't use gift giving willy-nilly in an effort to push people into liking you. Your best bet, if you are the gifting type, is to base it on how frequently they contact you as opposed to you chasing them down all the time.

Your other option, especially for those of you seeking entry-level positions, is to fall back on the thank you note. The same benefits apply to recruiters and even placement agencies you feel are trying to give you some personalized attention. After all, these companies aren't staffed by robots.

The general rule should be that if anyone helps you on your quest to get work, you should send that person a note showing your appreciation. Just like with HR departments, don't wait to send the note, or it won't have the impact you want when it does arrive. Unlike other cases, better late than never is not a good rule to operate by.

If you are friendly and nice, thank people in a personal manner in a timely fashion and stay in contact with people who have helped you along the way (never forgetting to add people to your LinkedIn network, of course), you will build an excellent cadre of people who speak well of you in no time.

Part V

The Part of Tens

Enjoy an additional Part of Tens chapter at
www.dummies.com/extras/gettinganithelpdeskjob.

In this part . . .

- ✔ Find out ten things you shouldn't do during an interview so that you can nab the job.

- ✔ Discover ten books you should own to further advance your IT career.

- ✔ Know which ten tools can make your life on the IT help desk easier.

- ✔ Find out which ten resources can help you in your job.

- ✔ Continue your learning in ten areas to keep your IT help desk skills top notch.

- ✔ Enjoy an additional Part of Tens chapter on interviewing for an IT help desk job at www.dummies.com/extras/gettinganithelpdeskjob.

Chapter 14

Ten Things Not to Do

In This Chapter

▶ Establishing a basis in the reality of working with people

▶ Covering the don't that most people . . . don't

▶ Discovering the actions and behaviors that can make you unpopular

*I*n this chapter, I share with you the things that you should not do as an IT help desk engineer. Think of each of these items as a kind of story moral spoiler. I've broken most of these rules and have worked with others who have broken those I have not violated. I have seen the fallout that comes from such violations and hope that you can learn from my words without having to experience them yourself.

Don't Touch Anyone

This advice is vaguely odd and creepy, but you may not realize that people unconsciously touch people all the time. It's a humanizing behavior that gives a human connection to those you feel some kinship to. You may, in fact, be unaware that the person you're patting on the back in consolation and commiseration may not feel any level of kinship with you, and that your touch may not be welcome, no matter how sincere your feelings.

Touchy-feely people are not popular, so don't be one of them. That doesn't mean you can't ever touch anyone again, but you need to be self-conscious about it. You may feel that you are comforting other people, they in turn they may get the impression that you are trying to intimidate them or to initiate actions that neither party wants to engage in.

Shake hands if offered and you can touch people whom you've made friends with over a year or two of working together. Just keep your mitts off everyone else.

Don't Yell at Anyone

Frustration is easy to come by when helping people use technology. One of the deepest and most treacherous pitfalls presents itself in the form of pride and superiority. You must avoid this pitfall at all costs. Like you, the people you are helping are human beings. Everyone has something they are good at, and not everyone has nerd chops. If they did, they wouldn't need IT departments.

I used to get upset, and I took it out on people who didn't always deserve it. Some time ago, however, I had an epiphany, but not a new one. I had learned that old chestnut, "You attract more flies with honey than vinegar." In other words, people respond better to pleasant attitudes than to sour, bitter, condescending personalities.

Anger is never the solution to any problem, and computers do not understand human emotions. To that end, getting frustrated won't change anything, so just don't bother. If you stay calm, cool, and collected, you will better survey the situation and figure out what's going on. Over time, you will learn how to help others who are frustrated to become calm, at which time you can enlist them into your effort to solve the problem.

In a related sense, if you have to yell to get someone's attention, use that energy to walk over there. It's rude to shout inside, even if the purpose is innocent.

Don't Try to Teach Customers the Technology

I've seen it countless times. Engineers walk into an office and proceed to explain what they are doing to users. The associated verbiage gives away the plot every time; they think it will calm users' fears. News flash, people! This will not do what you think. In fact, user personalities are very complex, and this tactic can backfire with a few of them.

You also don't need to talk to users while you are at their desks. Some will watch over your shoulder, while others will make suggestions that appear technically sound, but they will never really need to know the details of what you are working on.

The thing you must understand is the difference between educating users for success and educating users to pass the time. The former is not done one-on-one at a desk when a problem occurs, and the latter offers up too many chances for you to put your foot in your mouth.

It's best to just leave the stick alone and let the beast sleep. If you need something to do while you are already doing something, then run through the possible issues in your mind. Also, if the user's personality supports it (for example, the user says something like, "I'll just be over here reading if you need me."), then feel free to suggest he go take an early lunch or grab a coffee.

Don't Try to Do Everything Yourself

You are not a super hero. You do not have super powers. You are not vastly superior to everyone else. You may be a skilled technician and know a lot about computers and whatnot, but you also do not have a dozen arms, the ability to be in more than one place at a time, or a repository of all technical knowledge in your head. This fact may be annoying, but it's better to just accept it as truth.

In the vast majority of cases where you work with customers or users, you will have teammates, superiors, and other departments to draw on. You can even call on your contemporaries at other companies and take advantage of online resources.

My general rule is that if a line of attack does not present itself in the first 15 to 20 minutes, get some help. There's no shame in asking for help, and if others give you grief, feel free to point out all the times they needed help.

Now, in some instances you don't exactly have access to resources, but even working alone doesn't mean you're alone. Even an old phone or dial-up connection to the Internet can get you more information than you could ever need.

Don't Ignore the Forest for the Trees

It's a really bad idea to ignore things like fires burning all around you while your tree isn't in flames. This metaphorical concept illustrates that it's a bad idea to fix one user's machine while letting others issues go unanswered. Like the U.S. Forest Service, you have to keep an eye on everything at the same time you're fixing what's broken.

This task is not impossible. It just requires some active organization skills and willingness. It doesn't hurt to have a few friends on hand, either.

Don't Forget to Say "I Don't Know" When You Really Don't Know

This one is related to "Don't try to do everything yourself," and I've found that it is personally liberating. An enormous amount of freedom can be had from these three little words. I was always under the impression that if I didn't know something, I'd be dismissed on the spot. Quite the contrary happened. In fact, it was rather anticlimactic. Someone asked a question, I said I didn't know, and they said, "Well, let's look into it, then."

Hmm. That didn't sound angry or disappointed. Could it be that not knowing everything is actually not a crime? It turned out that was the case, after all. I was able to say I didn't know something, and we just turned around and figured it out on the spot. No drama. No loss of faith. Eventually, I morphed my "I don't know: into "I don't know, but I can research it for you."

Feel free to use that. No charge.

Don't Leave People Hanging

Nothing annoys me more than calling a technical support service, being asked if I can be called back, and never hearing from anyone again. I'm rather surprised how frequently I have to call back to remind the service representatives that they were fixing something I'm paying to use. I'm sure you don't like the feeling, either. If so, then spare your customers and users that same feeling.

If you're going to have to leave what you are doing, it better be for a darn good reason (fresh donuts in the break room do not count), and you'd better head back and finish up as soon as you can. The more people you leave hanging, the more of a reputation you will collect. Word gets around, and before you know it, you're being canned for performance reasons.

If you're having a hard time keeping track of the things you're working on, then get some help. Make notes, use a task tracker, setup a Kanban board, and ask one of your colleagues for help. Something. Anything!! Just get help and don't make anyone call you to remind you that you weren't done with some task you were assigned.

Don't Trash Talk Your Coworkers

This one will be a difficult temptation to avoid, but you must do whatever you can to avoid talking junk about your colleagues, even if they deserve it. Unfortunately, trash talk happens far too often. I had our cable service come in to troubleshoot a problem. The third technician to come over in as many weeks said that the previous tech had done shoddy work, and that was our problem. The sad thing is that it wasn't the problem. It turned out to be the cabling from the street to the building. That tech disparaged his colleague for nothing.

Speaking badly of others that are supposed to be your equal, or at least in the same general ballpark, has a rotting effect on an organization. Like rot in an apple, eventually it spreads to the entire fruit and ruins it all. Leave that apple in a crate of fresh apples, and they will rot, too, and sooner than they should. Trash talk has the same effect on people and organizations. Soon, you will build an impression of distrust and unhealthy competition between technicians. Others may get the impression that you are trying to knock others down to advance yourself.

If anything, follow that old saw about not saying anything if you can't say something nice. If the previous technician did make a mistake, suck it up, work it out, and when you have some alone time with the offender, let him know. Don't call him on the carpet in front of everyone. Give him the benefit of the doubt, and maybe he'll work it out. You never know. Someday, someone may do the very same thing for you.

No one is immune to making mistakes.

Don't Leave Something You've Started Unfinished

Not leaving something unfinished seems like a simple idea. You start something, and you finish it up. In the immortal words of Jeremy Clarkson, how hard can it be?

I know from personal experience that it can be quite hard. The hardest place to try to finish anything is the client site of a consultant. You aren't there every day, so people stockpile issues and bombard you with them when you appear on the appointed hour.

You can't let them phase you, and you can't let yourself get swamped to the point where you aren't sure what to do. You have to buckle down and triage everything. Put them into the order they need to be done, estimate times to completion, and stand firm. Then, make sure you go back and get everything done that you started.

If at all possible, never leave one job to start another unless it is life-threatening. Because very few things in IT are life-threatening, then you should have plenty of time to finish everything up.

Don't Make Customers Feel That They Are the Problem

It's terrible to talk badly about colleagues or superiors, but it's even worse to give customers the impression that the problems they are having are some-how their fault, even if it is. It is truly a rare thing that someone deliberately causes issues or requests technical support with the sole intention of griev-ing the support staff.

The takeaway from this one should be that, no matter what you think other people should know, they are calling for help because they do not know something. Do not be incredulous that they don't get it. Do not chuckle and say, "Wow, that's a first." Don't compare them to other employees to suggest that they could do better if they wanted.

Technical support staff have an unspoken social contract with their users. If they say it doesn't work, they are stating their truth. You need to make it work for them, not you, and it's not fair for you to suggest that they should know better. Treat people with respect, and they will respect you back. Treat them as if they are stupid, and they won't like you.

And when people aren't liked, they tend to get caught up in layoffs or restruc-turings or even just let go for compatibility issues. No, it's not legal, but companies still do it anyway.

Chapter 15

Ten Books You Should Own

In This Chapter

▶ Discovering new technologies and directions of thought

▶ Expanding your horizons through the simple act of reading

▶ Planting the seeds for your future with new, uncharted territory

*I*n this chapter, I list ten books you should have in your personal library and why. Books are great resources. Just look at this one! You can refer back to them over and over again, and you know that someone, like myself, took the time and care to put as much information in for the subject covered. These ten books are mostly from Wiley, of course, but they are not all *For Dummies* books. Just settle in and plan to pick up copies of everything listed.

Raspberry Pi For Dummies, 2nd Edition

If there's one little gadget you could own that you could experiment with endlessly, it would be the Raspberry Pi. This is a complete computer (mostly) the size of a credit card. This tiny little computer, from the Raspberry Pi Foundation (yes, a nonprofit charity organization), with an impulse buy price tag is a work of genius. You can get an A+ for a mere $20, and if you really want to splurge, you can get a B+ for a staggeringly paltry $35. It was developed to make learning computer science affordable to just about anyone anywhere on Earth. I think the group achieved its goal.

This tiny little computer is powerful and durable, and because there's very little cost involved in getting one, all possible reasons to avoid learning Linux are conveniently eliminated. *Raspberry Pi For Dummies,* by Sean McManus (Wiley) walks you through everything you need to know about the Pi and starts teaching you the basics of programming.

Windows 8.1 Bible

I'll admit it. *Windows 8.1 Bible* by Jim Boyce, Jeffrey R. Shapiro, and Rob Tidrow (Wiley) is coauthored by my writer pal Jim, and he's a good egg. Windows 8.1 itself, on the other hand, is sadly maligned and has not had adoption rates to Microsoft's liking. Yes, Windows 8.1 has two distinct and frustrating personalities and removed some of the most iconic aspects of Windows that people know really well, but it is a significant advancement over Windows 7 when it comes to performance and reliability, and it's not going anywhere soon.

The Bible series is a complete rundown of everything Windows 8.1, and it's worth your time if you're going to be supporting Windows users. Windows 8.1 isn't like Vista. There are millions of users out there, and the game has changed.

On Writing Well: The Classic Guide to Writing Nonfiction, 30th Edition

You may not believe me at first, but you will be writing. Technology is brimming with the written word. You'll write guides on how to use a piece of software, reports on large projects, emails to colleagues, and countless other pieces, and you will stand out if you write well.

On Writing Well: The Classic Guide to Writing Nonfiction, 30th Edition by William Zinsser (Harper Perennial) can help you do just that, and it's well worth the price of admission. Just ask any of the millions of people who have bought the book since it was first published 30 years ago. Yes, this book is that good.

Cloud Computing and Electronic Discovery

The concepts of cloud computing and what is termed eDiscovery is a fascinating and complicated world built on the back of the Internet, and it's not an easy set of ideas to wrap one's mind around. Cloud computing, however, is a fundamental element of the growing Internet of Things and is invading more and more of computer-based lives every day.

Reading *Cloud Computing and Electronic Discovery* by James P. Martin, Harry Cendrowski (Wiley), you will gain a fully rounded and deep understanding of not only the technological concepts that surround cloud computing and eDiscovery, but also the legal and operational impact it will have on business and, by extension, lives. If that wasn't enough, there are fascinating dissertations on legal cases that have shaped what is known and what is unknown about data and how it can and cannot be used.

This book is not light reading. It can be complex and, at times, difficult to understand, but anyone who dedicates time to understanding these concepts will surely have a leg up. It's well worth your time.

Designing the Internet of Things

Speaking of the Internet of Things, it is this very idea that is very likely going to be the next big thing in business over the next decade, and the book *Designing the Internet of Things* by Adrian McEwen, Hakim Cassimally (Wiley), discusses this topic. The Internet of Things has not only started to change the way people operate in today's world, but it will have a significant impact on most everything that has yet to be touched by the global network. In part, people already live in a world filled with Internet-enabled things. Computers, laptops, tablets, phones, watches, media players, video game consoles, exercise tracker bands, and even cars are all a part of the Internet of Things, but that is far from a complete list.

There are so many more "things" that make up our connected world, and in the next few years that number is expected to explode significantly. In essence, a node on the Internet of Things is anything that uses an internet connection (it doesn't matter how) to transfer data somewhere else where someone will use it for some purpose. A webcam is one such object, but then so are embedded systems that monitor the temperature in a server room or a device that keeps track of vibrations in heavy machining equipment.

There are numerous co-habiting devices that enable this new world, as well. RFID tags are the single most common form now, little objects that have some form of embedded data that can be read by another "thing", which then transfers that data to other systems. When you go to a big box store and purchase a DVD or Blu-Ray disc, the box has an RFID tag inside to personally identify that particular product. When the cashier scans it, the tag is identified, and the database is updated to indicate a sale. Later, if there is something wrong with the disc, that same tag is used to identify it, and the database gets updated again. I'm sure you can imagine some ways that information might be helpful.

The Gartner Group estimates that by 2020 there will be billions of nodes on the Internet of Things, all sending a wide range of data to and fro, all to be interpreted for one purpose or another. Livestock is tracked so owners know where they are. Actuators are used to determine if lights are on and allow users to turn those lights on or off remotely. There are scales that can keep track of your weight and even seen a tweet to let your "friends" know. There's even a Bluetooth egg tray that can let you know how many eggs you have and when they've gone bad.

One of the key elements to the growth of the Internet of Things is miniaturization. Functional, even powerful, computers are getting smaller and smaller, and the data they need to handle is well within their capabilities. This leads us back to the Raspberry Pi. At a mere $20-35, depending on model and features, these little boards, about the size of a credit card, are allowing a range of professional and private hackers to find all manner of new uses, or just the chance to build something with their own hands. Knowing how these devices work and expanding your awareness of the potential uses for them can really give you a leg up at a job.

The Innovator's Path: How Individuals, Teams, and Organizations Can Make Innovation Business-as-Usual

Having a clean, clear, defined path ahead of you can be an indispensable tool in your daily struggle to perform your assigned tasks, work with others, and prove yourself a valuable asset in the eyes of management. One way to do that is to get into the minds and hearts of management. Madge M. Meyer's book, *The Innovator's Path* (Wiley), leads you through the eight disciplines of companies that value categorical growth.

From the individual perspective, readers will gain insight into the processes that can be solid stepping stones along the path from idea to fruition, and that's no small thing. The worst thing you can do is to propose an audacious plan as an up-and-comer and fail just before reaching the finish line. This book will help you focus your efforts, spot potential blind spots, and turn yourself from hero to zero. All it requires is effort and dedication.

In addition, you will learn more about the values I have worked hard to instill in you throughout this book. The first step is to listen. You should do this as long as it takes for you to feel confident you can start offering ideas for innovation. There's no need to be in a rush. With tenacity and a proven track record of success, you will be offered a leadership role, and when you do, listening will become one of your most powerful tools.

Agile Project Management For Dummies

I cover Agile in some rather good detail in this book, but there's a lot to it that I just didn't have room to cover. Had I taken the time, this book may just have been called *Agile For Dummies.* Fortunately, there's already a book that covers that subject, and likely does a better job than I can. *Agile Project Management For Dummies* (or APMD, to save space) by Mark C. Layton (Wiley) is just that book. As you walk into more and more companies these days, you will find that they are likely using some form of Agile to manage their projects. In order to leverage your abilities, it helps to come forearmed with as much knowledge of the process as possible. After all, you will likely be asked to join in, and there's nothing less fun that being surprised with something on your first day.

I'm not going to cover Agile again here, but there is one thing that you should come to understand before walking in and proclaiming that you are already an Agile pro. You are not. Reading this book will not make you one. Understanding the concepts and linear process of Agile will not make you one. Knowing all of the lingo and being able to use the various common tools will not make you one. Like anything else, hands-on, practical experience is the only way to become proficient at a skill, and there's no difference with Agile. Learn all you can, develop your awareness, but be prepared to have your applecart upturned when you are presented with your new company's version of the process.

Just be confident in your overarching, horizontal knowledge and work hard to get it under control as soon as possible.

How to Deal with Difficult People: Smart Tactics for Overcoming the Problem People in Your Life

Everyone gets one. You can't avoid it. There are too many difficult people in life to avoid, and one or more will eventually be your boss or coworker. In his book *How to Deal with Difficult People: Smart Tactics for Overcoming the Problem People in Your Life* (Capstone), Gill Hasson says don't avoid them, work with them or, if that's not possible, channel their negative energy in a different direction. Gill's book is really like an expanded version of my guide to personalities.

This book helps you understand them and gives you the tools you need to manage them with the aim of reducing stress in your own life. I mean, really. Who needs more stress in their life? Certainly not IT people! You already have enough stress dealing with every little problem that comes down the pike.

This short and sweet guide gives you the power to deal with unreasonable people reasonably, and that's no small feat. After all, once you understand a problem, or difficult person, you can no longer be surprised or caught off guard by their antics.

The Practice of Professional Consulting

For those of you reading *The Practice of Professional Consulting* by Edward G. Verlander (Pfeiffer) to find yourself work in the endlessly exciting world of consulting, you will be hard pressed to find a better book on the subject. Consulting is a ridiculously complex and diverse world filled with a cavalcade of unique and interesting characters, and you need some guidance on how to navigate that world, or risk washing out entirely. In the IT arm of consulting, companies around every corner are offering the same basic services. What you need is an edge. A leg up. A helping hand.

What you need is a complete system of guidelines, boiled down into its component parts, and stitched together in a wide-ranging collection of scenarios that can help you prepare for all manner of situations. Mark my words, you will be challenged every day (and then some) for your first few years. How you handle that stress and diversity will define the path you take from that first step into the abyss.

Heed the advice, padawan. It will serve you well, or you will end up being the one served. Yes. Terrible pun.

Mindfulness Pocketbook: Little Exercises for a Calmer Life

Last but not least, I am presenting a little book that you can take anywhere and refer to any time you need it. I am also highlighting a second book from Gill, *Mindfulness Pocketbook: Little Exercises for a Calmer Life* (Capstone) and you'll see why. If you only buy one book from this list (and I don't advise that), it should be this one. Nobody likes stress. At least I don't know anyone who does. Well, maybe one or two, but they aren't happy, and I think they are happy that they aren't happy, but I digress.

The key to this book's power is that it is full of little exercises you can perform to put yourself into the mindset you seek in the circumstances that require said mindset. This is not an easy thing, but it is helpful to have someone (or in this case, something) with you to guide you through difficult times. It will require some effort on your part to figure out which chapter-let fits your issue, as well as the mindfulness to perform the exercises, but your efforts will pay off.

Just to make sure you get it all in, you should read the book in its entirety before using it as an incidental guide for the rough patches life offers. No situation is ever without flaws. You can't escape the laws of the universe. Something will go wrong. You just need to be prepared, calm, cool, collected, and aware. Don't discount your colleagues. Don't prejudge. Don't get mad.

And, whatever you do, don't lose yourself.

Chapter 16

Ten Tools You Should Own

. . . .

In This Chapter

▶ Examining the author's personal toolkit so that you can prepare to build your own

▶ Finding out more about the number and low cost of lots of indispensable tools

▶ Discovering that being prepared is one of the best tools you can ever have

. . . .

I've tricked you. This chapter is more about a few categories of tools than just ten individual tools. You will find a number of options for useful programs helpful when engaging in technical support work. Think of this chapter as a collection of ten things you will find indispensable.

You're not going to see a lot of Mac OS X utilities on this list, mostly because Macs don't need a lot. A lot of capable tools are already built into Mac OS X, and there aren't a lot of things that go wrong in the first place. I just don't want you to feel like I've left Apple out on purpose. To that end, you aren't going to see any Linux tools here.

Don't just count on this list, however. As you work on a wide range of issues, you will discover the need for a number of different tools and add them to your collection. This one should get you started.

Malware Tools

The most common emergency you will face on a regular basis is likely malware-related. Some of them are a real pain to deal with, too. These tools will come in handy:

> ✔ **MalwareBytes** (http://malwarebytes.org): While there is a paid version, the free version is just about the best tool there is for cleaning up stray issues. Make sure to get the latest version and try to have Internet access from the affected machine to get fresh updates.

✔ **SpyBot Search & Destroy** (`http://safer-networking.org`): Malware generally installs a lot more stuff than you'd like. Unfortunately, MalwareBytes cannot always clean up everything. Having SpyBot on hand gives you a second option.

✔ **RKill** (`www.bleepingcomputer.com/download/rkill`): One of the methods that malware uses to insinuate itself into systems is to disable common types of executables. RKill can stop many malware processes so that you can clean them out.

✔ **Mac Rogue Remover** (`www.bleepingcomputer.com/download/mac-rogue-remover-tool`): Most malware is targeted at Windows, but some out there are for Mac OS X. This tool handles a common series of malware for Macs.

✔ **ComboFix** (`www.bleepingcomputer.com/download/combofix`): As a last possible resort when cleaning out infected systems that contain recalcitrant viruses, ComboFix can usually clear them out.

✔ **Ubuntu** (`http://ubuntu.com`): This one may seem like an odd inclusion, but it's actually quite useful. Ubuntu can be downloaded as an ISO and written to a DVD-R. Once booted from the Live DVD, you can access and modify files on the system you boot up on.

Disk Management Tools

Dealing with hard drives and storage systems is a common task in IT departments. There is all manner of preparation, formatting, repair, and whatnot that you must manage in order for various laptops, desktops, servers, and storage systems to work. The following tools, all of which are free except Paragon's Hard Disk Manager Pro, are helpful in managing drives:

✔ **Microsoft Disk Management:** This built-in tool is actually quite good at dealing with volumes attached to the system you want to manage, as long as they are NTFS drives. It even supports rudimentary drive striping, though I strongly suggest you go the hardware route for RAID management.

✔ **Apple Disk Utility:** Mac OS X has its own drive management tool. Disk Utility is capable of dealing with HFS+ and FAT32 formatting and can even create and mount drive images. If you create an image of a CD or DVD, you can even mount it on the desktop, which is a useful trick for installs and updates or the newer Macs that do not have optical drives.

✔ **Paragon Hard Disk Manager Professional** (`http://paragon-software.com`): No. It's not free, but it's well worth the cost for a comprehensive drive management tool for Windows. It can handle partitioning, backups, imaging, archiving, and migration, comes with a tool to create bootable recovery media based on Linux or WinPE, and works fast and efficiently. It now has an Express mode, which doesn't really fit in with a Professional application, but it comes in handy on occasion.

✔ **GNOME Partition Editor** (`http://gparted.sourceforge.net`): If you aren't into the whole money thing, check out Gparted, an open source tool based on the GTK+ window tools and GNU's Parted tool to make a GUI-based pairing. While it runs only in Linux, the project does offer a Live CD/USB image that you can boot on any system. In fact, performing drive management functions while the disk being worked on is offline is considered the safest method.

✔ **ImgBurn** (`http://imgburn.com`): IT people burn a lot of CDs and DVDs for backups, install images, driver archives, and whatnot. Windows and Mac OS X have very basic tools for making discs, but ImgBurn is a free tool for Windows that gives you everything you need to image discs and create discs from images. While I'm not keen on the recent addition of optional adware, it's far from the worst I've seen (I'm not naming names, IzArc) and can easily be disabled. It is a very capable tool and worth the mild annoyance.

✔ **MagicDisc** (`www.magiciso.com/tutorials/miso-magicdisc-overview.htm`): This tiny, itsy bitsy, little tool's only job is to mount disc images on your desktop, just like you stuck the disc into your optical drive. MagicDisc can be ridiculously handy if you work with a lot of images from Microsoft's MSDN, manage a lot of virtual machines, or perform a lot of testing. It hasn't been updated since 2009, but it's free and works just fine on all versions of Windows.

System Cleaning Tools

Both Mac OS X and Windows systems need cleaning for different reasons. Windows is good about having uninstallers, but doesn't clean up well after itself. Mac OS X does not have uninstallers, but instead, you just drag the app to the trash, which doesn't always take all of the extras with it. There are also a wide array of caches, update directories, and databases that just get gummed up over time. The following is a selection of tools that are good at cleaning up when the operating systems are not:

✔ **CCleaner** (`http://piriform.com/ccleaner`): Windows can be an enormous pain in the rump when trying to clean it up. There is no way to do so manually without dedicating a week of your time to the task.

CCleaner is both a free and commercial application that does it all for you, knows all the nooks and crannies, and rewards you with tons of detailed information. It also just happens to not be bloated out of proportion. It also has business editions.

✔ **Defraggler** (`http://piriform.com/defraggler`): Another tool from Piriform, Defraggler is an excellent, compact defragmentation tool that can be scheduled and even limited to performing only certain tasks. Aside from being able to defrag at boot time (also referred to as offline), it can defrag certain folders and even specific files.

✔ **AppCleaner** (`http://freemacsoft.net`): I've always found it both convenient and frustrating that on a Mac I could drag an app to the trash to uninstall it. I would then find that it had left stuff behind elsewhere in the system. That's because a script is running in the background when you drag an app to your drive and then run it. It installs things where they belong seamlessly. Unfortunately, it leaves a mess. In that mess, however, is a log of everything it installed and connects to. That's where AppCleaner comes in. Drag the app onto AppCleaner, and it finds all the bits associated with it and offers them up for sacrifice to the Trash Gods. This one is free, but you can pay for ones that do the same job.

✔ **AllDup** (`http://alldup.de/en_index.htm`): A huge problem with storage costs frequently comes down to duplicated files. All of those copies start to pile up after a while, especially the media files. AllDup is a fast, free, and easy utility that helps you track down those darn clones and get rid of them.

Networking Tools

One regular task involves taking a look at the local network and Internet connections. You never know when you may need to correct an issue, and these tools can . . . ahem . . . save your bacon.

✔ **ServersCheck Monitoring** (`http://serverscheck.com`): While it's not super complete with agented monitoring, it is a remarkably complete monitoring suite. In fact, ServersCheck Monitoring sells agentless as if it were somehow better, but that's beside the point. It is very good, as long as you have a Windows Domain-based network to apply administrator credentials against in order to implement complete monitoring. That leaves out Macs, and machines that are not domain members must have their credentials manually added. Did I mention it's free? Also, you can pay for hardware module that adds SMS alerts using a GSM modem on the AT&T or T-Mobile networks.

✔ **SoftPerfect Network Scanner** (`www.softperfect.com/products/networkscanner/`): For something a lot less complicated than

ServersCheck Monitoring and still very useful, check out Network Scanner. This simple tool scans the network your computer is connected to. It's great for tracking down everything on a network at a client location. It will even work with Windows Domain administrator credentials to collect detailed information on active nodes.

✔ **Creatly** (`http://creatly.com`): Diagramming network layouts can be a pain, but fortunately some great tools are around. Take Creatly, for example. This online tool has a collection of simple network shapes that you can add. A free account is available, but I suggest you go with the Personal for $5 a month or Team 5 for $25 a month, each of which allows you to store unlimited private diagrams. Fiddle around with the free version if you aren't convinced.

Data Recovery Tools

If you have ever inserted a CD, DVD, USB flash drive or most any other kind of media into a drive or USB slot and got nothing, then welcome to the club. ISOBuster (`http://isobuster.com`) is rather awesome. I've recovered discs that appeared to be unrecoverable. It's an excellent tool and well worth every penny.

System Imaging Tools

Back in the day, Norton Ghost was the tool. Unfortunately, Symantec led Ghost off to the boonies back in 2010. Fortunately, some alternatives do work quite well. Imaging tools are used to make exact copies of drives so that they can be written to other drives as clones.

Disk imaging copies the block-level data on the drive from top to bottom instead of reading data. The process is simple enough. You configure a machine exactly the way you want it and then boot it up with the imaging software. You direct it to make an image of the system drive onto an external drive or network resource. You can then boot up a machine with identical hardware and write that image to it. Voilà. Instant clone.

Here are a few helpful system imaging tools:

✔ **Acronis True Image** (`http://acronis.com`): This commercial software package is about as good as you can get these days. It is fast, well supported, and flexible. It has pulled my bacon out of the fire on a number of occasions.

✔ **Clonezilla** (`http://clonezilla.org`): If a budget is important, then this open source project is a popular alternative. It's smart and fast and can perform block-level for familiar file systems and sector-by-sector copies for unfamiliar file systems to achieve perfect clones.

✔ **Cobian Backup** (`http://cobiansoft.com`): This freeware package is an example of perfection if Windows is all you care about. Cobian is particularly skillful at making bare-metal backup images of Windows systems, including server installations.

✔ **Carbon Copy Cloner** (`http://bombich.com`): The Developer, Mike Bombich, has been developing CCC for a very, very long time, and it has been Mac only since day one. CCC is an extremely competent drive imaging application and, over the years, has added a number of features. It is also one of the only packages on any platform that can create a bootable backup. That's right. You back up your Mac, and you can actually boot up the backup.

Helpful Hardware Tools

The best tools aren't always software or online. Sometimes they're actual tools. You know, like the ones in your real toolbox. Some of these tools are big. Others are small. All of them cost something, but they all have value. Here's a list of items that are helpful to have on hand:

✔ **A compact toolkit:** I prefer Syba kits, but you can get anything that suits your needs. You want screwdrivers, needlenose pliers, wire cutters, a crimper, a bunch of RJ-45 tips, and some microdrivers. Don't just get Philips and flathead, but also torx.

✔ **A USB to SATA drive adapter:** These come in countless formats from cable sets for 2.5-inch drives all the way to desktop docks. SATA is a standard for hard drive and solid-state drive connections, and these adapters make them work like USB external drivers.

✔ **A USB to PATA drive adapter:** Just in case.

✔ **A 2TB or larger external USB drive:** It's a good idea to have a lot of free storage available. You never know when you might need to transfer data.

✔ **A box dolly:** Lots of gear boxes are quite heavy. These make short work of moving them around.

✔ **A furniture truck:** These little wheeled platforms are fantastic for moving around really heavy things like uninterruptible power supplies.

✔ **A Fluke MicroMapper:** These terrific little gadgets aren't cheap (about $100), but they are excellent. It comes with a little remote that you can use to identify ports on the breakout board.

✔ **A USB to Serial port adapter:** It's surprising how many devices still use a serial interface for configuration. It's also hilarious how many computer do not have a serial port.

Tool Bag Gadgets and Gear

The ubiquitous "bag of tricks" wasn't just conjured into being from thin air. There is a large amount of truth to that old phrase. In order to be well prepared, you must have prepared well, and that means having some of the following bits and pieces on hand when you need them:

✔ **Flashlights:** It can be dark behind some racks and in some network closets.

✔ **Ethernet cables:** I've carried as many as five, but generally you only need one CAT-6e patch cable and one crossover cable for switch configuration.

✔ **USB cables:** It's a good idea to carry around various types of USB cables, just in case. There's B-type, Mini, and micro. Also get an extension cable. You never know when you might need an extra three feet.

✔ **Assorted general cables:** An audio patch cable (3.5mm stereo), a serial cable, a standard ungrounded power cable (the tip is shaped like a figure-8), and a standard grounded power cable that fits in PC power supplies.

✔ **A power strip with a breaker:** I like the ones that have sockets widely separated to accommodate wall warts.

Random Utilities

Some tools just come in handy or are nice to have. Here's a few of my personal favorites:

✔ **F.lux** (`http://justgetflux.com`): Nerds spend a lot of time looking at displays. At night, that can wear you out fast as your eyes compensate. F.lux deals with that issue by automagically adjusting the color temperature. When you first start using F.lux, it just makes your screen look yellow, but give it a few minutes, and it just starts to look warm as your eyes adjust. It's entirely free and is available for Mac, Windows, and Linux, as well as a number of mobile devices.

✔ **GreenShot** (`http://getgreenshot.org`): Taking screenshots of various things comes in real handy for troubleshooting and writing documentation. There are lots of utilities, and Windows itself has the Snipping Tool and the classic Print Screen function. GreenShot has them trumped. This small, free utility sits in the System Tray and waits. When you press Prt Sc button, it leaps into action. I have it set up to capture a selected region and then to choose what to do with the image. GreenShot will tie into network services and even has a built-in editor.

✔ **IrfanView** (`http://irfanview.com`): Image files are common to a lot of work and personal endeavors, and IrfanView is the editor for images of all types. It's been around for years, is very capable, and is well trusted. It's also quite free.

✔ **VLC** (`http://videolan.org`): VLC is like IrfanView for video files. VLC can open and play almost anything on the planet. It can also play almost any audio file type.

✔ **Oracle VirtualBox** (`http://virtualbox.org`): VB is the only free virtualization application available any more, ever since VMware's Player added a Professional license model. VB allows you to run just about any OS in a window on your computer. With a little effort, you can even get Mac OS X to run in Windows.

✔ **Xmarks** (`http://xmarks.com`): Xmarks, acquired by Marvasol several years back, is an add-on to most popular browsers that stores and syncs your bookmarks. If you are using bookmarks to collect important information and guides and whatnot, then you'll definitely want Xmarks.

✔ **LastPass** (`http://lastpass.com`): LastPass, another company owned by Marvasol, does for passwords what Xmarks does for bookmarks. Unlike a lot of cloud-based companies, LastPass has not been penetrated by hackers (knock on wood). It's great at generating strong passwords, filling in complex forms, and unlocking resources you don't access often. If you get the Pro version for $12 a year, you also get access to the mobile versions of the app. For $24 a year, you get you both LastPass and Xmarks Pro — a worthy combo.

Other Useful Tidbits

Finally, you will find all kinds of stuff that you want or need that may only present itself when you really, really need them. I list them here because

I have needed them at one time or another and would like to help you avoid that horrible feeling of not having it on hand:

- ✔ **Sticky notepads:** These notepads are great for marking things temporarily. One little trick I use is to cut the nonsticky parts off with scissors. These make remarkably good cable labels.

- ✔ **A pair of scissors:** Aside from cutting sticky notes down to size, they come in handy for all manner of tasks, including, but not limited to, cutting old zip ties.

- ✔ **Zip ties:** Packs and/or cases of zip ties are dirt cheap, come in different colors and sizes, and are almost infinitely useful. Not only can you bundle stuff together, but you can also hang or secure bits and pieces. Neaten up the look by trimming the tail after you tighten them up.

- ✔ **Retractable permanent markers:** Regular permanent markers are fantastic, but you can lose the caps, and they dry out. Get a few of the retractable kind that you just click closed like a ballpoint pen. Slick.

- ✔ **Electrical tape:** Get the kind that comes in a closeable tin, or the gooey adhesive gets all over everything.

- ✔ **A pair of USB-powered speakers:** You'd be surprised how frequently these speakers come in handy. Logitech makes a pair that sound awfully good. They get their power from USB and sound from the headphone jack. I picked up a pair of Z110 for $20.

- ✔ **Blank media:** Get a few of those huge spindles of CD-R and DVD-R discs, but also grab a spare 25 disc spindle. The small spindles make fantastic go anywhere holders for different kinds of writable optical disc. Mix and match as needed.

- ✔ **Paper clips:** You'd be shocked at how often CDs get stuck in drives and the only way to get them out is with an unbent paper clip . . . that you just don't happen to have.

- ✔ **General office supplies:** Pens, notepads, and cellophane tape are all good to have on hand.

- ✔ **Screen-cleaning gear:** The single best microfiber cloth I have ever used is not for sale. They are black and come in the box with Apple monitors, iMacs, and a few other Apple products. The next best thing is Toddy Gear's Smart Cloth (`www.toddygear.com`). It's not cheap at $10, but these things are remarkably effective.

Chapter 17

Ten Resources You Should Use

• •

• •

There's nothing more important to someone working in technology than resources. People just don't have the capacity to know everything, so they compensate. When they need to do something and can't recall how, they use resources to fill in the gaps.

In this chapter, I run down the top ten resources you have available to you. Some may seem obvious, and others require some capital expense, but all of them are useful. These items are not listed in any particular order of importance.

Other People

So, to be clear, I did say that these resources are all important, but this one is special. Other people are always going to be your best resource. These resources aren't limited to your colleagues, though. All kinds of people can help you. You just need to know how to use what they can tell you. You also need to develop a bond with certain people, whether it's just one of professional courtesy or a real friendship. Here's a closer look at some of the types of people you'll work with and ideas on how you can best integrate with them:

   ✔ **Your colleagues:** The people you work with can all be helpful resources. Those who have been working at your company longer than you know all of the inner workings of that company. They know people and can make introductions, pass on helpful details, share information on personalities, and help guide you through the emotional battlefield that dots most any company like a mine field.

Forging alliances when you are first hired is both a tool for helping you integrate quicker and to limit the potential negative relationships you may form.

One of the biggest mistakes you can make on a new job is to have a beef with one or more people. It's just the numbers, but you can't make friends with everyone, but you can be civil. It's an imperative.

✔ **Your superiors:** In an entry-level position, you will have numerous superiors. The closer they are to you, the more important it is to forge positive relationships with them. You will, however, have the rare occasion to provide services directly to those who inhabit the higher levels of the hierarchy. When these opportunities present themselves, be sure to act in an exemplary fashion, and you'll imprint yourself on the memory of those you have helped.

For your immediate managers, you must always perform your duties, report in on a regular basis when acting independently, and follow all rules. After all that, you can take some time to forge kinships with them. Learn about what they like, spend time engaging in work-related social gatherings, and be there when they need you. All these things help foster good feelings toward you with your leadership.

✔ **The people you serve:** Now, there are those whom you actually help. If you think they can't be resources, then you are mistaken. One of the methods I've found most helpful when providing internal help desk support is to make rounds. On a regular basis (whatever best supports your daily schedule), move around and ask everyone who doesn't appear to be too busy if everything is all right. Don't do it too often, or you may get annoying, though.

Over time, you will make a regular impression on all the people you help, especially if you remember the problems they have and check back in later to make sure that your fixes are making them happy. That's personal service, and personal service makes pleasant thoughts spring to mind when they talk about IT. They will speak well of you, and that will filter around. You can't buy that kind of good will, not for any amount of money.

Sure, the people you serve can be resources by telling you what their problems are, but the best thing they can do for you is enjoy receiving services from you. If you remain patient and diligent, you will reap the rewards of your efforts.

Microsoft's TechNet Community

MSDN is Microsoft's Developer Network, and it provides programmers of Microsoft products with the resources they need to get their jobs done and done well. For an annual fee, you get access to a wide range of powerful tools, resources, and software. I only bring this up because not long ago, Microsoft also offered IT people a version of this program called TechNet. That's all gone now, but it's not. That statement may be confusing, but it's actually a reason to rejoice.

Since Microsoft cancelled the paid TechNet programs, it has made all the resources of TechNet free and have migrated it all into a new, thriving, huge community resource pool everyone can participate in and draw help from. An astounding amount of detailed information is in TechNet, and Microsoft hasn't just handed it off to everyone else to manage to save itself some money. It has an entire staff working the sites and providing IT professionals with assistance they need when they need it.

Sure, all the included software is now no longer available in the form that it was before, but it's really the collected knowledge, endless scads of detailed documentation, and access to people who really know their business that's the real gem at the bottom of the muddy pond.

The Help Desk Institute

I'll say this. There are lots of groups for IT people, but there aren't that many for just technical support people. The one that stands out is HDI. Here's what they say about themselves:

> In 1989, HDI became the first membership association and certification body created for the technical service and support industry. Since then, HDI has remained the source for professional development by offering the resources needed to promote organization-wide success through exceptional customer service. In other words, we help professionals in service management better connect with customers, and that's just good business.

That HDI has been one of the only consistent resources for help desk engineers and for fostering strong and positive direction in help desk operations for corporations for the past 25 years says quite a lot. It goes to show that HDI has found who it is because it was able to see that technical support was going to become something very important to the computer industry as a whole. In hindsight, it's not all that surprising. When asked why, HDI, HDI says this:

> Members of the HDI community elevate the customer experience, which in turn makes business more productive. We stress the importance of understanding the customer's emotional reactions to a problem and how to differentiate that from the customer's technical problem.

Wow. Someone had a long time to think about how to really say this succinctly and with crystal clear clarity. Technical support is about the customer and making sure that customer is ultimately pleased with their investment in the products you support, be that internal support for staff of a company or products your company sells to customers.

I strongly suggest that anyone who can afford the annual membership fees of $75 do so. It is well worth it to have access to that significant library of support documents alone, and the fellowship is critical, too.

Product Documentation

One of the best places to look, but the least looked at, is product documentation. I personally know very few technically skilled people who spend any real time examining documentation. I can't speak for others, but in my experience, I know that this comes from my innate talent for being able to figure things out quickly and then explain it to others in easy-to-understand terms.

Another issue may be that not all product documentation is any good. That's not particularly surprising, considering the quality of instructions that come with build-it-yourself furniture, small appliances, matchbooks, or cotton swabs. I don't want to call anyone out in particular, but certain kinds of software projects lack decent software because the developers consistently overestimate the potential audience.

Not to mention, people just don't like to read instructions. Video games are a prime example. Back when Nintendo made its mark on the badly bleeding video game industry (stabbed in the heart by Atari, in case you were wondering, but that's another story) with its Nintendo Entertainment System, all games came with an instruction booklet. As the games grew more complex, the booklets gained pages. Some games even have what may qualify as a book inside the box.

The video game companies discovered that people didn't really read the manuals, though, and started to integrate the instructions into the games. Now, its commonplace for any game you play on most any platform to offer some form of training or walkthrough to help you learn the controls. Unfortunately, this approach isn't something the computer software industry has really emulated. On occasion, you'll see pop-ups in web-based applications that show you new features or point out the basics, but it's not the same.

It may surprise you then that most quality software actually has usable documentation that explains how things work, why certain actions behave the way they do, or just what to expect when using a function. Fortunately, one of the best known applications on the planet, Microsoft's own Word, has really good documentation. Once Microsoft introduced the Command Ribbon to replace traditional toolbar arrangement, much to the ongoing befuddlement and frustration of its users, people found it difficult to locate the commands they had spent years learning.

One of the least liked and most maligned efforts to offer more help to users of software was Microsoft's Clippit (often times, and erroneously, called Clippy), an anthropomorphic paper clip that made an appearance in Office 97 for Windows and Office 98 for MacOS. People were so annoyed by the little animated helper Microsoft disabled it in Office XP and removed it entirely in 2007. This failure didn't stop Microsoft from trying again with the release of Windows XP, where it used a little animated puppy for the desktop search function. I wrote about the complex process to disable it, and in an update, Microsoft made it easier. I don't know if I influenced Microsoft, but I like to think I did. There were also a number of other characters, including carica-tures of William Shakespeare and Albert Einstein, a little robot, and even a talking Mac called Max. The whole idea was so grating on users everywhere that even Microsoft mocked them, going so far as to include Clippit as a dead character in Office 2010: The Movie (don't worry, it's only two minutes long).

Apple is not immune to this weirdness, either. You likely wouldn't know that Apple's Disc Utility, an application designed to format and manage drives, is also a repository for Disc Image (DMG) files and even copies of commonly used CD-ROM or DVD-ROM discs. Disc Utility's hidden trick is that it can even mount an image of an optical disc on the desktop, just like you had stuck it into the drive itself. A quick scan through the online documentation for Disc Utility would reveal that information and show you how to use it.

The one thing you do not want to do is look at the documentation when you are in front of the client. This mistake can be forgiven in a few rare instances where the user has asked you to show him how to use some software that is not approved for use, you've never seen it, and he is going to use it for personal purposes, but this delves into company policy territory. In general, do all of your research outside of the review range of users. You do want to make them feel confident in your abilities and those of your compatriots.

Now, I'm not suggesting that you read the manuals for all software, but it's a good idea to be familiar with as much as possible, even if you have to look it up again. At least you'll know where to look when you do. You may be sur-prised how much you'll learn from the official documentation.

Google and Bing Search

Google first and then Bing second are great places to search for error messages. It's not that I don't like Bing. I do. I use it every day, but there are some things that Google is just better at organizing and providing links to deep searches that Bing just doesn't do. That's not to say you don't use Bing, though. Regardless of the tool you choose, though, solutions to problems just aren't available through traditional means can often be tracked down with some creative search terms.

For Google, here are some tips for advanced searching:

- ✔ **Add a minus (–) sign before a word that you do not want to appear in the results.** You will find that with common terms that are used to describe a lot of things, you'll get more junk. Minus out the keywords that reflect unhelpful items.

- ✔ **Add a plus (+) sign before a word that must appear in the results.** The plus sign helps make sure that certain words that may not regularly be included get preferential treatment.

- ✔ **Use an underscore (_) between two words to tell Google they should be linked.** For example, sometimes people refer to Active Directory as ActiveDirectory, so to search for those instances, use active_directory.

- ✔ **Insert terms in quotes so that their order is preserved.** Otherwise, Google just counts the number of instances each term appears in the document. You may need to find an "error code" and not all pages where "error" and "code" appear.

Bing uses the quotes, plus, and minus operators, but falls back on Boolean terms for most search operators:

- ✔ **Use the "near" operator to specify how close the following term must be to the preceding word.** For example, search for "windows linux", and you'll get a lot of pages that have these terms all over the place and are likely unrelated. Windows or Linux may appear in the body of the piece, and the other may be in an unrelated sidebar item. Instead, search like this to return only results that have Linux appear five or less words adjacent to Windows, giving you more accurate results:

  Windows near: 5 Linux

- ✔ **Use the "site" operator to limit the search scope.** For example, if you know that you saw an article on Gizmodo.com, but cannot find it using its search tool, try the following on Bing to return results only from Gizmodo that match the search terms within the parentheses:

  "helpful keywords" site: Gizmodo.com

Here's a helpful tip when searching for information from a Windows error dialog box. You know the ones, the kind that disappear and you're not sure how to get it to show up again. While nothing says that you can do it, you can use the Copy keyboard shortcut (Ctrl + C) to place the entire text of the dialog box into the Clipboard, including the title bar and button text! Open up Notepad.exe and paste it in to take a better look, and you can copy out what you need to use in a search.

Product Technical Support

When it comes down to it, an excellent resource is just like you: technical support. Whenever you need to deal with a problem that nobody else can solve, get on the horn, hop on chat, or even pen an email (depending on the urgency of the issue, of course). Because they are like you, they deserve respect and patience, at least to a degree. I'm not suggesting you let incompetent people (I'm not making it up — they exist) decide for you that a problem cannot be solved. Just make sure to give them the benefit of the doubt and let them do their job in a stress-free environment.

It may take some extra effort, but I bet they'll surprise you.

Most technical support people will bend over backward because, just once out of their miserable day, you came on the line and were nice. Not just nice, but understanding. It doesn't take a lot to get someone to help. Just some kind words and tolerance of their corporate-imposed limitations will typically do. I used to crank it up from stern to angry the minute I didn't get something taken care of immediately for a client. It took me a few years, but I learned a hard lesson. A vendor who dealt with a number of hardware manufacturers for the company I worked for told me that his people didn't like dealing with me and could they get someone else.

That really hurt, but after I steamed about it for a while, a friend told me that honey attracts more flies than vinegar. I already knew this, but I hadn't been applying it. I trusted that friend, however, so I made an effort to change. It was difficult at first, but I maintained my cool on every communication, and over time, it just became natural. It was easy to step into their shoes and hear me raging on the other end and knowing how annoyed I would be had I been required to deal with myself. I was like the jerk version of Captain Kirk in *Mirror, Mirror.*

I can't stress enough the importance of forging positive relationships with the people you work with and deal with. It doesn't matter if you interact several times a day or only a few times a year; their feelings matter. Be aware of them as real, emotional people who have responsibilities of their own and treat them with respect, and you will be well on your way to having an endless cadre of real, valuable, reliable resources.

Your Own Intuition

Don't count yourself out. You are a rock star. I don't mean that in a condescending manner, either. You, as a technical person, are on the leading edge of the future. It is people like you, with your skills, who are the jocks of today. Not everyone can be like you, and yet everyone needs what you have. If that doesn't make you a rock star, I don't know what does. Don't count yourself out, but don't let it go to your head, either.

This is the dangerous place nerds can get stuck: an overblown sense of self-importance. Yes, not everyone can be you, but there are more of you than I'm sure you'd like to admit. As such, you can't go around acting like you own stuff or are better than others. That's no way to win over people to your side when you need them most, and you will need them. One day. Even so, you have skills and can learn more. You can be a resource for others, and if you let them be a resource for you, that common ground will afford you a space to forge a lasting relationship.

So, it's best to believe in yourself and the real talent you have as someone who can work with technology. Look at it this way. You know those people who are so good at something they make it look easy? That's how nontechnical people look at you. If the HR department didn't believe in you, it wouldn't have hired you. If the manager didn't think you could cut it, he wouldn't have asked HR to have you back for another interview.

You have chops. Believe in yourself enough to be confident that you can solve problems and be an asset to the team.

Community Support Forums

I don't think it's possible to count all the sites and people involved with those sites where there are discussions of technology. I think it's safe to assume that millions of people from all around the world are talking about technology on the Internet. A lot of those people are just fans of gear and gadgets and whatnot, but a lot of people work in the IT world, and they have a tendency to share their knowledge. One of the more common forms of this is the community support forum.

Community support forums come in all forms and sizes, but they all share a common format. Some people ask questions, and others answer those questions. Why would people do this? Primarily because they can, but there's more to it than that. There is a shared bond nerds have with other nerds. Sure, some self-absorbed, better-than types are out there, but they either move to Wall Street or get stuck in some dead-end job where people don't have to deal with them. Most nerds are good people who are happy to share their knowledge with others. At some point, someone helped them.

It's a kind of paying it forward.

Like anywhere you interact with people, most forums demand that you be civil, and if you cannot, you get booted. If you're good to go, however, there will be times when no amount of searching will give you the results you need, and that means you need to ask. This usually happens when you have some kind of esoteric issue that has never been seen or is rare.

For example, I had a client for whom I was managing her legacy Mac OS web server, and she was having consistent issues where it would drop off the network at the cohosting location. Because the machine was over a decade old and the OS it ran had long been supplanted by Mac OS X, I had nothing to draw on. Technology had moved on, and there were no resources. I ended up tracking down one of the developers attached to the development of the web server software and talking to him about the problem. It turned out that all I needed to do was to filter a flag from incoming packets that caused an error in the TCP/IP stack used in MacOS of that era. I had the colocation staff install a small firewall device and configure it to filter out the offending bits, and the server has remained stable for well over a year now.

I stepped out into the community of the Internet, asked my question, and found an answer. Even when I had the specific information about what was causing the problem, I couldn't find anything helpful using Google or Bing. That's how out there this issue was.

The lesson that I'm aiming to illustrate here is that, once you have exhausted every other resource within a reasonable period of time, it's time to head out into the wilderness and trust that someone, somewhere has what you need. With the millions of nerds out there dealing with millions of iterations of your systems, it's reasonable to believe that someone out there may have a lead on a solution for you.

Another benefit to community forums is a bit less concrete, but still no less helpful. Every once in a while, when you have a particularly noisome problem to battle and you can't find anything helpful, you find something similar. These kinds of related issues and their proffered solutions can often suggest paths to a solution you may not have previously considered.

Error Logs

Operating systems themselves can also be excellent resources. While I am personally fond of Windows and Mac OS X roughly equally, I do prefer Windows when it comes to logging system events. All currently supported versions of Windows (that's Vista, 7, and 8) have some form of the Event Viewer, an application that gives users access to the logs created by the system itself and the applications that run on the system. It is in these logs where you will find much of the information you need to solve problems or, at the very least, figure out what's causing them.

Error Messages

Not everything gets logged, however. That can pose a problem, especially when the issue is intermittent. In the section "Google and Bing Search," earlier in this chapter, I offer a simple tip. Even though there are no menu items for it, you can copy the contents of a dialog box to the clipboard using the Ctrl-C keyboard shortcut. You can then paste it into Notepad.exe and take a closer look at it. Like the logs, error messages can give you insight into problems for applications that don't offer logs, or at least usable ones.

Chapter 18

Ten Things You Should Learn

*E*ducation is one thing. Education helps you establish levels of expertise in the panoply of academic standards and your chosen major and minor disciplines and prepares you for working with people, meeting deadlines, and being generally responsible (acknowledging that college students also act irresponsibly). It's the self-education part that I'm interested in in this chapter.

There are great benefits to be derived from branching out from your planned collegiate or other core educational path. After all, degree courses give you a rather specific series of classes aimed at teaching you a skill or trade. Unfortunately, the job market sees technical people as all-in-one, jack-of-all-trade types, capable of performing an array of tasks. What is also unfortunate is that these expectations are not reasonable, but that doesn't stop them from having said expectations.

As a service to you, I've written this chapter to give you information on ten or so things that I think you should learn about. Don't worry if you are already taking courses for some. You can delve into the others. I'm sure that you'll find a number of these ideas compelling as I'm making them as interesting as I possibly can. They really are quite interesting.

Virtual Machine Technology

Virtual machines have become a standard technology all throughout industry worldwide. There are a large number of benefits enterprise derives from the implementation of VM technology.

What exactly is a virtual machine?

In case you don't know what a virtual machine is, here's the rundown. A *virtual machine,* VM for short, is what amounts to a software-based version of a PC. First, you need a system that is capable of virtualization, also called VT-x. Most modern Intel Core series and AMD CPUs have VT-x support, but not all of them. If you have a computer with VT-x support, then you'll need a *hypervisor,* an application that automagically manages your systems resources and offers them to virtual machines. Finally, you need a virtual machine, which you create inside of the hypervisor.

When you first create a VM, you name it, allocate some space on your hard drive for a drive image, and configure the hardware resources it will use. Because a VM uses the same resources your PC uses, you need to allocate less than you have, but most hypervisors keep that in check for you. VMs can be run in windows or expanded to fill the screen.

In order for VMs to completely integrate with the desktop host they are running on, most hypervisors have specialized driver packages that enable some special features, mostly having to do with interaction. The mouse drivers allow the pointer to seamlessly move from host to guest. The keyboard drivers allow the appropriate shortcuts to be applied. The video drivers allow the guest OS to dynamically adjust apparent screen resolution depending on window size or if full-screen mode is activated.

There are hypervisors for all major platforms. VMware's Workstation and Player applications are available for Windows and Linux. The popular open source project QEMU is available for Windows, Mac OS X, Linux, and BSD. There is VMware's Fusion and Parallels Desktop for Mac OS X. For servers, there's VMware's vSphere, Citrix's Xen, and Microsoft's Hyper-V. Desktop hypervisors are applications while server hypervisors are installed against the bare-metal server, typically making them rather compact.

A reduction in electricity usage

In a traditional server environment, one hardware server is allocated for each server task. Each one of those hardware servers generates BTUs, a measurement of heat output, during normal operation. Say, as an example, you have a small company that has a domain server, a mail server, two application servers, two storage servers, and a web server. As a matter of course, there would also be a switch or two, a firewall device, some form of tape-based backup, a few uninterruptible battery backup devices, and other sundry server room gadgets.

Out of the seven servers, none of them ever max out their installed RAM or bump up against their CPU capacities. In fact, only the application servers use any more than a quarter of their operational capacity. Virtualization could reduce these seven physical machines down to the one domain server (Microsoft strongly urges against virtualizing domain controllers), combine the two application servers into one, combine the web and mail servers into one, and consolidate the two storage servers into one, turning seven into four.

Do the math. Assuming that each server has redundant 750W power supplies, that's 750 x 14, which gives you 10,500 watts. At maximum output, that gives you 35,805 BTUs per hour. It takes one ton of Heating, Ventilation, & Air Conditioning (HVAC) to handle 12,000 BTUs, so all seven servers requires approximately three tons of HVAC. Virtualization shifts the wattage down to 6,000, which generates 20,460 BTUs per hour, so now only two tons of HVAC are needed.

Unfortunately, it's impossible to offer any numbers on actual cost because there are significant variances between regional requirements for cooling as well as cost per kW hour based on the utility providing the power. The point is, however, that this company no longer has to pay for the extra ton of HVAC capacity and 4,500W less of server power consumption. Over time, those savings build up, and as a company scales upward, those savings can be in the millions.

Less space required for less hardware

Virtualization also impacts the amount of space required to hold those servers, which also impacts HVAC operational volumes. A smaller space to keep cool and offset the BTUs generated requires less cooling to maintain safe operating temperatures. It's not just HVAC that benefits, though. It's actual special volume that can be reduced.

Say that you have two 42U racks that each have 21 Dell PowerEdge 2950 Gen II servers each running its own OS and performing its own duties. Because those are circa 2006, upgrades have long been neglected, so you have a budget to spend. You decide to pick up 10 Dell PowerEdge R820, consolidate storage, virtualize your backup domain controller and failover DNS into one machine, virtualize your database servers into another machine, and then redeploy four development servers on each of the remaining servers. That leaves you single machines for your primary domain controller, mail, and web servers.

Now, 10 machines are running what used to require 21. Nice job!

Speedier server deployment

One of the things you learn first when starting to work with virtual machine technologies is that cloning is a ridiculously easy affair. The concept is simple. You start with a desktop hypervisor like VMware's Workstation and create a virtual machine. Once that VM is complete and configured the way you prefer, you can create a clone, which can then be deployed. It works something like a template in a word processor.

So, if it took you a few hours to install, update, and set up your server image, then I bet you'd be happy to hear that it takes only a few minutes to create a new instance from that clone. If that wasn't cool enough, the entire process can be automated using various tools, both free and commercial. Heck, even a Windows Batch script can be used to create new instances with just a click.

The most common way of managing virtual machine servers, however, is through the server manager. Generally, the more advanced the feature set, the higher the cost will be.

Additional options for disaster recovery

Traditional forms of backup are typically tape-based. Tapes are not exactly speedy, and high capacity tape libraries are not cheap. It can take a long time to restore an entire image from tape. In recent years, as drive capacities have risen and prices have dropped, multiterabyte storage devices have become more affordable. While backups are faster than tape, it still takes some time to restore backups, and extra steps always need to be taken in order to facilitate a restore, regardless of backup media.

Virtual machines, however, have a neat trick up their sleeve, and they're called snapshots. A *snapshot* is a kind of digital backup of a point in time of the VM. You can even make snapshots of live VMs. What makes them so much better than standard backups is that they can be restored in a very short period of time, anywhere from 10 to 20 minutes. If, for any reason, something happens to a VM during operation, it can be restored in short order. Because storage is cheap and snapshots are small, it's smart to make daily snapshots of all VMs.

Increased flexibility for systems configuration

Due to the fact that new VMs can be provisioned quickly and that you are only limited to the number of VMs you can have running by your installed

RAM and CPU capacity, you don't have to run out to get new hardware to try something new. This level of flexibility is an extraordinarily powerful tool. Need a new database server? Provision a new one from a baseline master VM. Does the development team need a new web server to test new software? Provision one of them, too.

If you are running short of hardware resources, when you do purchase a new server, it won't be limited to just one role. It can host a number of new guest VMs. The cost savings derived from being able to segment a single server can be enormous.

Improved reliability and consistency

Because you can make snapshots, move VMs around from host to host, and create new VMs at a moment's notice, the reliability factor of virtual machine environments increases significantly. Of course, that doesn't mean you can ignore other reliability factors, such as HVAC, power, hardware, and network redundancy, and off-site backups. With a well-planned system, however, you can put together a reliable and consistent virtual machine environment that offers superior redundancy, recoverability, and efficiency.

Faster interactions between virtual servers

One of the more interesting side effects you get from VMs is that when they are running on the same host, network interactions between them are significantly faster than via traditional network connections. In VMware's vSphere hypervisor, administrators can create virtual switches on each host server so that guest OS can talk with each other without having to send traffic outside the host, through a switch, and back.

In order to take advantage of this functionality, it's important to plan your VM deployments with the improved networking capabilities in mind. If you need speedy interactions between database servers, deploy them on the same host. If you need fast traffic between the web server and an application server, deploy them on the same host. You get the idea.

More effective use of available CPU cycles

Because most server processes aren't pegging the CPU anywhere near maximum, and the Dell R820's have dual 8-core Xeon processors, so there's quite a bit of room to play. The only thing you'll need to upgrade before starting is RAM. Linux-based systems can run on 265 to 1024 MBs just fine, depending on the expected load. Windows servers should be allocated no less than 1GB and preferably 2 to 4GBs. VMware's vSphere hypervisor needs at least 4GBs of RAM for itself and a few small VMs, so plan for what is necessary.

For the R820s I'd install no less than 32GBs of RAM. If you allocate four cores to each of four VMs, you can then allocate 8GBs of RAM to two VMs and 4GBs of RAM to the other two VMs. The R820 is capable of having four CPUs installed, expanding the total number of cores to 32. With a maximum RAM capacity of 384GBs, there are a significant number of configurations possible on such a server. The Performance model of the R820 costs around $7,500 (at least when this book was published), meaning a server with 4 VMs costs about $1,875 per VM.

If, when virtualized, you can reduce every four machines into one, you can reduce overall system load, cool air needing to be pushed, and electrical power consumption by 75 percent. That's not too shabby.

New administration functions not available for hardware-only environments

Virtualization is like a gift that gives you something new every time you open the box, and that doesn't stop when it comes to administration. When it comes to creating VMs for use in VMware's vSphere, you would use VMware's Workstation desktop application. From Workstation, you can transfer VMs to individual virtual hosts or to a vCenter server. vCenter allows you to centrally manage vSphere servers, and there's all manner of neat things you can do, depending on which paid packages you have acquired.

Some of the more awesome things you can do is move VMs from one host to another. You can even move active VMs from one host to another without any downtime! Try doing that without virtualization. You can also dynamically reallocate resources without having to restart servers, in some cases. All of this is on top of comprehensive monitoring, logging, and resource management. It's a very attractive proposition.

WordPress

In October 2014, Matt Mullenweg, the face of WordPress, stood in front of the WordCamp audience and announced a range of statistics about the popular blogging platform. Worldwide, 23.2 percent of all websites run WordPress, and that number is trending upward year after year. The WordPress project has 785 contributors who have made over 1,000,000 commits to the code base in the last year. There are just over 34,000 plugins and nearly 2,800 themes. WordPress is no joke, and it has established itself as one of the standard web publishing tools of Web 2.0+.

WordPress was originally created to be a PHP-based blogging system with a MySQL database backend, and it didn't have a lot of features. Over the years, WordPress (colloquially known as WP) became very popular because it's easy to use, quick to set up, has loads of third-party support, and is well documented. The WP universe is a thriving and dynamic one, and it doesn't appear to be stopping anytime soon. One of the more interesting aspects of WordPress is that the code was donated to the WordPress Foundation, a non-profit organization whose charter is to make sure that WordPress remains an open source project and to promote ongoing development.

WordPress was created by Matt Mullenweg and Mike Little. Automattic Inc., was formed in 2005 and is a for-profit web development company with WordPress as its centerpiece offering. In addition to contributing to WP development and acting as gatekeepers for all things WordPress, they have developed a wide range of products and services, both free and fee-based. One of their largest products is WordPress.com, a free blogging network based on WordPress that offers paid upgrades and supports around 60 million blogs.

WordPress itself is designed using HTML5, JavaScript, and PHP and uses MySQL for database operations. WordPress works by using special tags that call data from the database and display it on pages. WordPress has a comprehensive organizational structure for managing pages, and it's all controlled through the management dashboard. The visual appearance of a website is controlled by the active theme, and additional features can be added by installing plugins. As a convenience, there are catalogs for both themes and plugins, and you can install them with just a few clicks.

One of the great things about WordPress is that you don't need to be a developer to install, maintain, and modify it. It just takes a little elbow grease and diligence to understand the structure and operation of the system. The first place to start is with directory structure. The only part you need to become familiar with is the wp-content directory, which looks like this:

wp-content

plugins

themes

upload

index.php

As a security measure, all directories have an index.php file, which prevents web browsers and misconfigured web servers from having directory access to those folders.

As the directories suggest, the organization is quite obvious. You put plugins in the plugins folder and themes in the themes folder. The upload folder is used for media files that are uploaded using WordPress' media management tools. Themes and plugins are typically compressed in a ZIP file, which WordPress is able to open during the install process. Installation can be performed from the plugin and theme galleries that are built into WordPress, manually via the ZIP upload function, or via FTP access, if you have it.

In a nutshell, establishing a strong level of familiarity with how WordPress works, how it can be modified, how to manage it, and even how to install it, can give you a significant edge. Many companies use WordPress as an application framework, as suggested by the growth of that kind of work by respondents to the annual survey. Knowledge of WordPress and the magic of its inner workings can really help you advance in new directions, if you apply your skills carefully.

HTML 5 and CSS 3

As you work in WordPress to develop a comfortable level of expertise, you will find yourself looking at documentation for HTML (short for hypertext markup language) and CSS (short for cascading style sheets) to help solve various formatting issues or to modify the appearance of a theme. These two standard technologies, more than anything else, form the foundation of the Internet of today. Getting to know at least the basics of how HTML and CSS work will give you a leg up. If you become comfortable with HTML and CSS, you may even want to look into adding JavaScript to your repertoire.

HTML is a loosely structured markup language that is used as the building blocks for web pages. HTML 4.01 looks like the following:

```
<!DOCType HTML PUBLIC "-//W3C//DTD HTML 4.01 Transitional//EN"
          "http://www.w3.org/TR/html4/loose.dtd">
<html lang="en"><head>
<title>Example page</title>
<meta http-equiv="Content-Type" content="text/html; charset=windows-1252">
</head>
<body>
<h1>This is a heading</h1>
<p>This is an example of a basic HTML page.</p>
</body></html>
```

Each of the elements that are enclosed in brackets, like `<code>`, are called *tags*. The `<h1>` tag in the preceding example tells the web browser that the text the tag encloses is to be displayed using the Heading 1 formatting. The `</h1>` tag at the end of the line tells the web browser where that formatting ends. HTML is processed in a linear fashion, starting at the top of the page and working down until the end.

As you can imagine, HTML's linear qualities offer only limited formatting opportunities. In the old days, interesting formatting was performed with tables, often nested within more tables. For many years, however, CSS has been the formatting tool of choice for HTML files. CSS is a highly structured language that defines how text, images, and other objects are displayed in web pages. There are two primary parts to CSS; the style sheet and the extensions to HTML that apply the styles indicated.

Functionally, an HTML page is configured to reference an external style sheet or the CSS is inserted inline with the HTML. The former has many benefits over the latter. It's easier to read, and when you make modifications in one document, those changes are reflected in all HTML pages that reference the style sheet. It is rare that inline CSS is used these days, as it's very time consuming to manage. Inline CSS looks like this:

```
<!DOCTYPE html>
<html>
<head>
<style>
p {
    text-align: center;
    color: red;
}
</style>
</head>
<body>

<p>Every paragraph will be affected by the style.</p>
<p id="para1">Me too!</p>
<p>And me!</p>

</body>
</html>
```

In the preceding sample, the style for paragraphs, indicated by the letter p, is define inside the style tags. The style is applied when text is enclosed inside of paragraph tags. If this same styling were to be applied from an externally referenced style sheet, the HTML document would look like this:

```
<!DOCTYPE html>
<html>
<head>
<link rel="stylesheet" type="text/css" href="style.css"
</head>
<body>

<p>Every paragraph will be affected by the style.</p>
<p id="para1">Me too!</p>
<p>And me!</p>

</body>
</html>
```

Here, the stylesheet is indicated in the `link` tag. All CSS to be used would then be placed inside the style.css file. That file's content would look like the following:

```
p {
    text-align: center;
    color: red;
}
```

You may note that there is no `<style>` tag used in the stylesheet. The `style` tag is only used in HTML to indicate that CSS styling information is available and should be applied to any elements that match.

Aside from simple formatting, CSS has a number of different applications. You can define the appearance links, lists, tabled, borders, and text, but you can also define positioning, spacing and padding, alignment, and how various elements are rendered in a web browser. One very common use of positioning in CSS is defining where the header, footer, sidebar, and content areas appear in a page. In the HTML, each of these areas would be identified using a DIV tag that has a class, like so:

✔ **DIV tag:-** `<div>`

✔ **DIV tag with an ID:** `<div class="header">`

Figure 18-1 shows you an example of how CSS can be used to position regions on a web page for better control, a cleaner look, and consistent features.

In Figure 18-1, the headers class might be `header`, the sidebars class might be `sidebar`, and so on. Any CSS that is defined within that class is then applied to the elements that appear inside the DIV tag that is marked with that class. A simple declaration for the sidebar to make it appear to the left may be

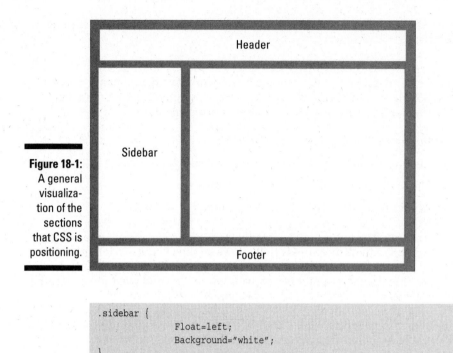

Figure 18-1:
A general visualiza-
tion of the sections that CSS is positioning.

```
.sidebar {
        Float=left;
        Background="white";
}
```

Of course, this section isn't meant to be an in-depth tutorial on HTML and CSS, just enough to give you a basic understanding of how they work. In the preceding section, I discussed WordPress, and that's a great place to see how it works.

Cross-Platform Domain Integration

Apple has long been on the road of success, especially with its popular iPhone and iPads. There are plenty of systems integration technologies for mobile devices, but desktops and laptops are another matter. While it's easy to add Android, BlackBerry, iOS, and Windows Phone devices into a corporate domain, with all of the rights and permissions management features, desktops operating systems are still more complex.

This issue is steadily becoming more common as more and more new companies and startups buy into the Apple ethos. From a corporate standpoint, leaving Mac OS X systems to fend for themselves outside of corporate policy controls is simply unacceptable. Centralized management becomes even more critical in companies with security requirements or government contracts.

I'm sure it will be no surprise that Windows systems are the easiest to integrate with an Active Directory domain, but you may not know that Apple's Mac OS X has a built-in solution as well. Once integrated, Mac OS X clients have similar administrative benefits to Windows clients:

✔ Centralized user account management

✔ Required adherence to Active Directory password policies

✔ Single sign-on access to Active Directory resources

✔ Access to network-based user Home folders

There are additional solutions. Centrify (www.centrify.com) offers a free product called Centrify Express that allows administrators to integrate Mac OS X systems with Active Directory, but it has some limitations. There is a paid version that adds a number of features well beyond what the integrated solution can offer. Centrify also offers a version for Linux.

No, I didn't forget about Linux. Standard tools for Linux that use the PAM (Pluggable Authentication Modules) architecture work quite well with SaMBa, an SMB file sharing framework for Linux, and its Winbind components that adds the ability for SaMBa to authenticate against a domain controller through LDAP (Lightweight Directory Access Protocol). Winbind also adds services for locating domain controllers and resetting passwords through RPC (Remote Procedure Call).

The best way to learn about integrating various non-Windows operating systems and mobile devices with domain controllers is to just do it. If you have the hardware resources at home, you can get demo copies of Microsoft Server 2008 R2. (You'll need to use at least Standard Edition for domain functionality.) You can even run them as virtual machines.

For clients, it will be easy to test Linux. According to DistroWatch (as of November 2014), the top three Linux distributions are all Debian-based. Mint tops the list (http://linuxmint.com), followed by Ubuntu (http://ubuntu.com), and then Debian itself (http://debian.org). They are free to download and use, but I talk more about that in the next section.

Mac OS X is going to be harder to deal with. There's no way around it. You need a Mac. Even if you had the resources to virtualize Mac OS X, you're legally required by Apple to run it on an Apple-branded Mac. In this case, you may be able to practice only with the Macs at work.

Linux, the Other Operating System

While most of the world chugs away on Windows and the rest on Mac OS X, millions of people around the world use Linux. Linux-based servers power a very large percentage of the Internet. According to W3Techs (www.w3techs.com), Linux runs 54.6 percent of all web servers, but numbers of desktop users are harder to come by. NetMarketshare (www.netmarketshare.com) says that in October 2014, only 1.41 percent of desktop users ran Linux.

What's important here, however, is that the lion's share of servers are Linux-based, and many corporations see the benefits of using an open source operating system for network operations because there is no cost to use it. That's not entirely true, though. You can download any one of dozens of popular Linux distributions and use them without paying licensing fees, but there is a cost for employing engineers who are well versed in Linux operations.

Conversely, organizations must spend money on technology regardless, so choosing Linux isn't necessarily a hard decision. You may be surprised to find who uses Linux: the U.S. Department of Defense, the Federal Aviation Administration, the U.S. Postal Service, and the U.S. Navy Submarine Fleet, the city of Munich in Germany, Spain, the French Parliament, and Macedonia's Ministry of Education and Science. One of the more well-known organizations to use Linux is the much publicized One Laptop Per Child organization (http://one.laptop.org), which claims to have distributed 2.4 million laptops to children worldwide. This is but a tiny number of countries, organizations, educational concerns, and governmental departments that have adopted Linux.

There are also a large number of corporate users of Linux, with Google the most well-known of them all. There are many more, such as Novell, IBM, Panasonic, Virgin America, Cisco, ConocoPhillips, Omaha Steaks (I know, right!), Amazon, Peugeot, Wikipedia, the New York Stock Exchange, Burlington Coat Factory, Toyota Motor Sales, and Travelocity. You may be shocked to know that Sony officially supported Linux running on its PlayStation 2 and PlayStation 3 game consoles, though Sony removed that functionality in PS3 update 3.21 and later.

If that's not enough to convince you that you should learn the basics of Linux, then I'm not sure what else to say. I do know, however, that once you start to dig into Linux, you will be compelled to learn more and more, and it will become a deep interest for you. This will become knowledge that you can carry forward with you as you advance.

Agile Project Management

I talk about Agile in great depth in Chapter 8. In a nutshell, Agile is a methodology for breaking development work down into small, manageable bits, distributing those bits around teams, meeting daily to work through problems and check on progress, and scheduling periods of work in a structured process that focuses on project awareness. Agile isn't just for development, though, and has been adapted to a wide range of tasks.

Agile is a very important part of the Internet economy and is used in an ever growing number of startups and small businesses. According to VersionOne's State of Agile report (`http://stateofagile.versionone.com/why-agile`), 73 percent of those polled claimed that Agile helped them complete projects faster, 92 percent indicated that it improved their ability to manage changing priorities, 87 percent reported an increase in productivity, 86 percent cited an improvement in team morale, and 82 percent claimed a reduction in risk.

Another interesting result from the VersionOne survey is that a full 55 percent of respondents use Scrum as their preferred implementation of Agile. Out of all of the many techniques that make up Agile, most teams use daily standups, iteration planning, unit testing, retrospectives, release planning, and burndown statistics the most. Agile Scrum is a comprehensive project management methodology and will take time to understand.

Adding Agile to your toolbox will give you an edge when working for companies that have some form of development team or teams or have adopted Agile to manage projects. In some cases, you may even be the one to bring Agile into your organization. Just be aware that it takes commitment and consistency to make Agile work.

Advanced Networking and Administration

I'm not going to go into detail in this section, but suffice it to say that networking and network administration are critical to all organizations. Without networks, after all, the Internet economy would not exist.

You should spend time learning two primary aspects of networking. One is networking itself, involving TCP/IP (Terminal Control Protocol/Internet Protocol), DNS (Domain Name Services), IPv4 (the old form of Internet addressing), IPv6 (the new form of addressing), HTTP (Hypertext Transfer Protocol), and a range of other technologies.

The other is administration, which gets a little more complicated, mostly because the administrative side of networking is controlled by a number of hardware vendors. You may have heard of Cisco, but there are also a number of other vendors, all serving various different levels of the networking marketplace. Many of these vendors, such as the aforementioned Cisco and Juniper Networks, HP, Brocade, Avaya, and many more, each have their own software to control devices such as routers, switches, and wireless networking systems.

If you develop a strong interest in networking, you can actually acquire older networking gear for cheap. Check eBay for great deals on gear that was formerly ridiculously expensive. Once you've gotten your testing system, you can start to dig into it. If that's not an option, simulators can help you learn the text-based administration commands. Check out GNS3, the Graphical Network Simulator (www.gns3.com) for Windows, Linux, or Mac OS X. It's important to note that GNS3 is only an emulator, so you'll have to supply ROM images for devices you want to populate your little networking universe with.

Server Administration and Hardware

Server administration and hardware is another subject that would be difficult to go into detail, so I'll just summarize things for you. You are likely already familiar with the concept of a server, but may have never had direct, hands-on experience managing one. A significant number of different technologies are involved in server operations, not to mention they can be extended in countless ways with various software packages. Each server does, after all, serve a specific role or roles, and that all needs to be configured and managed.

While you're dealing with the software end of things, you'll also invariably get your hands dirty (that's not entirely literal) working with the hardware. Even a small company with less than 100 employees can be supported by a good sized collection of hardware. There are servers, SAN and NAS storage devices, switches, a firewall, routers from your network provider, power supplies, cable management rails, server racks with either square or round holes and adapters from square to round, server mounting rails, management consoles, crash carts, backup systems, uninterruptible power supplies, Ethernet breakout panels, and all kinds of other gadgets.

It's a nerd's paradise — a veritable playground of technology.

Then there's hooking it all up. You have to learn about networking and cabling, power consumption requirements for hardware and not overloading your building power, doing the math on how long your servers will have on battery before shutting down gracefully or hard shutdowns, routing and bundling cables and power cords to make them easier to trace if something goes wrong, and about a million other things. It's a challenging environment, and you'd better have a good back (or a good back brace). Some of those UPS devices can weight around 100 lbs.

Then there's applying configurations to all of the gear so that it's capable of talking to each other. I liken the entire process to going to a race track for a race and finding that you need to build the car before you can head out on the track. Not only do you have to put it together, but it has to be sturdy enough to handle the entire race, or you'll be in the pit every other lap, if not down for the count. Note that I'm not yet talking again about the server software administration.

As you work with all of this gear, you'll get to know about all manner of components and technologies like Xeon processors, the weird way RAM gets installed in a server, whether or not you prefer Dell over HP or the other way around (for the record, I'm a Dell guy), and the real cost of getting a server room stocked. Speaking of cost, once you move over to software, if your company is a Microsoft shop, then you'll have to learn about managing licensing, contacting technical support, and when you'll need to get the boss to approve an expense for support after the expiration date (an excellent reason to maintain a service agreement, by the way).

After all that, there's yet more. Now you'll get involved with setting up primary and backup domain controllers, domain name, web, mail, application and development servers. There's database servers, too. Those are everywhere, which is why I talk about databases in the next section. There's setting up user accounts, applying policies, dealing with the Active Directory configuration, installing SSL certificates, blocking and unblocking access to services through the firewall, configuring remote access for administrators and users, and an endless list of a million other things.

It seems like it may just be chaos, but it's not. It's a joyous jumble of all manner of things technology, and it's a blast once you start feeling your chops. The server room is one of my favorite places to work, installing systems, getting things connected and configured, and walking out the other side with a successfully completed project, the bigger the better. It is very involved and requires a lot of dedication coupled with an insatiable need to never stop learning, but it's a great feeling when you have something that can be this complex in your back pocket.

Database Technologies

Not everyone likes databases. They're kind of dorky and the SQL syntax can be a real bear, but there's a truth here that can stand clarifying; almost everyone, everywhere uses one or more databases. You can't walk through some office without accidentally kicking a database server. The management and storage of data is one of the most powerful tools in business, and the power behind this data is the database server.

Head over to Amazon and check your orders? It's loaded from a database. Reading an article on a WordPress-powered website? It's loaded from a database. Filling out a form to get free tickets to see *The Late Show* with David Letterman? It's sent to a database. Heck, even a Microsoft Excel spreadsheet is form of database, what's called a flat file.

Technically, a database is nothing more than a structured collection of data. The most common form of database, which has been around since the late '70s, is the Relational Database, or RDBMS (Relational Database Management System). There are a few different kinds, like Microsoft SQL Server, the open source MySQL and PostgreSQL, and Oracle's 12c, but the one thing they all share is that they are SQL servers, which is sometimes pronounced as sequel.

SQL is more of a programming language than an actual database. It was designed to get, put, and manipulate data stored inside of a relational database, but most people just call the entire server SQL. A command in SQL is called a *query,* and it can contain all kinds of tasks for the server to perform with data, like calling it out, sorting it against other data, and matching data from one location to another. For example, you might fill out a form on a website that asks for your first and last name in separate fields. When that data is called out of the database for review, it will likely be formatted last name first, have a comma added followed by your first name, and then displayed in a list.

SQL isn't the only kind of database, though. There is one other, and I'm rather fond of it. It's called FileMaker, and it's made by a wholly owned subsidiary of Apple. FileMaker is a very user friendly form of RDBMS, but don't let its ease of use fool you. It's very powerful. Many companies around the world develop custom, in-house applications on FileMaker to manage all manner of things. FileMaker Pro makes it a great deal easier to compose a working database with a comfortable user interface without having to be a database expert. There's even a large developers community, and it's not just for Mac, but Windows, too.

Developing a deep understanding of how an RDBMS works, learning SQL, and understanding the management and recall of data can be a huge driver for your career in IT, so dig into it before you turn your nose up at the often misunderstood database. You might just be happy you did.

The Seeming Impossible: Inbox Zero

There is one last thing you can learn. It's not exactly a new technology. It's more of a methodology, but you will find it amazingly empowering. It's called Inbox Zero, and it means that your Inbox has nothing in it unless you are working on them. If you have anything in your inbox, you should work on it so that you can get it out of there and return your mental state to one of peace.

In a nutshell, Inbox Zero means just that: You have zero items in your inbox.

At first, the idea may seem counterproductive, but I think you'll be surprised. First, however, you need to make a rather final and difficult decision. Ask yourself whether Inbox Zero is right for you. Do you feel that you're sorting through email most of the day instead of getting any real work done? You sound like the perfect candidate for Inbox Zero.

After getting started with it a few years ago, I've become fully committed to living the lifestyle. It is remarkably difficult to start, but becomes ludicrously easy to implement over time. Even I don't employ a 100 percent Inbox Zero process, but I try to keep it close. The original idea was developed by Merlin Mann, the creator of the 43 Folders website, writer, speaker, and general gadabout. He had, you see, this idea.

He called it The Email DMZ. His idea was to create a separate inbox called DMZ that would take all of the collected cruft from the real inbox and get it out of sight. He was inundated with pleas to better explain his methods and/or madness, so he obliged . . . slowly. It took a while, but he eventually mapped out a keen plan to zero out his inbox. I'm not going to tell you about that, though. I'm going to tell you my process for paring back on your insanely huge inbox.

First, you must accept the fact that your inbox is out of control.

Second, you must come to believe that there is a better way of handling your inbox.

Third, you must take action in order to force your inbox into submission.

It's hard, but you may feel better once you start. As the old saying goes, you'll never know until you try. I've heard all manner of arguments against it as well, but I won't have any of it. People who insist that they must maintain the chaos through the rigorous maintenance of hundreds of filters or because they store all documents for their business as attachments to email may have just lost the thread for good, but if you can conceive of the idea that it is possible to wrangle your inbox, you can move on.

Your first step is to delete (yes, delete) all email from mailing lists of no importance to you. You'll be using your Search function, but scan through the list just to make sure other fruits aren't horning in on your racquet. You will be surprised at the number of junk emails you have. You don't need them anymore. If you do find them helpful in the moment, create a filter to move those messages to another folder, but you'll find that you will be deleting them anyway. You just need to get them out of your daily email routine so you can deal with them after your important email.

Now you can keep deleting until you have found all mail that is delivered by robots. That should be reducing your inbox by a large amount, so you're about ready for the second step.

Now the second step is to get the rest of the email out of the inbox, but how? You aren't going to delete it. That wouldn't be good. You are going to archive it, just like Merlin's DMZ folder. Fortunately, clients like Outlook and Mailbird and online services like Gmail and Outlook.com all have the ability to easily archive email, a tool that will help you greatly in your quest.

So, Step 2 is to select all emails in your inbox, deselect only the emails you are actually working on or are important, and then archive the rest. Now, you should be down to 30 to 50 emails you have to deal with, and you're going to do that now.

First, look over anything that isn't work or family-related. Once you get what you can from it, delete or archive it.

Then, acknowledge that just accomplished something. Good work, you!

Now, start working through the rest. Did you respond to them? Are they expecting something back? Do they need an answer? Did you already give it to them? If you've dealt with it, it gets archived.

Now it's time for the rules and the first rule is that once an email arrives, you need to deal with it. Then:

- ✔ If it's important, deal with it immediately.
- ✔ If it's not, leave it in the inbox until you can.

Just don't leave stuff there too long. This is part of the beauty of a Zero Inbox. It makes you feel bad for not dealing with it and letting it get buried. It's just sitting there, staring you down.

Now, once you have it out of your hands and into someone else's, it becomes that person's responsibility to deal with. If you're asked about the project, you can say you sent whatever to whomever, and you're duties are being satisfied. It's no longer in your wheelhouse.

You'll see how good that feels.

Chapter 19

Ten Things You Should Never Say During an Interview

● ●

In This Chapter

▶ Knowing what's better left unsaid during an interview

▶ Discovering why some things shouldn't be said

● ●

T he human being is an interesting animal. Aside from loving food, cute and cuddly puppies and kittens, saucy news about attractive celebrities, and discussions of weather with total strangers, they love lists. It's not all that surprising. Lists are concrete, measurable collections of information, helpful or not, and people like them.

In this chapter, I give you ten things you should never say during an interview (unless you want to intentionally sabotage your hiring chances!).

The moral of these tales: Don't be creepy, obsessive, paranoid, inappropriate, and impatient, share too much information, focus on unimportant details, distracted, disorganized, or disinterested. None of these are positive traits and will not help you get a job.

"I Can't Help But Notice That You're Wearing a Pleasant Fragrance Today. Might I Get a Closer Smell So I Might Identify It?"

Rather stalker-ish, don't you think? Prepare yourself for a rather forcible removal, possibly by police officers.

"I've Been Counting the Ceiling Tiles in This Office, and I'm Pretty Sure That the One in The Back Right Corner Was Placed in the Wrong Position. Would You Like Me to Fix It for You?"

If you were planning on showcasing your Obsessive Compulsive Disorder as a feature, you may have derailed any possibility that the interviewer may find that a useful talent.

"Do You Ever Get the Feeling You're Being Watched?"

Paranoia is not a job skill, at least not outside of various agencies providing national security services.

"You Know, I Think We Had a Great Time Today and Was Wondering If You Were Free for Dinner?"

If they had just landed you a $100,000 per year position as an executive, this might be appropriate.

"Are We Done Yet?"

Yes. Yes, we are. Don't let the door hit you on the way out.

"Yes, I Have Been Fired from a Job. Why? For Hitting a Coworker. Is That a Problem?"

Violence isn't the answer, unless the answer you are seeking is that you don't have the job, but thanks for coming.

"That's Very Interesting and All, But Tell Me More about the Coffee Maker"

Perks are not the job. The job is the job. Perks are what you get to make the job you do more pleasant. The job is not something you have to do when you aren't using a perk. Clear?

"Yeah, I've Got These Nasty Bunions on My Left Foot. Do You Have Any Remedies 'Cuz I Could Really Use One?"

In case you hadn't noticed, this is a job interview, not your 10 a.m. appointment with your podiatrist on Wednesday. Nice win for focus there, Paul. Don't forget your axe.

"I've Got Another Interview in 20 Minutes, So If We Could Wrap This Up, That Would Be Great"

Excellent work scheduling there, genius. Let's hope that, unless you have another interview cross-scheduled with that next one, you'll be offered the job because you aren't getting this one.

"I'm Not Really Interested in This Job, But I Could Use the Money, and I Have Some Friends Who Work Here, So It Could Be Fun for a While"

Well, then. I hope that your next interview goes better for you, and you find that job that will pay you to be a slacker. Good luck.

Index

• D •

• E •

Notes

Notes

Notes

Notes

Notes

Notes

Notes

Notes

Notes

Notes

Notes

Notes

About the Author

Tyler Regas is a 20-year veteran of the technology trenches and has worked as enlisted and officer material roles in all of the job positions referenced in this book. Mr. Regas is also a professional writer, blogger, and freelance technical writer. He lives in Southern California with his wife of 18 years, daughter, a surprisingly loud scaredy cat, and a surprisingly silly sausage dog.

Dedication

I dedicate this book, and future editions, to my daughter, Leah Lucie Ellen Regas. You rock. Know this.

Author's Acknowledgments

I'd like to thank Katie Mohr and Kelly Ewing for putting up with me and my strange working hours. I would also like to acknowledge all of the people I have ever worked with for and on behalf of. Without you, I would never have been able to amass the widely diverse experience I can share here. I'd also like to thank my agent Carole and Waterside, the best agency there is, as they always go the extra mile for their writers no matter what. You guys are the best!

I will make three special acknowledgements, as well. First, to Darrin. You taught me a great deal about moving my consulting skills to the next level while allowing me an unprecedented level of autonomy. Second, to Chris. You gave me a renewed faith in the power of Apple technology in the workplace and the undying catchiness of most any track from just about any The Cars album. Third, but not least, to Erik. You were the best right-hand man a guy could have ever asked for. Our time was too short. Thank you.

Publisher's Acknowledgments

Senior Acquisitions Editor: Katie Mohr

Project Editor: Kelly Ewing

Copy Editor: Kelly Ewing

Editorial Assistant: Claire Brock

Sr. Editorial Assistant: Cherie Case

Project Coordinator: R. Kinson Raja

Cover Image: © iStockphoto.com / porcorex

Apple & Mac

iPad For Dummies,
6th Edition
978-1-118-72306-7

iPhone For Dummies,
7th Edition
978-1-118-69083-3

Macs All-in-One
For Dummies, 4th Edition
978-1-118-82210-4

OS X Mavericks
For Dummies
978-1-118-69188-5

Blogging & Social Media

Facebook For Dummies,
5th Edition
978-1-118-63312-0

Social Media Engagement
For Dummies
978-1-118-53019-1

WordPress For Dummies,
6th Edition
978-1-118-79161-5

Business

Stock Investing
For Dummies, 4th Edition
978-1-118-37678-2

Investing For Dummies,
6th Edition
978-0-470-90545-6

Personal Finance

Personal Finance
For Dummies, 7th Edition
978-1-118-11785-9

QuickBooks 2014
For Dummies
978-1-118-72005-9

Small Business Marketing
Kit For Dummies,
3rd Edition
978-1-118-31183-7

Careers

Job Interviews
For Dummies, 4th Edition
978-1-118-11290-8

Job Searching with Social
Media For Dummies,
2nd Edition
978-1-118-67856-5

Personal Branding
For Dummies
978-1-118-11792-7

Resumes For Dummies,
6th Edition
978-0-470-87361-8

Starting an Etsy Business
For Dummies, 2nd Edition
978-1-118-59024-9

Diet & Nutrition

Belly Fat Diet For Dummies
978-1-118-34585-6

Mediterranean Diet
For Dummies
978-1-118-71525-3

Nutrition For Dummies,
5th Edition
978-0-470-93231-5

Digital Photography

Digital SLR Photography
All-in-One For Dummies,
2nd Edition
978-1-118-59082-9

Digital SLR Video &
Filmmaking For Dummies
978-1-118-36598-4

Photoshop Elements 12
For Dummies
978-1-118-72714-0

Gardening

Herb Gardening
For Dummies, 2nd Edition
978-0-470-61778-6

Gardening with Free-Range
Chickens For Dummies
978-1-118-54754-0

Health

Boosting Your Immunity
For Dummies
978-1-118-40200-9

Diabetes For Dummies,
4th Edition
978-1-118-29447-5

Living Paleo For Dummies
978-1-118-29405-5

Big Data

Big Data For Dummies
978-1-118-50422-2

Data Visualization
For Dummies
978-1-118-50289-1

Hadoop For Dummies
978-1-118-60755-8

Language &
Foreign Language

500 Spanish Verbs
For Dummies
978-1-118-02382-2

English Grammar
For Dummies, 2nd Edition
978-0-470-54664-2

French All-in-One
For Dummies
978-1-118-22815-9

German Essentials
For Dummies
978-1-118-18422-6

Italian For Dummies,
2nd Edition
978-1-118-00465-4

Available in print and e-book formats.

Available wherever books are sold. **For more information or to order direct visit www.dummies.com**

Take Dummies with you everywhere you go!

Whether you are excited about e-books, want more from the web, must have your mobile apps, or are swept up in social media, Dummies makes everything easier.

Leverage the Power

For Dummies is the global leader in the reference category and one of the most trusted and highly regarded brands in the world. No longer just focused on books, customers now have access to the For Dummies content they need in the format they want. Let us help you develop a solution that will fit your brand and help you connect with your customers.

Advertising & Sponsorships

Connect with an engaged audience on a powerful multimedia site, and position your message alongside expert how-to content.

Targeted ads · Video · Email marketing · Microsites · Sweepstakes sponsorship

21 Million Monthly Page Views & 13 Million Unique Visitors

Dummies products make life easier!

- DIY
- Consumer Electronics
- Crafts
- Software
- Cookware
- Hobbies
- Videos
- Music
- Games
- and More!

For more information, go to **Dummies.com** and search the store by category.

FOR
DUMMIES

A Wiley Bran